Y0-BUD-539

sto

G

Simple Family Favorites

Simple

Family Favorites

by Jean H. Shepard

 STEIN AND DAY/ *Publishers* / New York

First published in 1970
Copyright © 1970 by Jean H. Shepard
Library of Congress Catalog Card No. 76-127234
All rights reserved
Published simultaneously in Canada by Saunders of Toronto, Ltd.
Designed by Bernard Schleifer
Printed in the United States of America
Stein and Day/*Publishers*/7 East 48 Street, New York, N.Y. 10017
SBN 8128-1342-1

1566469

To my sons
Lance and Brad

Contents

Introduction

This book is for hungry teens, campus queens, career guys and gals, young marrieds, busy new mothers, older moms who cook for older children and their friends, and all others who like to cook and eat young.

Its purpose is to combine variety with simplicity, speed, and economy and to provide those recipes especially geared to the ravenous appetites, unspoiled palates, and sound digestions of this delightfully food-oriented group. So to anyone who wants to bridge the generation gap—at least at the table—read on!

10 Basic Rules for Safety in the Kitchen

1. Keep at least 2 small emergency fire extinguishers in handy and visible areas of the kitchen—one preferably near the stove. The foam variety is best for extinguishing fat fires. (*Never pour water on a fat fire*: use salt if fire extinguisher is not available.)
2. Keep antiseptic burn ointment readily accessible in kitchen. When burn occurs, immediately hold part under cold running water or apply ice cube. Pat dry and apply ointment. To prevent blisters, renew several times as ointment dries. (If burns are severe, exposing raw flesh, *do not apply anything*: see doctor immediately.)
3. If fat fire occurs in broiler or oven, simply close door and turn off heat. Flames will go out.
4. Beware of steam burns: they are also serious and painful. Remove pot covers away from face to divert rising steam.
5. Never switch electrical appliances on or off or touch their cords with wet hands or with one hand in water. *Water conducts electricity.*
6. Replace worn and frayed electric cords immediately to avoid short circuits and flash fires.

13

7. Be sure to turn off oven, broiler, and gas burners *all* the way. Check burners after spillage.
8. Never put head into oven to investigate difficulties in lighting it. Always keep face well away.
9. Keep handles of pots and pans turned to the inside of stove so they cannot be accidentally knocked off.
10. When not in use, keep pot holders on wall hook—not on stove where they may catch fire from the burners.

I

Main Course Specials— Under-Thirty Style

Main courses or their elements may run the gamut from pizza to shish kebab and vary infinitely with mood or fad. The following, however, are tried and true favorites with many innovations that appeal to the younger crowd's tastes. They are quick and easy to prepare.

BURGERS AND DOGS

CHEESEBURGERS

2 pounds ground beef
Salt and pepper
8 slices American cheese or sharp Cheddar cheese

Shape and season 8 hamburger patties and place in hot, salted, ungreased skillet. Brown one side (about 3 to 4 minutes), turn, place slice of cheese on top of each, and continue panbroiling until cheese has begun to melt.

Alternative

Try a topping of crumbled blue cheese with a sprinkling of chopped parsley. This is a delightful and reasonable facsimile of the delicious "lionburger" served at the Columbia University Club in New York City, where the original recipe is a well-guarded chef's secret.

Other Toppings

Catsup	Top before turning.
Mustard	Top before turning.
Garlic or lemon butter	Mix softened butter with lemon juice or garlic powder to taste.
Sautéed mushrooms	Cook sliced mushrooms in melted butter until tender.
Sautéed onions	Cook sliced onions in melted butter until soft and transparent. Stir occasionally to keep from browning.

SAUCY HAMBURGERS

2 pounds ground beef
Salt and pepper

Shape meat into 8 patties; sprinkle with salt and pepper. Broil, panbroil, fry, or grill. Brush with Spicy Barbecue Sauce and turn to brown both sides while cooking. Serve with extra sauce. (Makes 8 servings.)

Spicy Barbecue Sauce

Heat ⅓ cup corn oil in skillet. Add 1 medium-sized minced onion, and cook over low heat, stirring often, until tender. Stir in ½ cup dark corn syrup, ½ cup catsup, ½ cup water, ⅓ cup vinegar, 2 tablespoons each prepared mustard and Worcestershire sauce, 2 teaspoons salt, and ½ teaspoon pepper. Simmer 15 minutes; stir occasionally. (Makes 2½ cups.)

GOURMET BURGERS MUSCOVITE

2 pounds chopped beef
Salt and pepper

1 pint sour cream
1 (4-oz.) jar red caviar

Shape and season 8 hamburger patties and cook in hot, salted, ungreased skillet, turning once to brown. Serve topped with a dollop of sour cream and a spoonful of red caviar. (Makes 8 servings.)

GRILLED ONIONY HAMBURGERS

2 pounds chopped beef
Salt and pepper
1 envelope dry onion soup mix

Lightly mix beef and dry soup mix. Shape into 8 patties. Pan-broil, broil, or fry patties; or for special goodness place them in a hinged grill and cook over charcoal. (Makes 8 servings.)

CHILI BURGER BUNS

2 pounds ground beef
1½ teaspoons salt
½ teaspoon pepper
½ cup dark corn syrup
½ cup prepared mustard

4 tablespoons vinegar
4 tablespoons Worcestershire sauce
1 cup chili sauce
¼ teaspoon chili powder

Sprinkle beef with salt and pepper; brown in skillet over medium heat, stirring to break up pieces. Mix syrup, mustard, then vinegar, Worcestershire sauce, chili sauce, and chili powder. Add to meat; heat. Serve hot in hamburger rolls. (Makes 8 servings.)

HOT TUNA BURGERS

1 (7-ounce) can tuna, drained and flaked
½ cup finely shredded Swiss cheese
1 cup chopped celery
¼ teaspoon salt

Dash pepper
¼ cup mayonnaise
2 tablespoons catsup
1 teaspoon lemon juice
4 hamburger buns

Combine all ingredients except buns. Cover and chill in refrigerator until serving time. Spoon tuna mixture into buns. Wrap each bun in aluminum foil and heat on grill over glowing charcoal, turning frequently, about 15 minutes; or in 350° F. oven 15 minutes. (Makes 4 servings.)

CHILI BEAN BURGERS

1 (1-pound) can red kidney beans
½ cup mayonnaise
2 tablespoons chopped onion
½ teaspoon chili powder

1 pound ground beef, seasoned as desired, and shaped into 4 patties
4 hamburger rolls, split and toasted
4 tomato slices

Drain beans; combine with mayonnaise, chopped onion, and chili powder. Broil hamburger patties, turning once, until done as desired. Top each with small amount of chili mixture. Broil 6 inches from heat 1 to 2 minutes or until lightly browned. Serve on toasted rolls, garnished with tomato slices. Serve with remaining chili mixture. (Makes 4 servings.)

* QUICK HAMBURGER PIZZA ON TOAST OR BUN

Cooked ground beef (leftover hamburgers)
Sandwich bread or split buns

Pizza sauce (tomato purée seasoned with garlic and oregano)
Shredded Cheddar cheese

Arrange bread slices or buns on pan and toast lightly. Brush with pizza sauce. Chop cooked hamburger and sprinkle over toast or buns. Top with shredded cheese. Heat in 425° F. oven 5 to 8 minutes, or heat under broiler until hot. (Two slices pizza toast or 2 pizza bun halves per serving.)

QUICK-GRILLED FRANKS

Brown gently scored frankfurters in skillet in 1 tablespoon hot oil for 4 to 5 minutes, turning often.

POT-BOILER FRANKS

Drop franks in boiling water. Cover, reduce heat, and *simmer* 5 minutes.

MANUEL'S RED-EYE DOGS

Place Pot-Boiler Franks in toasted buns and top with Red-Eye Sauce.

* asterisk is explained in acknowledgements at end of book.

Red-Eye Sauce

½ pound hamburger beef	½ teaspoon chili powder
¼ cup sliced onion	½ teaspoon salt
¼ cup water	½ teaspoon monosodium gluta-
1 clove garlic, minced	mate
1 (8-ounce) can tomato sauce (seasoned)	

Cook beef slowly, separating thoroughly with fork. Add other ingredients and simmer 12 to 15 minutes. (Makes 10 servings.)

FRANKLY FAVORITES

Pot boil franks, drain, and place in a pan. Mix equal parts dark corn syrup and chili sauce or catsup, and pour into pan with franks. Heat until glazed.

* DOGS OLIVER

Grill, broil, or simmer franks. Slice, and place them on a plate. Top with a scoop each of potato salad and cottage cheese.

* RYEZERS

Grill, broil, or simmer franks. Spread large oval slices of rye bread with mustard. Add slice of cheese. Split frank lengthwise and place on one side of each slice of bread. Fold over and fasten with toothpicks. Brush with melted butter and bake in 350° F. oven for 10 minutes.

* SALTY DOGS

Grill, broil, or simmer franks. Dip them in cheese sauce and roll in crushed potato chips. Place in hot dog buns.

* STEAK HOUSE DOGS

Grill, broil, or simmer franks. Place in hot dog buns. Top with a teaspoon of steak sauce and a sprinkling of canned French-fried onion rings.

* FRANK TANKER

Split 2 grilled franks lengthwise. For each tanker, arrange 2 franks, slices of American cheese, green pepper rings, tomato, onion, and pickle slices on buttered, split hard rolls.

* BOULEVARD DOG

Grill, broil, or simmer franks. Place in hot dog buns. Top with a spoonful each of horseradish, seasoned sour cream, and sautéed sliced mushrooms.

* FRANKFURTER CLUB

Split 2 grilled franks lengthwise and place on a slice of toast. Add second slice of toast. Top with slice of American cheese, 2 or 3 tomato slices, and 2 crisp bacon strips. Top with third slice of toast.

FRANKFURTERS DELUXE

8 frankfurters	1 tablespoon finely chopped onion
¼ pound liverwurst	8 slices bacon
⅓ cup mayonnaise	8 toasted frankfurter buns
2 tablespoons finely chopped pickle	

Split frankfurters lengthwise, cutting only partway through. Mash liverwurst; mix in mayonnaise, pickle, and onion. Stuff into frankfurters. Press together and wrap each with a bacon slice. Fasten with toothpicks. Broil 3 inches from heat for 8 minutes or until bacon is crisp. Serve on toasted buns. (Makes 8 servings.)

BOARDWALK FRANKS

2 tablespoons butter
½ cup chopped onion
1 pound frankfurters, cut in thirds
1 can undiluted tomato—rice soup

⅓ cup water
1½ tablespoons bottled steak sauce
1 teaspoon prepared mustard
4 drops Tabasco sauce

Sauté onion in butter until tender and transparent. Add franks, soup, water, steak sauce, mustard, and Tabasco. Bring to boil slowly and cook uncovered for about 12 to 15 minutes or until sauce is rich and thick. Stir occasionally and spoon into buttered, toasted buns. (Makes 8 servings.)

RAE'S PIGS IN BLANKETS

1 cup flour
2 teaspoons baking powder
½ teaspoon salt

4 tablespoons shortening (room temperature)
½ cup milk
Cocktail wieners

Mix dry ingredients together. Cut in shortening with pastry blender or knife. Add milk gradually to make soft dough, using a fork to mix well. Toss on a well-floured board. Roll out very thin. Cut in strips. Place wieners on strips of dough, roll dough over to cover, close each end. Place in ungreased shallow pan in 450° oven and bake 10-12 minutes. (Makes about 2 dozen.)

LUAU FRANKS

5 frankfurters, sliced
1 (8-ounce) can pineapple slices
½ cup chopped onion
2 tablespoons butter
1 green pepper, sliced
1 beef bouillon cube dissolved in
⅓ cup hot water

1 tablespoon cornstarch
1 tablespoon brown sugar
2 tablespoons vinegar
1 tablespoon soy sauce
Salt

Sauté onion and green pepper in melted butter in large, deep skillet; cover and cook slowly over low heat 5 minutes. Combine cornstarch, brown sugar, salt. Add syrup from canned pineapples, vinegar, soy sauce, and bouillon, and pour over sautéed onion and green pepper. Stir thoroughly and cook until mixture thickens. Add frankfurters and pineapple slices and heat through. Serve open-face on toasted buns or over hot rice. (Makes 4 servings.)

GLAZED APPLES AND FRANKFURTERS

¼ cup margarine	4 frankfurters
1 tablespoon prepared mustard	2 tart apples, peeled and quartered
½ cup dark or light corn syrup	

Melt margarine in skillet; blend in mustard and syrup. Add frankfurters and apples. Cover. Simmer over low heat 10 minutes or until apples are tender. Arrange frankfurters on serving plate and surround with apples. Pour syrup over all. (Makes 4 servings.)

FRANKFURTERS GERMAN STYLE

1 medium onion, sliced	Freshly ground pepper
1 clove garlic, minced	10 frankfurters split in half
1 cup cooked rice	1 (16-ounce) can sauerkraut

Combine sauerkraut, rice, onion, garlic and pepper and place in large casserole or Dutch oven. Arrange frankfurters on top. Cover and bake in 350° F. oven 40 minutes. (Makes 4 servings.)

PORK-BEAN DOGGIES

10 frankfurters	2 tablespoons mustard with horse-
10 frankfurter buns, split	radish
2 (1-pound) cans pork and beans	2 tablespoons minced onion
1 (14-ounce) bottle catsup	2 tablespoons green pepper flakes
½ cup pancake and waffle syrup	1 teaspoon Worcestershire sauce
2 tablespoons wine vinegar	Grated Parmesan cheese

Heat frankfurters and buns. Meanwhile, combine pork and beans, catsup, syrup, vinegar, mustard, onion, green pepper, and Worcestershire sauce in medium saucepan. Heat. Place frankfurters in buns. Spoon bean mixture over each. Sprinkle with Parmesan cheese. (Makes 8 to 10 servings.)

POTATO PIGGIES

2 cups cooked mashed potatoes
8 frankfurters, halved crosswise
½ cup corn-flake crumbs
½ cup dark corn syrup

1 cup canned French-fried onion rings
Parsley flakes (optional)

Spread potatoes completely around each frankfurter half with wide spatula or knife. Roll in corn-flake crumbs. Arrange in lightly greased 8-inch-square baking dish. Drizzle with syrup. Sprinkle with onion rings and parsley flakes. Bake, uncovered, in 350° F. oven 20 to 25 minutes or until well browned and crisp. (Makes 4 servings.)

BEEF

MARINATED BEEF

⅔ cup tarragon vinegar
½ cup light corn syrup
¼ cup corn oil
2 tablespoons Worcestershire sauce
1 teaspoon salt

½ teaspoon prepared mustard
¼ teaspoon pepper
2 pounds sliced cooked beef
2 onions, thinly sliced

Combine vinegar, syrup, corn oil, Worcestershire sauce, salt, prepared mustard, and pepper. Pour over beef and onions in shallow dish. Marinate in refrigerator at least 3 hours. Remove beef and onions from marinade. Serve cold. (Makes 8 servings.)

TANGY-TOPPED MEAT LOAF

Prepare your favorite meat loaf recipe and bake as recipe directs. During baking, baste often with Tangy Sauce. Serve any remaining sauce hot with meat loaf.

Tangy Sauce

1 (8-ounce) can tomato sauce
¼ cup dark corn syrup
1 tablespoon vinegar

1 tablespoon minced onion
2 teaspoons Worcestershire sauce

Combine tomato sauce, syrup, vinegar, onion, and Worcestershire sauce in saucepan. Bring to boil, then simmer about 5 minutes, stirring occasionally. (Makes about 1¼ cups sauce.)

SWEET AND SOUR BEEF

2 tablespoons margarine
3 cups cooked beef, cut into ½-inch cubes
3 tablespoons flour
1½ cups water
½ cup vinegar

⅓ cup dark corn syrup
1 envelope onion soup mix
⅓ cup firmly packed brown sugar
1 teaspoon dry mustard
Cooked rice

Melt margarine in large skillet. Add beef; brown on all sides over medium heat. Stir in flour; then gradually stir in remaining ingredients. Bring to boil, stirring constantly. Simmer 20 minutes. Serve with rice. (Makes 4 to 6 servings.)

BEEF TERIYAKI

1 (2-pound) flank steak
1 cup pineapple juice
¼ cup dark corn syrup
¼ cup soy sauce

1 clove garlic, minced
1 tablespoon chopped candied ginger
2 tablespoons corn oil

Trim excess fat and membrane from steak, and score surface of both sides. If desired, treat with meat tenderizer as package directs. Mix pineapple juice, syrup, soy sauce, garlic, ginger, and corn oil in large, shallow pan. Stir to blend. Place steak in pan; spoon marinade over it. Let stand at least 3 hours or overnight in refrigerator. Turn steak 3 or 4 times. Remove from marinade. Preheat broiler or grill. Broil steak 2 to 3 inches from heat for 3 to 4 minutes on each side. Carve diagonally across grain into thin slices for serving. (Makes 4 to 5 servings.)

FONDUE BOURGUIGNONNE
(Beef Fondue)

Corn oil
Margarine
2 pounds beef tenderloin or sirloin,
  cut into cubes

Assortments of sauces such as curry, tomato, mustard, hollandaise, or sour cream

Fill fondue pot about ½ full with combination of oil and margarine. (Use about ½ cup margarine to every 2 cups of oil.) Heat oil mixture over medium heat to 375° F. Place fondue pot over heating element in fondue stand that is on plate or tray. To serve: each person spears and cooks own meat in hot oil mixture to desired doneness. Then, using dinner fork, dips cooked meat into desired sauces. (Makes about 4 servings.)

Note: 2 pounds medium size shrimp, raw, shelled and deveined, can be substituted for beef.

CANTONESE BEEF

⅓ cup dark corn syrup
¼ cup soy sauce
¼ cup cooking sherry
2 tablespoons cornstarch
2 tablespoons water

¼ teaspoon ginger
2 pounds beef chuck, cut in ½-inch cubes
1¼ cups water

Combine syrup, soy sauce, sherry, ginger in shallow dish. Add meat; marinate 1 hour in refrigerator, stirring occasionally. Mix meat and marinade with 1¼ cups water in saucepan. Cover; simmer 1 hour or until meat is tender. Blend cornstarch with 2 tablespoons water; stir into meat mixture. Simmer 2 minutes, stirring constantly. Serve on hot, cooked rice. (Makes 6 to 8 servings.)

BEEF STEW

2 pounds stewing beef
2 tablespoons corn oil
1 tablespoon paprika
6 tablespoons water
1 envelope onion soup mix

2 cups water
1 (10½-ounce) can tomato purée
4 to 6 medium potatoes, pared and cubed

Cut beef into 1-inch cubes. Heat corn oil in deep skillet or Dutch oven. Add beef; cook until lightly browned on all sides. Sprinkle with paprika; add 6 tablespoons water. Cover; simmer 45 minutes. Stir in onion soup mix, 2 cups water, and tomato purée; simmer 15 minutes. Add potatoes; cook about 15 minutes or until tender. (Makes 4 to 6 servings.)

LAMB AND VEAL

CARAWAY SHISH KEBABS

½ cup corn oil
¼ cup light corn syrup
¼ cup chopped onion
1 tablespoon lemon juice
1 teaspoon oregano
1 teaspoon caraway seeds
½ teaspoon salt

2 pounds lean lamb, cut into 1-inch cubes
6 small white onions, parboiled
6 whole mushrooms
1 green pepper, cut into 1½-inch pieces and parboiled
1 tomato, cut into wedges

Combine corn oil, syrup, onion, lemon juice, oregano, caraway seeds, and salt. Pour over lamb cubes in bowl. Marinate in refrigerator at least 3 hours, turning meat occasionally. Arrange meat, onion, mushroom, green pepper, and tomato alternately on metal skewers. Broil 5 inches from source of heat for 15 to 20 minutes. Brush occasionally with marinade and turn once. (Makes 6 servings.)

VEAL SCALLOPINI

3 pounds veal steak, pounded thin
   (¼ inch thick)
½ cup flour
1 teaspoon salt
Dash pepper
2 teaspoons paprika
1⅓ cups (6-ounce can) broiled
   sliced mushrooms

1 beef bouillon cube
1 cup (8-ounce can) seasoned
   tomato sauce
¼ cup chopped green pepper
Parmesan cheese (grated)

Coat veal well with mixture of flour, salt, pepper, and paprika. Brown in hot fat. Place in rectangular baking dish. Drain mushrooms; add water to mushroom liquid to make 1 cup. Heat to boiling; dissolve bouillon cube in hot liquid and pour over meat. Bake in 350° F. oven 30 minutes. Combine mushrooms, tomato sauce, green pepper; pour over meat and continue baking for 15 minutes more. Serve with generous topping of sauce and sprinkle with Parmesan cheese. (Makes 8 servings.)

PORK

ORANGE BAKED PORK CHOPS

4 pork chops, cut 1 inch thick
2 teaspoons salt
⅛ teaspoon pepper
2 tablespoons corn oil

⅔ cup light corn syrup
2 cups finely chopped oranges
2 teaspoons cornstarch

Sprinkle chops with salt and pepper. Brown in hot corn oil in large skillet, turning once. Remove chops, drain off excess fat, and add syrup and oranges to skillet. Bring to boil; boil 1 minute. Arrange chops in single layer in ovenproof dish. Pour sauce over chops. Bake at 350° F. for 1 hour or until meat is tender. Baste often. Remove chops to serving dish and keep warm. Stir cornstarch into 2 tablespoons water, then into sauce; cook and stir until mixture boils. Serve hot over chops. (Makes 4 servings.)

PORK CHOPS POLYNESIAN

4 pork chops, cut 1 inch thick	½ cup dark corn syrup
1 (11- or 12-ounce) package mixed dried fruit	1 teaspoon salt
	½ teaspoon curry powder
¾ cup pineapple juice	Hot cooked rice

Brown chops on both sides in large skillet over medium heat. Drain off excess fat. Combine fruit, pineapple juice, corn syrup, salt, and curry powder; pour over chops. Cover and simmer 1 to 1¼ hours, turning chops occasionally, until chops are cooked. Serve over rice. (Makes 4 servings.)

PORK CHOPS WITH SPICY PEACHES

6 pork chops, cut ¾ inch thick	1 teaspoon lemon juice
1 teaspoon salt	¼ teaspoon cinnamon
¼ teaspoon pepper	¼ teaspoon ginger
1 (1-pound) can peach halves in syrup	⅛ teaspoon ground cloves
	2 teaspoons flour
½ cup light corn syrup	¼ cup water

Using a skillet, brown pork chops on both sides over medium heat. Pour off excess fat. Sprinkle chops with salt and pepper. Drain peaches, reserving ¼ cup syrup. Combine reserved syrup, corn syrup, lemon juice, cinnamon, ginger, and cloves. Pour over chops. Cover. Cook over low heat about 45 minutes or until pork is completely cooked. Add peach halves to serving platter; keep warm. Blend flour and water. Stir into liquid in skillet. Bring to boil, stirring constantly. Spoon over chops. Serve immediately. (Makes 6 servings.)

FRUITED LOIN OF PORK

1 cup dried apricots
½ cup sherry
1 (3-pound) center-cut pork loin, with backbone cracked

½ cup dark corn syrup
1 tablespoon grated orange rind
¼ cup orange juice
½ teaspoon soy sauce

Combine apricots and sherry in saucepan. Cover and cook, stirring occasionally, until apricots are plumped with all the sherry. Cut deep slits between chops in pork loin. Insert 3 or 4 apricots in each. Insert meat thermometer. Place pork in roasting pan. (Do not add water or cover.) Roast in 325° F. oven about 2 hours or until pork temperature reaches 185° F. (allow about 40 minutes per pound). Meanwhile, combine syrup, orange rind, orange juice, and soy sauce in saucepan. Bring to boil, then cook 3 minutes. Brush on pork several times during last 30 minutes of roasting time. Do *not* baste pork with drippings in pan. (Makes 6 to 8 servings.)

CURRANT-GLAZED HAM

1 (5-pound) canned ready-to-eat ham
¾ cup red currant jelly
½ cup dark corn syrup

1 teaspoon vinegar
¼ teaspoon powdered cloves
Whole cloves

Trim and heat ham. Meanwhile, combine jelly, syrup, vinegar, and powdered cloves in saucepan, and cook over medium-low heat, stirring constantly, until jelly is melted and mixture is smooth. Remove ham from oven; score diagonally, making cuts about ⅛ inch deep, about ¾ inch apart, across fat surface of ham. Stud with whole cloves, placing one in center of each diamond. Pour part of glaze over ham. Bake in 325° F. oven about

45 minutes, basting frequently with remaining glaze, until ham is well-coated and all glaze is used. Serve with pan juice as a sauce. (Makes 15-20 servings.)

CHILLED APRICOT-GLAZED HAM

¼ cup dark corn syrup	2 tablespoons lemon juice
1 tablespoon cornstarch	1 (8-pound) canned precooked
¼ teaspoon ground cloves	ham
1 cup apricot nectar	

Combine syrup, cornstarch and ground cloves in saucepan. Stir in apricot nectar and lemon juice. Cook over medium heat, stirring constantly, until mixture thickens and comes to a boil. Boil 1 minute. Spread on chilled ham. Refrigerate several hours before serving. (Makes 25-30 servings.)

Note: For improved flavor ham can be baked in 300° F. oven for 1 to 2 hours, then cooled.

SLICED HAM WITH RAISIN SAUCE

1 tablespoon cornstarch	2 tablespoons vinegar
⅛ teaspoon salt	¼ cup water
½ teaspoon dry mustard	⅓ cup raisins
¼ cup brown sugar, firmly packed	1 tablespoon margarine
1½ cups dark corn syrup	6 slices cooked ham

Measure cornstarch, salt, mustard, and sugar into small saucepan. Gradually stir in syrup, vinegar, and water. Add raisins and margarine. Cook and stir over medium heat until mixture boils. Simmer 15 minutes, stirring occasionally. Pour over ham slices in shallow baking dish. Bake in 325° F. oven about ½ hour. (Makes 6 servings.)

APPLE UPSIDE-DOWN HAM LOAF

1 pound ground lean ham
½ pound ground beef chuck
1 egg, slightly beaten
¼ cup milk
½ cup fine dry bread crumbs
¼ cup chopped celery
2 green onions with tops, chopped

½ teaspoon dry mustard
⅓ cup light corn syrup
¼ teaspoon ground cloves
⅛ teaspoon cinnamon
1½ cups canned sliced apples, drained

Put ham and beef through meat grinder together. Combine egg and milk. Add bread crumbs to meat, then egg and milk, then celery, onion, and mustard. Combine syrup, cloves, and cinnamon. Spread in bottom of 9 x 5 x 3 inch loaf pan. Arrange apple slices in syrup mixture. Pack meat mixture firmly on top, filling spaces between apple pieces. Bake in 350° F. oven 1 to 1¼ hours or until done. Let set about 5 minutes to absorb some juices; then tip mold and pour off excess. Unmold onto serving platter. (Makes 6 servings.)

APPLE AND SPICE SPARERIBS

3 pounds spareribs, cut from ends
   partway to base
1 teaspoon salt
2 cups (1-pound can) applesauce

½ cup dark corn syrup
⅛ teaspoon paprika
Dash ground cloves

Sprinkle ribs with half the salt. Broil about 10 minutes on one side; turn, and broil 10 additional minutes or until brown. Remove from broiler; pour off fat. Sprinkle with remaining salt. Place ribs in single layer in roasting pan. Bake uncovered in 350° F. oven for 20 to 30 minutes. Meanwhile, combine applesauce, syrup, paprika, and cloves. Spoon onto ribs. Continue baking about 20 minutes or until ribs are tender and done. (Makes 4 servings.)

APPLE-GLAZED SPARERIBS

4 pounds spareribs, cut into 4- or
    5-rib portions
1 teaspoon salt
1 cup apple juice
½ cup dark corn syrup
2 tablespoons vinegar

2 tablespoons margarine
1 teaspoon grated lemon rind
2 tablespoons lemon juice
½ teaspoon ground ginger
4 medium cooking apples, pared
    and sliced

Place ribs in shallow baking pan. Sprinkle with salt. Bake in
450° F. oven for 30 minutes. Drain off excess fat. Meanwhile,
heat apple juice, syrup, vinegar, margarine, grated lemon rind,
lemon juice, and ginger in saucepan. Arrange half the ribs in a
13 x 9 x 2 inch baking dish. Top with half the apple slices. Repeat.
Pour half the syrup mixture over all. Cover and bake in 350° F.
oven for 1 hour, basting with remaining syrup mixture every 20
minutes. Uncover. Continue baking about 30 minutes or until
ribs are tender and well-browned. (Makes 4 to 6 servings.)

CHICKEN

COCONUT ISLAND CHICKEN

2 pounds chicken thighs (thaw if
    frozen)
Salt
3 tablespoons margarine
⅔ cup dark corn syrup

1 (3½-ounce) can flaked coconut
5 to 6 slices canned pineapple,
    drained
1 (11-ounce) can mandarin orange
    sections, drained

Sprinkle chicken with salt. Melt margarine in shallow roasting
pan. Turn each chicken piece in margarine to coat. Arrange in
pan in single layer. Bake in 400° F. oven about 45 minutes or
until golden brown. Combine syrup and coconut; set aside. Remove chicken from roasting pan. Arrange pineapple slices in
drippings. Place about 2 chicken pieces on each slice. Spoon
syrup mixture over chicken. Bake about 15 minutes or until coco-

nut is browned. Garnish with mandarin orange sections. (Makes 5 to 6 servings.)

SAVORY GRILLED CHICKEN

Allow half of 1½ to 2 pound broiler per serving. Cook chicken pieces on grill, slowly, until tender. Turn often, baste with sauce.

To Oven-Broil Chicken

Cook chicken pieces on oiled broiler rack set about 4 inches from heat, until tender. Turn often and baste with sauce.

Sauce

½ cup dark corn syrup
2 tablespoons prepared mustard
⅓ cup vinegar
2 tablespoons Worcestershire sauce
1 teaspoon Tabasco sauce
¼ cup minced onion
2 (8-ounce) cans tomato sauce

Combine all ingredients in a saucepan. Bring to a boil; boil 2 minutes. (Makes about 3 cups.)

HERB-GLAZED CHICKEN

3 pound frying chicken, cut in serving pieces
2 tablespoons margarine
1½ teaspoons salt
¼ teaspoon pepper
¼ teaspoon marjoram
1 teaspoon grated lemon rind
Juice of one lemon
½ cup dark corn syrup
¼ cup water

Brown chicken in melted margarine in large skillet with oven-proof handle. Sprinkle with salt, pepper, and marjoram. Blend lemon rind, juice, syrup, and water, and pour over chicken. Place skillet in 350° F. oven. Bake 45 minutes or until chicken is tender. (Makes 4 servings.)

LEMON-LIME CHICKEN 1566469

Juice of 2 lemons	¼ teaspoon pepper
Juice of 2 limes	½ cup corn oil
1 garlic clove, crushed	½ cup dry white wine
1 teaspoon salt	2½ to 3½-pound fryer, cut into
1 teaspoon crushed tarragon leaves	serving pieces

Combine lemon juice, lime juice, garlic, salt, tarragon leaves, pepper, corn oil, and white wine in large bowl. Place chicken in marinade. Cover and refrigerate for 8 hours or overnight. Remove chicken from marinade and arrange in shallow roasting pan. Bake in 425° F. oven, basting occasionally with marinade, 55 to 60 minutes or until chicken is tender. (Makes 4 servings.)

FISH AND SHELLFISH

BROILED FISH FILLETS WITH SAUCE

2 tablespoons margarine	1 tablespoon Worcestershire sauce
2 tablespoons chopped green pepper	1 teaspoon salt
¼ cup chopped onion	¼ teaspoon garlic powder
1 (8-ounce) can tomato sauce	Pepper
¼ cup lemon juice	2 pounds fish fillets (flounder,
¼ cup dark corn syrup	halibut, or sole)

Melt margarine in skillet. Add onion and green pepper. Sauté about 5 minutes or until tender, stirring occasionally. Stir in tomato sauce, lemon juice, syrup, Worcestershire sauce, salt, garlic powder, and pepper. Simmer 5 minutes. Pour over fish fillets in shallow pan. Marinate in refrigerator 30 minutes, turning once. Remove fish from marinade. Broil 6 inches from source of heat 8 to 10 minutes or until fish flakes easily with fork. Baste occasionally with marinade. Pour remaining sauce over fish to serve. (Makes 6 servings.)

PINEAPPLE SHRIMP

1 (1-pound, 4-ounce) can pineapple chunks, drained, with ½ cup syrup reserved
¼ teaspoon salt
¼ cup dark corn syrup
1 tablespoon soy sauce
¼ teaspoon ground ginger
1½ tablespoons cornstarch

⅓ cup vinegar
1 medium green pepper, cut into strips
1 medium onion, sliced and separated into rings
1 pound cooked shelled shrimp, halved lengthwise
Hot cooked rice

Combine reserved ½ cup pineapple syrup, corn syrup, soy sauce, salt, and ginger in large saucepan. Blend cornstarch and vinegar. Stir into mixture in saucepan. Bring to boil over medium heat, stirring constantly. Stir in green pepper strips, onion rings, and pineapple chunks. Cook 3 minutes. Add shrimp and heat, stirring constantly. Serve on hot rice. (Makes 4 servings.)

BEANS

GINGER BEANS AND CANADIAN BACON

1 teaspoon ginger
1 tablespoon minced onion
½ cup dark corn syrup

2 (1-pound) cans baked beans
½ pound Canadian bacon, sliced

Mix ginger, onion, and corn syrup, and pour over beans in a 2-quart ovenproof casserole. Stir to mix well. Arrange Canadian bacon slices over top of beans. Bake in 400° F. oven about 1 hour or until beans are hot and bubbly. During baking, baste bacon slices often with juices in casserole to glaze. (Makes 6 servings.)

BAKED KIDNEY BEANS WITH TOMATOES

1 pound dry red kidney beans	1 medium onion, finely chopped
1 (1-pound) can tomatoes	⅓ cup catsup
4 slices bacon, cut into ½-inch	1 tablespoon salt
pieces	1 tablespoon dry mustard
2 apples, finely chopped	1 clove garlic, minced
½ cup dark corn syrup	

Soak beans overnight in water to completely cover. Discard all but 1 quart water, and gently boil beans about 30 to 35 minutes or just until tender. (Add more water, if needed.) Drain, reserving 1 cup cooking liquid. Combine beans, reserved 1 cup liquid, and remaining ingredients in 2½-quart casserole. Partially cover. Bake in 300° F. oven for 2 hours. Uncover and bake 1 hour longer. (Makes 6 to 8 servings.)

SNAPPY BAKED BEANS

2 (1-pound) cans pork and beans	¾ cup finely crushed ginger snaps
¼ cup dark corn syrup	(about 20)
¼ cup catsup	¼ cup crumbled cooked bacon
2 tablespoons chopped onion	(about 4 slices)

Combine all ingredients. Turn into lightly greased 1½-quart casserole. Heat in 375° F. oven about 30 minutes. (Makes 6 to 8 servings.)

FIRESIDE BEANS

½ cup dark corn syrup	2 (1-pound) cans baked beans
1 tablespoon grated onion	½ pound Canadian bacon, sliced
1 teaspoon ground ginger	

Combine corn syrup, onion, and ginger. Spoon baked beans into 2-quart ovenproof casserole. Stir in syrup mixture. Arrange slices of Canadian bacon on top. Bake in 400° F. oven for 1 to 1½ hours, basting frequently until bacon is well glazed. (Makes 6 servings.)

GINGER-PEACHY BAKED BEANS

Follow recipe for Fireside Beans, substituting 1 (1-pound, 3-ounce) can peach halves, drained, for Canadian bacon.

VEGETABLES

Unlike meat and fish, vegetables have never been extremely popular with the young crowd or with husbands of any age. The following new recipes are sure to disguise the "sameness" and "flatness" of flavor so often complained about.

STRING BEANS PIQUANT

> 3 cups cooked or canned string beans, drained
> Sauce Piquant

Add hot sauce to beans. Bring to a boil, stirring constantly. Serve at once.

Sauce Piquant

5 slices bacon, diced	1 teaspoon salt
¼ cup light corn syrup	Pepper
¼ cup vinegar	Paprika

Fry bacon until crisp, stirring often. Add light corn syrup, vinegar, salt, and a few grains each of pepper and paprika. Bring to a boil, serve hot over vegetables. (Makes 4 to 6 servings.)

CABBAGE PIQUANT

> 1 medium head cabbage
> Sauce Piquant

Shred cabbage. Cook until tender but crisp, then drain. Add hot sauce; stir to mix well. Serve at once. (Makes 4 servings.)

WILTED LETTUCE

> 1 medium head lettuce
> Sauce Piquant

Wash lettuce, and cut in small pieces into salad bowl. Add hot sauce, and toss lightly. Serve at once. (Makes 2-3 servings.)

GLAZED VEGETABLES

Vegetables—1 pound or 4 medium onions, carrots, parsnips or sweet potatoes or 2 acorn squashes	2 tablespoons margarine ¼ cup dark corn syrup Salt Pepper

Wash and pare vegetables. Cut in halves, quarters, or slices as desired for serving. Cook in boiling salted water until tender. Drain. (Sweet potatoes can be cooked first, then pared, if desired.) Arrange cooked vegetables in a greased ovenproof casserole. Dot with margarine, then add corn syrup. Sprinkle with salt, pepper, and other seasonings as desired. Spices and herbs add flavor interest. Bake in 400° F. oven 15 minutes or until vegetables are well glazed. Baste often with syrup mixture in casserole.

To Prepare Without Pre-cooking

Arrange pieces of pared, cut-up vegetables in greased ovenproof casserole. Dot with margarine, add syrup and seasonings as above.

Cover tightly. Bake in 400° F. oven 35 to 50 minutes or until vegetables are tender. Uncover and bake 15 minutes more, basting often with syrupy mixture in casserole.

ORANGE BEETS

8 small raw beets	2 tablespoons light corn syrup
Juice of one orange	1 teaspoon salt
1 teaspoon grated orange rind	1 tablespoon margarine

Wash beets well. Peel and grate, or chop finely. (There should be about 3 cups.) Add water to orange juice to make 1 cup liquid. Mix with beets in saucepan. Stir in orange rind, syrup, salt, and margarine. Cover pan tightly; bring mixture to boil. Simmer gently 15 minutes or until beets are tender. Serve hot. (Makes 4 servings.)

SAUCY BAKED TOMATOES

6 medium tomatoes	½ teaspoon salt
⅛ teaspoon pepper	2 tablespoons margarine

Remove skins from tomatoes and cut out hard center cores. Place in baking dish and sprinkle with salt and pepper. Dot with margarine and bake in 375° F. oven 20 minutes. Meanwhile, prepare sauce and pour over hot tomatoes. Serve hot. (Makes 6 servings.)

Sauce

2 stalks celery ⎫	1 tablespoon cornstarch
½ green pepper ⎬ finely chopped	1 teaspoon salt
1 small onion ⎭	1 tablespoon lemon juice
½ cup brown sugar	1 tablespoon water
½ cup dark corn syrup	

Combine finely chopped celery, pepper, and onion with brown sugar and corn syrup. Cook over low heat 10 minutes, stirring occasionally. Mix cornstarch with salt, lemon juice and water.

Stir gradually into vegetable mixture. Cook and stir over low heat until sauce is slightly thickened and smooth. (Makes about 1 cup.)

SWISS POTATOES LUCERNE

2½ pounds potatoes, peeled	2 tablespoons margarine or butter
3 medium apples, peeled and cored	1 teaspoon salt
1 medium onion, chopped	3 tablespoons light corn syrup

Cut potatoes and apples into ¾-inch pieces and place in cold water to cover. Cook onion in margarine or butter in a skillet over low heat until tender. Drain potatoes and apples, saving ½ cup of the water. Add potatoes, apples, water, and salt to onions in skillet. Cover tightly, simmer ½ hour or until potatoes are tender. Stir once or twice during cooking. Stir in syrup, and cook, uncovered, 5 more minutes. (Makes 6 servings.)

SWEET AND SOUR GLAZED ONIONS

½ cup light corn syrup	½ teaspoon salt
¼ cup vinegar	2 (1-pound) cans small whole
¼ cup margarine	onions, drained
1 tablespoon grated orange rind	¼ cup toasted slivered almonds

Combine syrup, vinegar, margarine, grated orange rind, and salt in saucepan. Bring to boil and boil about 10 minutes, or until slightly thickened. Pour over onions in shallow baking pan. Broil 5 inches from source of heat 8 to 10 minutes. Sprinkle with toasted almonds. (Makes 6 servings.)

SQUASH TREAT

3 acorn squash	½ cup light cream
Salt	3 tablespoons brown sugar
Pepper	¼ cup margarine
½ cup dark corn syrup	

Parboil squash 15 minutes. Pare; remove seeds. Cut squash into ½-inch wedges and put into a 10 x 6 x 2-inch casserole. Season with salt and pepper. Combine syrup, light cream, and brown sugar. Pour over squash. Dot with margarine. Basting occasionally, bake in 350° F. oven for about 45 minutes or until squash is just tender. Then increase temperature to 400° F. and continue baking casserole 15 minutes. (Makes 6 servings.)

SWEET POTATO BALLS

2 (1-pound, 1-ounce) cans vacuum packed sweet potatoes
1 teaspoon salt
½ teaspoon lemon or orange rind, grated

3 tablespoons margarine, melted
⅓ cup light corn syrup
1⅓ cups flaked coconut, coarsely chopped

Drain potatoes, if necessary. Mash and beat until smooth. Add salt and grated rind. Gradually add melted margarine and syrup, beating after each addition, until fluffy. If necessary, chill until firm enough to handle. Shape into balls, using about ½ cup mixture for each. Roll in coconut. Arrange in greased baking dish. Bake in 400° F. oven 20 to 25 minutes or until coconut is lightly toasted. (Makes 8 or 9 servings.)

RICE

BOILED RICE

1 cup raw rice
2 cups cold water
½ teaspoon salt

Combine ingredients in 2-quart saucepan; cover tightly and bring to strong boil. Turn heat very low and cook 15 minutes. Do not stir or raise lid of saucepan. Remove from heat; keep tightly covered, and allow rice to steam another 10 minutes. (Makes 3 cups.)

Note: For instant rice just follow quick and easy directions on package or box.

RICE PILAFF

¼ cup corn oil	2 cups water
½ cup chopped onion	1 cup uncooked rice
¼ cup chopped green pepper	1 envelope chicken noodle soup
1 (16-ounce) can tomatoes	

Heat corn oil in saucepan. Add onion and green pepper; cook slowly until tender and lightly browned. Add tomatoes and water; bring to boil, then stir in rice and soup. Reduce heat when mixture boils again. Cover and simmer, stirring occasionally, 15 to 20 minutes, or until rice is tender. (Makes 6 servings.)

II

The Art of Frying: A Primer

Fried chicken, French-fried potatoes—indeed, anything fried, it seems, is extremely popular with active people. Therefore it is important that all frying should result in food that is perfectly browned, thoroughly cooked, and free of excess fat.

SAFETY FIRST

1. Use a pan or kettle that is well balanced and of proper depth and size.
2. Be sure that pan or container in which the oil is stored is free of moisture.
3. Keep pan handles turned away from edge of range.
4. *Never* cover while heating oil.

BASIC RULES

1. To prevent spattering: Before frying, dry potatoes, meat, fish, and other moist foods with a towel. Wipe moisture from frozen foods.
2. Cut foods into uniform pieces to cook and brown evenly.
3. Arrange foods to be coated for frying along assembly line idea. Starting at the left, place the food to be fried, then the seasoned crumbs, on waxed paper; next, place egg or milk in a shallow bowl; next, more crumbs on waxed paper; and at the right end, something to hold the coated food. Keep the fingers of the left hand dry for rolling the food in crumbs; use the right hand for dunking it in egg or milk.
4. Flour chicken, fish, or shellfish by shaking it with the seasoned flour in a clean paper bag.
5. Let coated croquettes stand for a while before frying them. This gives the crumbs a chance to adhere.
6. Dust foods with flour prior to batter dipping. Use tongs to dip food into batter and to place it in the hot oil.
7. After frying, drain food thoroughly by placing it on absorbent paper such as paper towels or unglazed brown paper.
8. Thoroughly clean frying equipment after each use. Wash it in hot, soapy water. Scour, if necessary, with steel wool or a stiff bristle brush. Rinse thoroughly and dry well. Follow

manufacturer's directions for cleaning all electrical frying equipment.

DEFINITIONS AND PROCEDURES

PAN FRYING—cooking in a pan with the addition of very little fat; just enough to keep the food from sticking; also called *pan broiling* or *sautéing* (an alternative term usually associated with such foods as onions, peppers, and mushrooms). *To pan fry,* use enough fat to cover the bottom of the pan (I prefer corn oil); thick and slightly uneven shapes like chicken or fish need about a depth of ¼ to ½ inch. Heat oil over medium heat before adding the food to be fried. To test, add a small piece of food and if it sizzles the fat is hot enough.

SHALLOW FRYING—frying in a fry-pan or skillet in fat about one inch deep. Almost anything you deep fry may be shallow fried. Southern fried chicken is always shallow fried. Electric skillets have now made shallow frying popular for many foods. *To shallow fry,* pour corn oil (or other fat) into a skillet or fry-pan to a 1-inch depth. Heat over medium heat to 375° F. on a deep-fry thermometer. Follow manufacturer's directions with an electric fry-pan.

OVEN FRYING—produces the effect of frying although it is not actually frying. It is cooking with a coating of fat in a hot (400° to 425° F.) oven. Foods most successfully oven fried are chicken and fish.

DEEP FRYING—frying in deep kettle ⅓ filled with hot fat. A frying basket for lowering foods into the oil and for draining is helpful. A long-handled fork, a slotted spoon, or tongs are handy for turning foods during frying. *To deep fry,* use a sturdy flat-bottomed kettle of adequate size, or an automatic electric deep fryer. Fill kettle ⅓ full (or follow directions for electric deep fryer) of corn oil (or other fat), thus allowing for sufficient cooking space when the food is added to the hot corn oil. For example, in a 3-quart kettle, use one quart corn oil.

For accuracy, *use a deep-fry thermometer.* Always read the thermometer at eye level or as the manufacturer directs. *Wait until the correct temperature is reached before adding the food. Maintain the frying temperature at all times.* It is a good practice to fry only one layer of food at a time. When frying croquettes, fritters, or doughnuts, keep them separated.

When frying large quantities of potatoes, it is best to use the 2-step method (*see below*). This way you fry the potatoes ahead, one layer at a time, then just before serving, brown the potatoes in much larger batches in hotter fat.

After frying, let the corn oil cool; then strain it through a strainer or funnel lined with 2 thicknesses of cheesecloth, into a clean, dry wide-mouth jar. Cover the oil and store in refrigerator for reuse in frying. Add some fresh corn oil each time the oil is used again. (Keep oil for frying fish separate to avoid giving other foods a fishy taste.)

For Deep or Shallow Frying

DIPPING BATTER—Sift together 1 cup flour, 1 teaspoon baking powder, and ½ teaspoon salt. Combine 1 slightly beaten egg, ¼ cup corn oil, and 1 cup milk. Add to dry ingredients and beat until smooth.

CORN MEAL BATTER—Sift together 1 cup flour, 1½ teaspoons baking powder, and 1 teaspoon salt. Add ½ cup corn meal. Combine 2 slightly beaten eggs, 2 tablespoons corn oil, and ¾ cup milk. Add to dry ingredients and mix until smooth.

BREAD CRUMB COATING—Coat foods to be fried with seasoned fine, dry bread crumbs. Then dip in beaten egg and coat again with the crumbs.

CHICKEN

Cut up frying chicken. Wash and dry. Coat with seasoned flour, or dust with flour and dunk in Dipping Batter or Corn Meal Batter, or coat with Bread Crumb Coating. Fry 15 to 30 minutes.

FISH AND SHELLFISH

Rinse and dry fish. Devein shrimp; clean soft-shelled crab. Leave fillets whole or cut into serving-size pieces. Dust with flour and dunk in Dipping Batter or Corn Meal Batter, or coat with Bread Crumb Coating. Fry 2 to 3 minutes.

POTATOES (1-STEP METHOD)

Wash and pare. Cut lengthwise into ½-inch strips. Soak in cold salted water 30 minutes. Drain and dry thoroughly. Fry 8 to 9 minutes.

POTATOES (2-STEP METHOD)

Wash and pare. Cut lengthwise into ½-inch strips. Soak in cold salted water 30 minutes. Drain and dry in towel. During the first frying period potatoes are cooked until tender but not brown; then they are browned during the second period. Step A may be done several hours in advance.

Step A—Fry 2 to 3 minutes until tender but not brown.

Step B—Fry 2 to 3 minutes or until brown.

VEGETABLES: (CAULIFLOWER, TOMATO, EGGPLANT, SUMMER OR ZUCCHINI SQUASH, ONIONS)

Separate cauliflower into flowerets. Cut tomato and eggplant into ½-inch slices. Cut squash and onions into ¼-inch slices. Separate onions into rings. Dust with flour, dunk in Dipping Batter or Corn Meal Batter, or coat with Bread Crumb Coating. Fry 2 to 5 minutes or until tender and brown.

FRUIT FRITTERS

Peel and cut into slices or halves, or use well-drained canned fruit. Dry, dust with flour, dunk in Dipping Batter. Fry 2 to 5 minutes.

III

SnackTime U.S.A.— Barbecue Cooking and Other Party Food

Young people are party people, and happiness is a successful bash—from the spontaneous snack party to the carefully planned formal dinner. Wherever young people assemble, they will munch, snack, sip, crunch, and nibble. So here are kicky snack foods, zippy dips, hors d'oeuvres, mile-high hoagie sandwiches, pizzas with pizzaz and a Mexican accent, frankfurters mounded up, up, and away, and barbecued everything. These fourth-meal foods can embellish the suggested party menus for everything from a beach barbecue to a backyard picnic.

HORS D'OEUVRES, DIPS, AND SNACKS

* WEE BARBECUED BACON BUNS

1 pound bacon
1½ cups Barbecue Sauce
8 miniature buns

Slowly pan fry bacon until thoroughly browned, pouring off fat as it accumulates. Add barbecue sauce. Cover and let simmer for 20 minutes, stirring occasionally. Serve on miniature buns. (Makes 4 servings.)

* Hot Barbecue Sauce

2 teaspoons Tabasco sauce
2½ cups bottled chili sauce
¾ cup cooking oil
½ cup lemon juice
2 tablespoons tarragon vinegar
1 cup chopped onion

2 garlic cloves, minced
1 tablespoon brown sugar
1 bay leaf, crumbled
1 teaspoon dry mustard
1 teaspoon salt

Combine ingredients with ½ cup water. Bring to a boil; then reduce heat and simmer for 15 minutes. Pour off surface fat and strain, using liquid only. Sauce may be kept covered in refrigerator for at least 1 week. (Makes about 4 cups.)

APPETIZER MEAT BALLS

½ cup soft bread crumbs
¼ cup milk
1 pound ground beef
1 tablespoon chopped onion
1 teaspoon salt

¼ teaspoon pepper
2 tablespoons margarine
¼ cup prepared mustard
¼ cup catsup
¼ cup dark corn syrup

Combine bread crumbs and milk. Toss lightly with ground beef, onion, salt, and pepper, mixing well. Shape into ¾-inch balls. Brown in melted margarine in skillet. Combine syrup, mustard, and catsup. Pour over meat balls. Simmer, stirring occasionally, about 10 minutes or until sauce thickens and meat balls are glazed. (Makes 4 dozen.)

*TURKEY APPETIZER BALL

1 cup cooked white meat of turkey, finely chopped
4 slices bacon, finely diced
¼ cup crumbled blue cheese

6 tablespoons dairy sour cream
Finely chopped pecans (½-lb. package)

Pan fry bacon until crisp; then drain. Combine turkey, bacon, blue cheese and sour cream. Chill. Form into ball. Roll in chopped pecans. Refrigerate until ready to serve. Serve with assorted crisp crackers. (Makes approximately 2 cups.)

SWEET AND SOUR SAUSAGES

2 (8- to 10-ounce) packages brown-and-serve sausages
2 tablespoons cornstarch
¼ cup cold water
1 (13½-ounce) can pineapple chunks, drained, with ½ cup syrup reserved

¾ cup dark corn syrup
¼ cup white vinegar
½ teaspoon salt
½ cup green pepper, cut into ½-inch squares
½ cup maraschino cherries, drained

Cut each sausage crosswise into thirds. Brown lightly in skillet. Blend cornstarch and water. Combine cornstarch mixture, pineapple syrup, corn syrup, vinegar, and salt in chafing dish or skillet. Bring to boil; simmer 5 minutes. Add sausage, pineapple chunks, green pepper, and cherries. Heat. To serve, spear chunks of food with toothpicks. (Makes enough for 10 to 15 appetizer servings.)

* CURRIED TURKEY SQUARES

8 slices cooked turkey
8 slices sandwich bread
¼ pound butter
¼ teaspoon curry powder

¼ cup shredded coconut
2 tablespoons minced onion
Chutney
Salted peanuts

Cut turkey slices into quarters. Trim crusts from bread and spread with mixture of butter, curry powder, coconut, and onion. Cut each slice of bread into quarters. Top with quarter slices of turkey. Grind or chop chutney and place about ¼ teaspoon on top of turkey. Chop peanuts and sprinkle on top of chutney. (Makes 32 appetizers.)

* BOLOGNA ROLLS

½ pound bologna, sliced thin
1 cup onion snack cracker crumbs

½ cup shredded Cheddar cheese
2 teaspoons prepared mustard

Blend all ingredients except bologna. Top each slice of bologna with approximately 1 tablespoon filling. Roll up and fasten with cocktail picks. (Makes 16 to 18 rolls.)

* TURKEY CRISPS

Bite-size pieces of roasted turkey
Bacon
Wooden food picks

For each Turkey Crisp, wrap a bite-size piece of cooked turkey meat in half a slice of bacon. Fasten with wooden pick. Bake in 400° F. oven for 12 to 15 minutes or until bacon is crisp. Drain and serve immediately. May be served with cocktail sauce.

Note: Turkey Crisps may also be prepared under the broiler instead of in the oven.

* BEEF BITS

1 (2½-ounce) jar sliced dried beef	¼ cup chopped parsley
2 (3-ounce) packages cream cheese, softened	1½ tablespoons minced onion
	1 teaspoon prepared mustard

Chop dried beef very fine and mix ⅓ of it with the remaining ingredients. Refrigerate until firm. Form into small balls and roll in the remaining dried beef. (Makes 24 appetizers.)

* HAM CUBES TO DIP OR DUNK

1 pound canned ham	2 tablespoons grated lemon rind
1 pint sour cream	1 tablespoon lemon juice
½ cup horseradish	

Cut ham in ½-inch cubes. Blend remaining ingredients. Cover serving platter with watercress sprigs. Center with bowl of dip. Place ham cubes around dip. Garnish with a few very thin slices of twisted lemon. Have cocktail picks in server on side. (Makes 2 to 3 dozen appetizers.)

* MINIATURE WIENER ROAST

1 small head green cabbage
2 (5-ounce) cans Viennese sausage

Rinse cabbage in warm water to soften outer leaves. Turn leaves back to form "petals." Cut hole in center of cabbage large enough to hold a container of canned heat. Spear each sausage with a wooden food pick and stick into the cabbage. Just before serving, light the canned heat and let each guest roast his own wiener. (Makes 14 appetizers.)

* SNACK BOWL

1 pound canned ham	1 pint midget sweet pickles
1 pound Cheddar cheese	Parsley flakes

Cut ham, cheese, and pickles in cubes. Toss together in large, flat bowl. Sprinkle with parsley. Serve for appetizers or snacks. Have food picks on side for spearing.

* TINY TURKEY SANDWICH SMORGASBORD

Spread rounds or slices of party-size rye bread with softened butter. Add thinly sliced roast turkey. Top with dollop of dairy sour cream. Garnish with salmon caviar, stuffed olive slice, beet horse-radish, slice of sweet or dill pickle, slice of hard-cooked egg, slice of radish, or cranberry relish. Finished platter should contain assortment of the above garnishes on sandwiches.

* HAM AND OLIVE DIP

(3-ounce) can deviled ham	⅛ teaspoon onion salt
1 cup sour cream	½ teaspoon horseradish
¼ cup chopped green olives	

Combine all ingredients and mix until well blended. (Makes 1½ cups.)

* TURKEY CUBES WITH CRANBERRY COINTREAU DIP

Cooked and cooled turkey meat, cubed
2 tablespoons Cointreau
1 (14-ounce) jar cranberry-orange relish

Mix Cointreau with relish. Serve turkey meat on picks with dip.

DILL DIP

½ cup mayonnaise
½ cup sour cream
1 teaspoon lemon juice
1 teaspoon grated onion or onion
   juice

½ teaspoon salt
½ teaspoon dry mustard
¼ teaspoon dill weed

Combine all ingredients. Chill. Serve as dip with shrimp, crisp
celery curls, cucumber fingers, or broiled flounder or boiled cod.
(Makes 1 cup.)

MOLDED BLUE CHEESE SPREAD

Margarine
½ cup minced parsley
¼ cup chopped nuts
1 (8-ounce) package cream cheese
¼ pound blue cheese, crumbled

½ teaspoon Worcestershire sauce
Dash cayenne
¼ teaspoon salt
¼ cup mayonnaise

Prepare a 2-cup round bowl or mold by generously brushing with
margarine. Press parsley around sides and sprinkle nuts over the
bottom. Combine cream cheese, blue cheese, Worcestershire
sauce, cayenne, and salt. Blend well. Stir in mayonnaise and mix
until well blended. Spoon gently into prepared dish. Chill. Unmold and serve with crackers. (Makes 1½ cups.)

QUICK PATE

½ pound liverwurst
¼ cup mayonnaise

½ teaspoon grated onion or onion
   juice
Dash salt and pepper

Mash liverwurst with fork. Blend with remaining ingredients.
(Makes about 1 cup.) Serve with toast or crackers.

58

Molded Pâté

Press pâté into small bowl or 10-ounce custard cup. Chill several hours, until firm. Blend 2 ounces (¼ cup) cream cheese and 2 tablespoons mayonnaise. Unmold pâté. Spread sides and top with cream cheese mixture. Chill. Garnish as desired.

CHEESE PUFFS

¼ teaspoon Worcestershire sauce
¼ cup mayonnaise
¼ cup finely grated American cheese

Dash dry mustard
1 egg white, stiffly beaten
12 toast rounds or squares

Combine mayonnaise, cheese, Worcestershire sauce, and mustard. Fold into beaten egg white. Lightly spoon onto toast rounds or squares. Place on ungreased cookie sheet. Bake in 350° F. oven 10 to 15 minutes or until puffy and golden brown. Serve hot. (Makes about 12.)

DEVILED EGGS

6 hard-cooked eggs, halved lengthwise
¼ cup mayonnaise
1 teaspoon vinegar

½ teaspoon Worcestershire sauce
¼ teaspoon dry mustard
Paprika

Remove egg yolks and mash. Mix with remaining ingredients until light and blended. Spoon into egg-white halves. Refrigerate until ready to serve. Sprinkle with paprika. (Makes 12 halves.)

GUACAMOLE

1 large avocado, peeled and seed removed
1 tablespoon lemon juice
⅓ cup mayonnaise

2 teaspoons grated onion or onion juice
Dash Tabasco sauce

Mash avocado with fork; add lemon juice. Mix in remaining ingredients well. Chill. (Makes about 1½ cups.) Serve as dip with corn chips.

(In Mexico Guacamole is also used as a salad dressing)

* PICKLE-O-RELISH

½ cup sliced stuffed olives   1 medium onion chopped
½ cup sweet pickles, diced   ¼ cup pickle juice

In bowl combine sliced olives, pickles, and onion. Pour pickle juice (drained from pickles) over mixture and toss lightly. Cover and refrigerate for several hours before serving. (Makes 1½ cups.)

* TACO PIZZA

1 (12½-ounce) package pizza mix   1 medium tomato, peeled and
1 (15½-ounce) can chili with   diced
   beans   1 cup freshly shredded Cheddar
¼ cup finely chopped onion   cheese
½ head lettuce, finely shredded   1 small avocado, peeled and sliced
   (about 4 cups)

Prepare pizza dough according to package directions. Spread on well-oiled jelly-roll pan or regular pizza pan to form a very thin layer. Spread chili evenly over dough. Top with pizza sauce (contained in pizza package). Bake in 425° F. oven for 20 minutes or until crust is golden brown. Remove from oven and top immediately with chopped onion, shredded lettuce, diced tomatoes, shredded Cheddar cheese, and avocado. Cut into pieces and serve immediately. (Makes 12 servings.)

CHEESE FONDUE DIP

½ cup milk   1 cup mayonnaise
¼ cup dry white wine   2 cups shredded Cheddar cheese
½ teaspoon Worcestershire sauce   French bread, cut into bite-size
¼ teaspoon dry mustard   pieces
Dash white pepper

60

Mix together milk, wine, Worcestershire sauce, mustard, pepper, mayonnaise, and cheese in 2-quart saucepan. Cook over low heat, stirring occasionally, about 20 minutes or until cheese is melted and mixture is hot. Pour into fondue pot or chafing dish. To serve: place chunks of French bread on fondue forks or on wooden picks and dip in Cheese Fondue Dip. (Makes 2 cups.)

CHEESE FONDUE DIP WITH MILK

Prepare Cheese Fondue Dip as directed, using ¾ cup milk and omitting wine.

* PAUL BUNYAN SANDWICHES

¼ cup butter	2 teaspoons salt
1 cup finely chopped onion	⅛ teaspoon pepper
1 cup finely chopped green pepper	1 teaspoon poultry seasoning
2 pounds ground beef chuck	1 teaspoon Tabasco sauce
1 cup chopped pitted ripe olives	1 teaspoon chili powder
2 (6-ounce) cans tomato paste	2 teaspoons Worcestershire sauce

Cook onion and green pepper in butter until onion is clear. Add beef and cook until meat is well browned. Add remaining ingredients and simmer, uncovered, for about 15 minutes or until flavors are blended. Serve at once over toasted hamburger buns.

Alternate Method

Allow mixture to cool. Spoon onto buttered bun halves, top with remaining halves, and wrap buns in aluminum foil, sealing ends well. Refrigerate foil-wrapped buns until ready to use and then heat in 375° F. oven for about 15 minutes before serving. (Makes 10 to 12 sandwiches.)

* DEVILED DRUMSTICKS

12 chicken drumsticks	½ teaspoon pepper
1 teaspoon salt	2 tablespoons lemon juice
1 teaspoon dry mustard	Corn-flake crumbs or cracker meal
2 tablespoons maple syrup	12 slices bacon
1 teaspoon salt	

Place drumsticks in large pan with one teaspoon salt and enough water to cover. Bring to a boil. Turn heat low and simmer for ½ hour. Cool slightly. Mix next five ingredients and brush over drumsticks. Roll in cracker meal or corn-flake crumbs. Arrange in baking dish. Wrap a slice of bacon around each drumstick. Place on rack in baking pan and bake in 400° F. oven 15 to 20 minutes or until bacon is brown. (Makes 12 servings.)

* SALAMI-SLAW RELISH

8 slices Genoa salami, cut into ¼-inch strips	1 teaspoon minced onion
	¼ teaspoon sugar
1 medium-size head crisp green cabbage, finely shredded	½ teaspoon salt
	2 teaspoons tarragon vinegar
⅓ cup chopped celery	1 teaspoon celery seeds
½ cup dairy sour cream	

In large bowl, combine cabbage and celery. In small bowl, combine sour cream, minced onion, sugar, salt, celery seeds, and vinegar. Pour sour cream dressing over cabbage mixture; toss lightly until cabbage is well coated. Add salami strips and mix again, lightly. (Makes 8 to 10 servings.)

SNACKS WITH FOREIGN FLAVORS

HEIDELBURGERS

1 pound pork sausage	4 Kaiser rolls
1 large apple	4 lettuce leaves
1 tablespoon butter	1 (4-ounce) can sauerkraut
1 tablespoon brown sugar	

Divide the pound of pork sausage into 4 patties. Pan fry for 20 minutes until browned on both sides. Meanwhile, core and slice an apple into (¼-inch) slices. Melt the butter in another pan and add the brown sugar. Glaze the apple slices in this mixture until tender. Assemble the sandwich by first slicing the Kaiser roll and placing a lettuce leaf at the base. Next add the browned sausage patty followed by the glazed apple slice and topped with a spoonful of sauerkraut. Serve immediately. (Makes 4 servings.)

* ITALIAN FRIED SANDWICH

Genoa salami	1 egg, well beaten
Mozzarella cheese	3 tablespoons milk
White bread	

Make sandwiches with slices of salami and cheese. Press slices of bread firmly together. Dip sandwiches into mixture of egg and milk. Pan fry in small amount of butter until sandwich is browned on each side.

* YARD-LONG RIVIERA HAM LOAF

2 (3-ounce) cans deviled ham	1 package (1 cup) shredded
1 loaf French bread	Cheddar cheese
¼ cup butter or margarine	¼ cup minced onion
2 tablespoons prepared mustard	Dill pickles

Cut French bread into ¾-inch slices down to, but not through, bottom crust. Cream together butter and mustard until light and fluffy and spread between bread slices. Spread alternate slices with deviled ham and sprinkle shredded cheese on remaining slices. Spoon chopped onion onto the deviled ham and insert thin slices of dill pickle into the cheese. Wrap loaf in aluminum foil and heat in 400° F. oven for 12 to 15 minutes or until bread is hot and cheese is melted. (Makes 6 to 8 servings.)

* MEAT LOAF CIRCLES, PIZZA STYLE

1 pound ground chuck	1 teaspoon salt
½ cup fine bread crumbs	⅛ teaspoon pepper
½ cup water	1 cup canned tomato sauce
¼ cup minced onion	½ cup shredded Mozzarella cheese
2 tablespoons Parmesan cheese	½ teaspoon oregano
1 egg	Sliced mushrooms and olives

Mix crumbs and water in bowl. Add beef, onion, Parmesan cheese, egg, salt, and pepper. Mix and pat into 2 pie pans. Bake in a 375° F. oven for 20 minutes. Remove from oven and spread half of tomato sauce over top of each meat circle. Sprinkle with Mozzarella cheese and oregano. Garnish with sliced olives and mushrooms. Return to oven for 5 minutes or until cheese is bubbling hot. Loosen meat circles from pie pans with spatula and slide onto bottom half of flat, round loaf of bread. Cut in wedges, and serve with sliced French bread. (Makes 6 servings.)

* SAUSAGE GONDOLAS

Sausage	Tomato sauce
Toasted frank buns	Shredded Cheddar cheese

Spread split toasted frank buns with tomato sauce. Cover with thin lengthwise slices of sausage. Top with shredded cheese and broil sandwich until cheese melts. Serve hot.

64

* VIENNESE OMELET BUNS

Hard salami, cubed
Egg mixture for omelet

Add cubed salami to egg mixture. When cooked, serve omelet on toasted sandwich buns.

BARBECUED EVERYTHING SUGGESTIONS— IN OR OUT OF DOORS

BARBECUED SPARERIBS

½ cup pineapple juice
½ cup dark corn syrup
2 tablespoons soy sauce

1 teaspoon salt
3 pounds spareribs, cut into 2- or 3-rib portions

Combine pineapple juice, syrup, soy sauce, and salt in large, shallow dish. Add spareribs and let marinate about 1 hour, turning occasionally. Roast ribs on rack in roasting pan in 350° F. oven 1½ hours or until meat is tender. Turn several times and brush with marinade. (Makes 4 servings.)

To Grill

Bake in oven about 1 hour; then remove to grill and cook about ½ hour longer or until meat is tender. Turn several times and brush with marinade. (Makes 4 servings.)

SHORTCUT BARBECUED CHICKEN

Broiler-fryer chickens
Bottled French dressing
Corn oil

Allow ½ chicken per serving. Halve, quarter, or cut chicken into parts. With halves or quarters, hook wing tip behind shoulder joint onto back. Pour French dressing over chicken. Cover, place in refrigerator, and let marinate in dressing about 1 hour. Adjust grill so that it is at least 6 inches from coals. Brush grill with corn oil. Place chicken skin-side-up on grill. Cook slowly until tender, turning frequently to brown and cook evenly. Brush frequently with French dressing.

GRILLED FISH

Fish fillets, steaks, or whole fish
Corn oil
Sliced onions ⎱
Butter or margarine ⎰ for whole fish only

Use a hinged grill or basket to make turning easy. Brush fillets and steaks with corn oil. Place in hinged grill and grill, turning frequently, about 3 to 5 minutes or until fish flakes easily when tested with a fork. Allow ½ pound fillet or steak per serving. With large whole fish, fill cavity with sliced onions and dot with butter or margarine. Brush with corn oil and place in hinged wire grill. (Do not clamp grill.) Grill, turning frequently, until fish flakes easily, about 30 to 45 minutes for a 5-pound fish. A 5-pound fish serves 6.

FISH BARBECUE SAUCE

½ cup olive oil
1 clove garlic
¼ teaspoon salt

½ teaspoon Tabasco sauce
3 tablespoons lemon juice

Soak garlic in oil overnight. Combine remaining ingredients and mix well. Baste fish with sauce liberally as it broils. (Makes ½ cup sauce.)

ALL-PURPOSE BARBECUE SAUCE

(This sauce may be used to baste hamburgers, chickens, steak, etc. before and during grilling.)

1 medium onion, chopped
⅓ cup corn oil
½ cup dark corn syrup
½ cup catsup
½ cup water

⅓ cup vinegar
2 tablespoons prepared mustard
2 tablespoons Worcestershire sauce
2 teaspoons salt
½ teaspoon pepper

Heat corn oil in skillet. Add onion and cook over low heat, stirring frequently, until tender. Add remaining ingredients. Simmer 15 minutes, stirring occasionally. (Makes about 2½ cups.)

SHASHLIK

3 pounds leg or shoulder of lamb,
    cut in 1-inch cubes
6 tomatoes, sliced
4 large onions, sliced
18 mushroom caps
¾ pound bacon
½ teaspoon pepper

½ cup corn oil
¼ cup lemon juice
3 tablespoons onion juice
1 teaspoon salt
1 clove garlic
¼ teaspoon mace

Combine oil, seasonings, and lemon juice, and marinate meat cubes and vegetables for about 4 hours in a cool place. Place meat, vegetables, and bacon (folded over twice) alternately on skewers. Broil, turning skewers frequently to allow even browning, until meat is done and tender to the fork. (Makes 6 to 8 servings.)

SHRIMP-ON-A-SKEWER

Peeled shrimp
Soy sauce

Pineapple wedges
Bacon

Marinate shrimp in soy sauce overnight. Drain and skewer with alternate wedges of pineapple and bacon (folded over twice). Broil over coals.

GRILLED SALMON STEAKS FOR SUMMER SUNDAY SUPPER

Salmon steaks	Salt
Lemon juice	Pepper
Flour	

Brush each side of steak with lemon juice, cover loosely with waxed paper, and refrigerate for about an hour. Dust with flour, salt, and pepper and grill until done.

BACKYARD LONDON BROIL

2½-inch sirloin steak
Melted butter or All-Purpose Barbecue Sauce

Broil steak over the coals. Serve in ½ inch slices, and top with melted butter or All-Purpose Barbecue Sauce.

CHICKEN LIVERS ON SKEWERS

24 chicken livers	Mushrooms
8 slices bacon	Bread crumbs
Salt	Melted butter
Pepper	Lemon juice
Olive oil	Chopped parsley

Clean, wash, and dry chicken livers. Season with a sprinkle of salt and pepper. Cut livers in half. Broil bacon slices 1 minute on each side and cut each slice into 6 pieces. Alternately spear liver slice, mushroom, and bacon on skewers. (Should cover 8 skewers.) Roll in oil, dip in bread crumbs, and broil over coals. Arrange on warm dish and top with mixture of melted butter, lemon juice, and chopped parsley.

HASTY SOFT-SHELLED CRAB

6 soft-shelled crabs
Melted butter
Lemon juice
Salt

Pepper
Cayenne
Bread crumbs

Dip crabs in butter and season with lemon juice, salt, pepper, and cayenne. Roll in bread crumbs and place on grill over coals. Broil 10 to 15 minutes.

OUTDOOR GRILLED LOBSTER TAILS

Frozen or fresh lobster tails
Butter
Salt

Pepper
Lemon juice
Chopped parsley

Dot lobster tails with butter, season with salt and pepper, and broil shell-side-down until shell browns. Turn and brown meaty side. Baste frequently with melted butter and serve with lemon juice, chopped parsley, and melted butter mixture.

GRILLED CORN-ON-THE-COB

Corn-on-the-cob
Butter
Salt

Husk corn. Spread with soft butter and sprinkle with salt. Roll loosely in foil without sealing (so corn will roast, not steam), and twist the ends. Grill 15 to 20 minutes or until tender. Turn frequently.

INDIAN STYLE ROAST CORN

> Corn-on-the-cob
> Heavily salted water
> Butter

Turn back husks and strip off silk. Dip in salted water. Draw husks back up and lay cobs on top of coals. Cook 8 to 10 minutes, turning frequently to prevent burning. Husks are dry and brown when done. Break off husks with barbecue glove and serve with butter.

VEGETABLE KEBABS

Sliced bacon
Cooked white potatoes
Cooked sweet potatoes
Small cooked onions
Whole mushrooms

Small whole cherry tomatoes
Salt
Pepper
Melted butter

Cut potatoes and bacon into 1-inch pieces. Pierce vegetables and bacon alternately on skewers. Sprinkle with salt and pepper and dip into melted butter. Brown, turning skewers to cook all sides evenly.

FRUIT KEBABS

Apples
Bananas
Pineapple chunks (fresh or canned)

Whole canned apricots
Melted butter

Cut apples into 1-inch chunks, and peel bananas into 1-inch pieces. Remove pits from apricots. Thread fruit alternately on skewers, repeating pattern until skewer is filled. Brush with melted butter and brown quickly and carefully, turning frequently to toast fruit evenly.

HONEY-CURED BANANAS

Bananas
Honey

Make a 3-inch-long shallow slit in banana skin (leaving peel on banana). Force 1 tablespoon of honey into the opening and let stand for about an hour. Place on grill and cook 8 minutes, turning frequently.

PARTY IDEAS

JULY 4TH VAGABOND PICNIC

Print invitations, complete with RSVP, with felt-tipped pen or marker on inflated red, white, and blue balloons. Deflate balloons and mail.

MENU

MELON IN SEASON

CHICKEN ALMOND SANDWICHES

CHEESE AND PIMIENTO SANDWICHES

CASSEROLE SALAD

POTATO CHIPS

ICE CREAM CONES

SODA

CHICKEN ALMOND SANDWICHES

1½ cups finely chopped chicken	Salt
3 tablespoons slivered almonds	Pepper
⅓ cup mayonnaise	12 slices white bread

Mix chicken and almonds. Stir in mayonnaise, salt, and pepper. Spread on 6 slices bread. Top with remaining slices, and cut diagonally in triangles. (Makes 12 sandwiches.)

CHEESE AND PIMIENTO SANDWICHES

1 cup firmly packed shredded Cheddar cheese	1 pimiento, finely chopped
3 tablespoons mayonnaise	12 slices whole wheat bread

Blend cheese, mayonnaise, and pimiento together. Spread on 6 slices of bread. Top with remaining slices, and cut in half. (Makes 12 sandwiches.)

CASSEROLE SALAD

½ cup corn oil	½ cup sliced celery
3 tablespoons lemon juice	2 cooked potatoes, diced
1 tablespoon sugar	½ cup finely chopped onion
1 teaspoon salt	1 cup diced bologna
¼ teaspoon pepper	¼ cup Swiss cheese, cut into strips
¼ teaspoon dry mustard	2 tomatoes, cut into wedges
2 tablespoons catsup	1 quart bite-size salad greens
1 green pepper, cut into strips	

In a large jar with a screw top, combine first 7 ingredients. Shake well to blend. Add green pepper strips, celery, potatoes, onion, and bologna. Cover and chill. In order given, place remaining ingredients in a large bowl or casserole. Cover and chill. At serving time pour dressing mixture over greens in bowl, and toss to mix thoroughly. (Makes 4 to 6 servings.)

BEACH OR POOL PARTY

Start the fire, and allow plenty of time for swimming and water games.

MENU

DUNKER'S DIP AND POTATO CHIPS

GRILLED ONIONY HAMBURGERS (SEE P. 17)

PICKLES

CORN-ON-COB ROASTED INDIAN STYLE (SEE P. 69)

COLE SLAW

FROSTED BROWNIES

SIMPLE PARTY PUNCH (SEE P. 194)

DUNKER'S DIP

1 pound cottage cheese
½ cup milk

1 envelope smoky green pea soup
6 stuffed olives, chopped

Blend cottage cheese and milk. Fold in soup and olives. Chill at least 3 or 4 hours. Serve with potato chips. (Makes 2½ cups dip.)

COLE SLAW

1 (3-pound) head of cabbage
¾ cup mayonnaise
¼ cup vinegar
½ green pepper, finely chopped

2 teaspoons sugar
1 teaspoon salt
Freshly ground pepper

Shred cabbage. Combine mayonnaise, vinegar, green pepper, sugar, and salt. Mix with cabbage. Pepper to taste. Cover and refrigerate until serving time. Carry to picnic in insulated container. (Makes 12 servings.)

FROSTED BROWNIES

Prepare 2 batches of brownies in 8- or 9-inch pans using a mix or favorite recipe. When cool, frost with a blended mixture of ⅔ cup chocolate-flavored syrup and ½ cup chunk-style peanut butter.

PORCH SMORGASBORD

For a Swedish touch to the buffet table, use a blue-and-yellow color scheme. Light the table with a profusion of candles. Provide plenty of plates so that guests can make several trips to the table, taking a fresh plate for each course so as not to mix hot and cold foods.

MENU

COLD PEA SOUP

SARDINES AND ANCHOVIES

SWEDISH RYE BREAD

CHICKEN SALAD

MARINATED VEGETABLES

BREAD AND BUTTER PICKLES

SWEDISH MEATBALLS

BOILED NEW POTATOES

CHEESE AND CRACKERS

RASPBERRIES AND CREAM

LACE WAFERS (SEE P. 239)

COFFEE, TEA, MILK

COLD PEA SOUP

2 envelopes smoky green pea soup
6 cups water

½ teaspoon onion juice
1 cup light cream

Mix dry soup with water, and prepare according to directions on envelope. Press through a strainer; chill 12 hours. Just before serving, add onion juice and light cream. (Makes 12 demi-tasse-cup servings.)

CHICKEN SALAD

1 cup mayonnaise
4 ounces cream cheese, softened
6 tablespoons milk
Dash hot pepper sauce
6 cups diced cooked chicken

1 cup finely diced celery
1 cup small stuffed olives, halved
Salt
Pepper

Blend mayonnaise, cream cheese, milk, and hot pepper sauce. Chill. Toss chicken, celery, and olives with mayonnaise mixture. Season to taste with salt and pepper. Chill. (Makes 10 to 12 servings.)

MARINATED VEGETABLES

2 bunches carrots, cut in strips and cooked
2 pounds asparagus, cleaned and cooked
2 pounds green beans, cooked
2 (17-ounce) cans sliced beets, drained
⅔ cup vegetable cooking liquid
2 tablespoons finely chopped scallions

2 tablespoons finely chopped green pepper
2 tablespoons finely chopped pimiento
1½ cups corn oil
¾ cup vinegar
2 tablespoons sugar
2 teaspoons salt
¼ teaspoon pepper

Arrange carrots, asparagus, beans, and beets in large, shallow dish or pan. Combine cooking liquid, scallions, green pepper, pimiento, corn oil, vinegar, sugar, salt, and pepper. Pour over vegetables. Cover; marinate in refrigerator at least 3 hours, basting occasionally. Remove vegetables and arrange on large platter. (Makes 12 servings.)

SWEDISH MEATBALLS

5 tablespoons corn oil	2⅓ cups water
¾ cup finely chopped onion	2 eggs
1½ pounds ground beef	2 teaspoons salt
¾ pound ground pork	¼ teaspoon pepper
1½ cups cold mashed potatoes	2 envelopes cream of mushroom
⅓ cup fine dry bread crumbs	soup
¾ cup cream	2 cups milk

Heat 2 tablespoons of the corn oil in skillet; add onion; cook over low heat, stirring frequently, until golden. Combine onion, beef, pork, potatoes, bread crumbs, cream, ⅓ cup of the water, eggs, salt, and pepper. Lightly mix; shape into 1½-inch balls. Heat remaining 3 tablespoons corn oil in large skillet; cook meatballs, 1 layer at a time, until well browned. Remove meatballs; pour off fat. Pour in 1 cup water; cook, stirring constantly, until blended. Mix remaining cup water with soup. Stir into skillet; mix in milk. Cook, stirring until thickened. Add meatballs, heat. (Makes 10 to 12 servings.)

BACKYARD PICNIC

Celebrate a holiday or any glorious occasion with a bang-up backyard classic picnic complete with kid games like Tug of War, Three-Legged Race, and Kick the Can.

76

MENU

PINEAPPLE BAKED HAM AND/OR FRIED CHICKEN (SEE P. 49)

MACARONI AND/OR POTATO SALAD (SEE PP. 119, 121)

GARDEN TOMATOES

DEVILED EGGS (SEE P. 58)

PICKLED BEETS

SOFT ROLLS AND BUTTER

DO-IT-YOURSELF STRAWBERRY SHORTCAKE

LEMONADE SPECIAL (SEE P. 195)

ICED TEA

PINEAPPLE BAKED HAM

1 (13-pound) ready-to-eat ham
1 cup dark corn syrup
1 teaspoon grated orange rind
1½ teaspoons dry mustard

1 (1-pound, 4-ounce) can crushed
  pineapple
Maraschino cherry halves
Whole cloves

Trim ham and place with fat side up on rack in roasting pan. Heat in 325° F. oven about 1¼ hours. Meanwhile, combine syrup, orange rind, mustard, and pineapple. Remove ham from oven, score fat, and brush ham with some of the syrup mixture. Bake, basting often, 45 minutes or until ham is well glazed and heated through. Remove from oven. Stick cloves through centers of cherry halves; insert one in each square scored on ham. Bake 10 minutes longer, basting several times. Serve extra sauce with ham. (25 servings.)

STRAWBERRY SHORTCAKE

Split biscuits
Sliced sugared strawberries
Whipped or pouring cream

Bring out makings for strawberry shortcakes, and let each guest fix his own.

ORIENTAL BARBECUE

Turn your backyard into a Japanese garden by hanging Japanese lanterns on bamboo fishing poles stuck in the ground. Seat your guests at a low table covered with inexpensive woven mats. Try your hand at an Oriental flower arrangement, or use Chinese water flowers. And don't forget the chopsticks—they're half the fun of eating Oriental-style.

MENU

EGG ROLLS

BEEF TERIYAKI (SEE P. 25)

RICE

GREEN BEANS WITH WATER CHESTNUTS

LEMON SHERBET (SEE P. 265)

LITTLE PASTRIES

TEA

EGG ROLLS

(Make one day in advance. Chill. Reheat in 400° F. oven, or in skillet on grill.)

1 cup sifted flour	¼ cup minced bamboo shoots
1 cup water	1 tablespoon minced onion
3 eggs	2 tablespoons corn oil
1 cup minced celery	Dash pepper
1 cup minced cooked shrimp	Corn oil
¼ cup minced water chestnuts	

1. Hold first chopstick in hand in a fixed position.

2. Hold.second chopstick like a pencil above first.

3. Pick up food by moving second chopstick to meet first.

How to use chopsticks

Combine flour, water, and 2 of the eggs. Beat 5 minutes; let set about 15 minutes. Mix celery, shrimp, water chestnuts, bamboo shoots, onion, 2 tablespoons corn oil, and pepper. Heat a heavy 8-inch skillet until drops of water bounce on it. Brush skillet with corn oil. Pour 2 tablespoons batter into skillet, tilting skillet so batter spreads evenly. Batter sets quickly. Cook until batter sets and edges curl slightly. Turn out onto dry dish towel. Continue preparing skins, brushing skillet with corn oil before cooking each skin. Put about 2 tablespoons shrimp mixture in center of each skin. Brush edges with remaining egg, beaten slightly. Fold nearest edge over filling; then fold sides in about 1 inch. Roll skin away from you; seal with beaten egg. Fill deep skillet ⅓ full with corn oil; heat to 375° F. Fry egg rolls, a few at a time, turning as needed until lightly browned on all sides, for about 8 minutes. Drain on absorbent paper. (Makes about 10.)

GREEN BEANS WITH WATER CHESTNUTS

1 tablespoon corn oil
3 cups diagonally sliced green
    beans
1 (5-ounce) can water chestnuts,
    sliced

1 scallion, sliced
¼ teaspoon salt
⅛ teaspoon pepper
1 tablespoon sherry or water
1 teaspoon sugar

Heat corn oil in large skillet on a grill until very hot. Add beans, water chestnuts, and scallion; cook about 3 minutes. Add salt, pepper, sherry, and sugar. Cover; cook 8 to 10 minutes, shaking pan occasionally. (Makes 6 servings.)

LITTLE PASTRIES

1 cup sifted flour
½ teaspoon salt
¼ cup sesame seeds
2 tablespoons brown sugar

¼ cup water
2 tablespoons corn oil
Peanut butter
Corn oil, for frying

Combine flour, salt, and sesame seeds in a mixing bowl. Bring sugar and water to boil over low heat, stirring until sugar is dissolved. Remove from heat; add 2 tablespoons corn oil. Add all at once to flour mixture; stir to blend. Shape into 15 small balls; cover with a damp cloth. Roll each ball of dough into a paper-thin circle; spread center generously with peanut butter. Moisten edges with water; fold over and seal edges with a fork. Fill deep skillet ⅓ full with corn oil; heat to 375° F. Fry pastries in hot oil about 3 minutes or until golden, turning once to brown both sides. (Makes 15.)

DINNER AT EIGHT ON THE PATIO

For state occasions plan a super-elegant and romantic patio dinner. To dine in style, set the patio table as carefully as your dining room table with white tablecloth and colorful cloth napkins, your best flatware and china. Arrange pots of red geraniums in the center of the table and replace them after dark with an oil-burning lamp or candles. For a real fairyland look, set flares around the edge of the patio.

MENU

SHRIMP PIQUANT

CHARCOAL GRILLED STEAK

MIXED VEGETABLE SOUFFLE SALAD

ONION BREAD

SLICED CHILLED WATERMELON TOPPED WITH BLUEBERRIES

GRAHAM CRACKER CRUNCHES

COFFEE, TEA, MILK

SHRIMP PIQUANT

2 pounds shrimp, cleaned and
   cooked
½ cup corn oil
½ cup lemon juice

1 teaspoon salt
⅛ teaspoon pepper
¼ teaspoon garlic salt
¼ teaspoon hot pepper sauce

Place shrimp in a dish. Combine remaining ingredients; pour over shrimp. Cover, refrigerate several hours, stirring once or twice. There are 45 to 50 medium shrimp in 2 pounds.

MIXED VEGETABLE SOUFFLE SALAD

1 cup hot water
1 (3-ounce) package lemon-
   flavored gelatin
½ cup cold water
4½ teaspoons vinegar
½ cup mayonnaise
¼ teaspoon salt
Dash pepper

⅓ cup shredded carrot
⅓ cup sliced radishes
⅓ cup diced celery
⅓ cup chopped greens (watercress,
   spinach, romaine, endive, or
   escarole)
2 tablespoons diced green pepper
1 tablespoon finely chopped onion

Pour hot water over gelatin in bowl; stir until gelatin is completely dissolved. Add cold water, vinegar, mayonnaise, salt, and pepper; blend with rotary beater. Pour into metal loaf pan. Chill in freezing unit until firm about 1 inch from edge of pan but still soft in center. Turn mixture into bowl and beat with rotary beater until fluffy and thick. Fold in vegetables. Pour into 1-quart mold or individual molds. Chill in refrigerator (not freezing unit) until firm. Unmold. (Makes 4 to 6 servings.)

ONION BREAD

2 (about 15-inch) loaves French bread
1 envelope golden onion soup mix
⅔ cup margarine

Cut bread into diagonal slices from top almost through to bottom crust. Blend margarine and powdered soup. Spread on cut surfaces of bread. Wrap loaves in aluminum foil. Heat on grill, or in 375° F. oven about 15 minutes or until hot. (Makes about 16 servings.)

GRAHAM CRACKER CRUNCHES

1¼ cups graham cracker crumbs
¼ cup sugar
½ teaspoon cinnamon
½ teaspoon nutmeg

½ cup peanut butter
⅓ cup light or dark corn syrup
Confectioners' sugar

Combine crumbs, sugar, cinnamon, and nutmeg. Stir in peanut butter and syrup, blending well. Roll into ½-inch balls. Chill. Roll in confectioners' sugar. (Makes about 2½ dozen.)

HOT BREADS, WAFFLES, AND
OTHER BRUNCHTIME FAVORITES

NUT TOAST

⅓ cup light corn syrup
⅓ cup firmly packed brown sugar
¼ cup margarine
⅛ teaspoon salt
½ teaspoon vanilla or imitation
  maple flavoring

1 cup ready-to-eat cereal flakes
  (any kind)
¼ cup chopped nuts
6 toast slices

Combine syrup, brown sugar, margarine, and salt in saucepan. Cook over medium heat, stirring constantly, until mixture comes to a boil and boils 1 minute. Remove from heat. Add flavoring. Fold in cereal and nuts. Arrange toast slices on cookie sheet. Spread evenly with cereal-nut mixture. Broil about 1 minute or until topping melts into toast slightly. Serve immediately. (Makes 6 servings.)

ORANGE CRUMB FRENCH TOAST

2 eggs
¼ teaspoon salt
⅔ cup orange juice
8 bread slices
¾ cup fine dry bread crumbs

3 tablespoons margarine
1 cup light corn syrup
1 teaspoon grated orange rind
¼ cup orange juice

Beat eggs, salt, and ⅔ cup juice together well. Dip bread slices into mixture, then into bread crumbs, coating evenly on both sides. Melt some margarine on hot griddle or in skillet; brown bread on both sides, adding margarine as needed. Meanwhile, combine syrup, grated orange rind, and ¼ cup juice in saucepan. Simmer 5 minutes. Serve French Toast with hot orange syrup and additional margarine. (Makes 4 servings.)

STICKY CINNAMON BUNS ⚹

½ cup dark corn syrup
2 tablespoons melted margarine
¼ cup brown sugar, firmly packed
1 package yeast roll mix

2 tablespoons melted margarine
2 tablespoons sugar
2 teaspoons cinnamon

Mix first three ingredients in large skillet, and spread to cover bottom. Prepare yeast roll mix by package directions and let rise. Roll dough into rectangle ⅛ inch thick; spread with mixture of margarine, sugar, and cinnamon. Roll as for jelly roll, cut into 12 slices, and place, cut-side-up, in skillet. Cover, let rise double in bulk. Bake in 375° F. oven 35 to 40 minutes. Invert pan immediately. Shake to remove rolls. Serve rolls hot.

QUICK AND EASY CINNAMON BUNS

2 tablespoons margarine
1 can (10) refrigerated pan-ready biscuits
¼ cup firmly packed brown sugar

¼ teaspoon cinnamon
¼ cup light corn syrup
¼ cup chopped nuts

Melt margarine in 1 (8-inch) layer cake pan. Snip biscuits into quarters with scissors. Scatter in pan of melted margarine. Roll pieces with fork to coat completely. Blend sugar and cinnamon in small saucepan. Add syrup. Stir over low heat just until sugar is melted. Stir in nuts. Drizzle over biscuit pieces. Bake in 400° F. oven or about 15 minutes until biscuits are well browned. Let stand 5 minutes; then invert on serving plate and remove from pan. To serve, break apart with 2 forks. (Makes 40.)

GRAHAM MUFFINS

1½ cups (18) graham crackers, finely crushed
2 teaspoons baking powder
½ cup milk

⅓ cup margarine, melted
¼ cup dark corn syrup
1 egg, beaten
½ cup chopped pecans

Stir all ingredients together, mixing well. (Batter will be thick.) Spoon into 12 paper-lined 2½ x 1¼-inch muffin cups, filling each ⅔ full. Bake in 375° F. oven about 20 minutes or until muffins test done. (Makes 12.)

SPICY APPLE PANCAKES WITH CARAMEL SYRUP

1½ cups pancake mix
1 medium apple, pared and finely chopped (about 1 cup)
½ teaspoon cinnamon
1 egg, well beaten

¾ cup milk
¼ cup light corn syrup
1 tablespoon corn oil
1 recipe caramel syrup

Combine pancake mix, chopped apple, and cinnamon in mixing bowl. Blend egg, milk, syrup, and corn oil. Stir into dry ingredients, blending well. Pour onto lightly greased skillet, spreading thin. Cook, turning once, until lightly browned on both sides. Serve with caramel syrup. (Makes 20 [3-inch] pancakes.)

Caramel Syrup

½ cup dark corn syrup
3 tablespoons evaporated milk or light cream

1 teaspoon margarine
¼ teaspoon vanilla

Combine syrup, milk or cream, and margarine in saucepan. Bring to boil. Remove from heat and add vanilla. (Makes about ¾ cup.)

APRICOT SNACK LOAF

½ cup chopped dried apricots
2 cups sifted flour
2½ teaspoons baking powder
1 teaspoon salt
½ cup chopped nuts

¼ cup margarine
½ cup sugar
1 egg, beaten
⅓ cup light corn syrup
⅓ cup orange juice

Soak apricots in hot water 15 minutes; drain. Sift flour, baking powder, and salt together into mixing bowl. Add nuts and drained apricots. Set aside. Cream margarine and sugar; blend in egg, syrup, and orange juice. Stir into flour mixture, mixing well. Turn into greased 8½ x 4½ x 2½-inch loaf pan. Bake in 350° F. oven for 60 to 70 minutes or until loaf tests done. Cool in pan 10 minutes before removing. Cool completely before slicing. (Makes 1 loaf.)

WALNUT SWIRL LOAF

Dough

½ cup milk	1 egg, slightly beaten
¼ cup margarine	⅓ cup sugar
1 package active dry yeast or 1 cake compressed yeast	1 teaspoon salt
	2½ cups sifted flour
3 tablespoons warm water (105° to 115° F.)	

Scald milk; stir in margarine. Cool to lukewarm. Sprinkle or crumble yeast into warm water, and stir until dissolved. Combine egg, sugar, and salt in mixing bowl. Stir in milk mixture, then yeast. Gradually add enough flour to form a soft dough; beat well. Grease top; cover. Let rise in warm place, free from draft, about 45 minutes or until doubled in bulk.

Filling

⅓ cup milk	1 cup finely ground walnuts
⅓ cup light corn syrup	½ teaspoon cinnamon
1 egg, slightly beaten	

(Prepare while dough is rising.) Scald milk. Combine syrup and beaten egg. Add to hot milk. Stir over low heat about 5 minutes or just until mixture begins to thicken. Stirring constantly, add nuts and cinnamon, and cook just until mixture reaches spreading consistency. Cool slightly.

86

Roll out dough on well-floured board or cloth to 22 x 9-inch rectangle. Spread evenly with walnut filling. Roll up jelly-roll fashion, starting at short side. Put into greased 9 x 5 x 3-inch loaf pan. Cover. Let rise as directed above until doubled in bulk. Bake in 350° F. oven about 45 minutes or until bread tests done. Remove from pan. Cool on wire rack.

QUICK PERFECT PANCAKES

2 eggs
2½ cups milk
2 cups biscuit mix

¼ cup dark corn syrup
¼ cup corn oil

Beat eggs until soft peaks form. Blend in milk. Add biscuit mix, syrup, and corn oil. Mix just until thoroughly dampened. Spoon about 2 tablespoons for each pancake onto hot griddle. When bubbles begin to break, turn to cook other side. Serve with pancake syrup. (Makes 3 dozen pancakes.)

PANCAKE SIZZLERS

Prepare pancakes following above recipe. Fold hot pancakes in halves, then in quarters. Set aside to reheat in sauce. May be wrapped and stored in refrigerator or freezer. (Makes 3 dozen pancakes.)

Sauce

¼ cup margarine
1 cup orange marmalade

1¾ cups light corn syrup
1 tablespoon orange extract

Heat margarine, marmalade, and corn syrup together in a large skillet, using medium heat. Heat pancakes, sprinkle with one tablespoon orange extract, and ignite. Serve when flaming stops. Vary sauce with different jams or preserves. (Makes 6 servings.)

GINGERBREAD PANCAKES

1¼ cups sifted cake flour
¾ teaspoon soda
¼ teaspoon salt
½ teaspoon ginger
½ teaspoon cinnamon

¼ teaspoon clove
1 egg, well beaten
⅔ cup dark corn syrup
⅓ cup strong coffee
¼ cup margarine, melted

Sift flour with soda, salt, and spices. Mix egg, syrup, coffee, and margarine. Stir into dry ingredients just until moistened. Batter should be lumpy. Bake pancakes on hot griddle, using ¼ cup batter for each. Turn once to brown both sides. Serve hot with pancake syrup. (Makes 8 pancakes.)

GERMAN APPLE PANCAKES

2 eggs, slightly beaten
1 cup milk
¼ cup light corn syrup
1¼ cups sifted flour
⅓ cup margarine (or more if needed)

2 apples, pared, cored, and thinly sliced
Sugar

Beat eggs with milk and syrup to blend well. Mix in flour until smooth. Melt 2 tablespoons margarine in large skillet over medium to low heat. Pour batter for several pancakes into skillet, using about ¼ cup for each. Top with apple slices. Cook, turning once until lightly browned on both sides. Place on serving dish, apple side up. Sprinkle with sugar, then roll up. Keep warm in very slow oven while baking additional pancakes to use all of batter. Add more margarine to skillet as needed. Sprinkle with sugar again to serve. (Makes 3 servings.)

WAFFLES DELUXE A LA MODE

2 eggs
2 cups sifted self-rising cake flour
1 tablespoon sugar
1¼ cups milk

¼ cup margarine
Vanilla ice cream
Strawberries in syrup

Beat eggs until foamy. Add self-rising cake flour, sugar, and milk. Beat until smooth; then beat in melted margarine. Bake in hot waffle iron. Serve with vanilla ice cream topped by a spoonful of strawberries in syrup. (Makes about 8 waffles.)

SHAKER MUFFINS

1 egg
1 cup milk
¼ cup corn oil

¼ cup sugar
2 cups unsifted self-rising cake
  flour

Grease 12 (2½-inch) muffin pan cups. Put egg and milk into 2-quart juice shaker. Cover tightly; shake vigorously 20 times, holding top and bottom of shaker securely. Add corn oil, sugar, and flour. Cover; shake 20 times. Pour batter into prepared pans, filling cups ⅔ full. Bake in 400° F. oven 20 to 25 minutes or until cake tester inserted in center of muffin comes out clean. Serve warm. (Makes 12.)

ORANGE SHAKER MUFFINS

Shaker Muffin Batter
2 teaspoons grated orange rind
2 tablespoons sugar

1 tablespoon margarine
½ teaspoon orange juice

Follow recipe for Shaker Muffins, adding 1 teaspoon grated orange rind with corn oil, sugar, and flour. Bake muffins 20 minutes. Meanwhile, mix sugar, margarine, the other teaspoon grated orange rind, and orange juice. Spread mixture on muffins. Bake 5 minutes longer.

CINNAMON SHAKER MUFFINS

Shaker Muffin Batter   1 tablespoon sugar
1 tablespoon margarine   ¼ teaspoon cinnamon

Prepare Shaker Muffin batter. Bake muffins 20 minutes. Meanwhile, melt margarine and mix sugar with cinnamon. Brush muffins with melted margarine and sprinkle with sugar-cinnamon mixture. Bake 5 minutes longer.

QUICKIE BREAD BUNS

Sliced bread   Cinnamon
Margarine   Dark corn syrup

Use one slice bread for each bun. Spread bun with margarine, sprinkle with cinnamon, and remove crusts. Cut slice in 4 squares. Place, cut-edge-down, in greased muffin pan. Bake in 375° F. oven 10 minutes. Remove from oven; pour 1 tablespoon dark corn syrup over each bun. Bake 5 to 10 minutes longer, or until tops are browned.

TAFFY TOAST

3 tablespoons syrup
1 tablespoon softened margarine
4 slices toast

Mix syrup with softened margarine, and spread over toast. Broil or heat in oven until syrup mixture bubbles. For variety, sprinkle the toast with raisins, chopped nuts, or stir ⅛ teaspoon cinnamon into syrup mixture.

QUICK AND EASY CARAMEL ROLLS

⅓ cup margarine
¼ cup brown sugar
⅓ cup pancake syrup

¼ cup nuts, halves or chopped
1 package (12) brown-and-serve
rolls

Bring margarine, sugar, and syrup to a boil in saucepan, stirring constantly. Boil and stir 1 minute. Divide mixture into 12 medium-sized muffin cups. Sprinkle nuts onto syrup; then gently press rolls into cups. Bake in 375° F. oven 15 minutes or until rolls are browned. Remove from oven, cool about 30 seconds, then turn upside-down onto waxed paper. Shake pan gently to remove rolls. (Makes 12.)

ORANGE ROLLS

½ cup light corn syrup
¼ cup sugar
2 tablespoons melted margarine

Combine corn syrup with sugar and margarine. Divide mixture equally into 12 greased muffin cups.

Dough

3 cups sifted flour
3 teaspoons baking powder
1½ teaspoons sugar

½ cup margarine
1 cup milk

Sift flour with baking powder and sugar. Cut in margarine until mixture is crumbly. (Or use 3 cups prepared biscuit mix.) Stir in milk. Roll out dough on floured cloth or board into rectangle ⅛ inch thick.

Filling

2 tablespoons melted margarine
2 tablespoons sugar
2 teaspoons grated orange rind

Spread dough with a mixture of melted margarine, sugar, and grated orange rind. Roll as for jelly roll; cut into 12 slices. Place slices cut-side-down in muffin cups. Bake in 375° F. oven 30 minutes or until biscuits are browned. Remove from pans at once and serve hot. (Makes 12.)

CORN BREAD

1 cup sifted flour
2½ teaspoons baking powder
1 teaspoon salt
¾ cup corn meal

1 cup milk
1 egg, well beaten
⅓ cup dark corn syrup
¼ cup corn oil

Sift flour with baking powder and salt; stir in corn meal. Combine milk, egg, syrup, and corn oil. Mix into dry ingredients just to moisten. Batter should be lumpy. Bake in greased 8-inch-square pan in 425° F. oven 30 to 35 minutes. (Makes 12 servings.)

ORANGE ALMOND COFFEE RING

¼ cup sugar
1 teaspoon grated orange rind
¼ cup margarine
¼ cup blanched almond halves

1 package ready-to-bake refrigerator
    biscuits
⅓ cup light corn syrup

Blend first three ingredients; spread in 8-inch ring mold to cover bottom and sides. Sprinkle with almonds. Arrange biscuits in mold, flat-side down, edges just touching. Bake in 450° F. oven 10 minutes. Remove from oven; reset oven to 400° F. Pour syrup over biscuits; bake 5 minutes longer. Cool 1 minute; invert pan onto waxed paper, and shake to remove ring.

CINNAMON-PECAN COFFEE RING

Follow recipe for Orange Almond Coffee Ring, but replace sugar with brown sugar, orange rind with ½ teaspoon cinnamon, almonds with pecans, and light corn syrup with dark corn syrup.

NUT PIZZA

1 recipe biscuits (made with 2 cups flour or mix)	¼ cup brown sugar
	⅓ cup pancake syrup
3 tablespoons margarine	½ cup chopped nuts

Prepare biscuit dough and press evenly into a 13-inch pizza pan. Make rim around edge slightly higher than center of dough. Blend margarine and brown sugar, then mix in syrup and nuts. Spread evenly over dough. Bake in 450° F. oven about 25 minutes or until crust is golden brown. Serve hot, cut in wedges. (Makes 12 servings.)

PINEAPPLE PIZZA

Follow recipe for Nut Pizza, omitting nuts. Use ½ cup drained, crushed pineapple in topping. Add 1 teaspoon grated orange rind, if desired.

Note: Baked pizza may be frozen, then reheated in hot oven to serve.

FIREPLACE FAVORITES—
FOR ROASTING AND TOASTING

FOILED ROASTED POTATOES

Scrub baking potatoes thoroughly and coat with vegetable shortening or salad oil. Wrap individually in foil and bake either on top of coals (turning occasionally) or buried in live coals for 45 to 60 minutes.

CAMPFIRE OYSTERS

Alternate one-inch pieces of bacon and drained oysters on skewers, or cut long green sticks with peeled and sharpened ends. Cook over fire until bacon is well broiled and edges of oysters curl. Slide off onto buns. Season with salt, pepper, and lemon juice.

SKEWERED ROLLS

Thread brown-and-serve rolls on skewers. Brush with melted butter and hold over coals, turning to toast evenly.

HOT BUTTERED POPCORN AND APPLES

Heat ¼ cup corn oil in long-handled popper or large, heavy kettle. Add ½ cup popping corn. Cover, leaving small air space at edge. Shake frequently over flames until popping stops. Salt generously. Melt butter and pour over popcorn. Serve with juicy fresh apples.

TOAST-MALLOWS SUPREME

Toast marshmallows on skewers over embers until well browned on outside and soft and runny inside. Slip each off skewer onto a brown-edge cookie on which a square of bar milk chocolate has been placed. Cover with another cookie.

CARAMEL APPLES

Insert sharp wooden skewer into blossom end of apple. Roast apple over live coals until skin peels off easily. Roll hot apple in pan of brown sugar, return sugared apple to the fire, and turn it slowly as sugar melts into candy coating.

IV

Sandwiches—
From Tea Sandwiches
to Heros

The all-time staple of the youth diet may not be all things to all people, but one sure thing is that plain or fancy, finger-size or Dagwood-size, sandwiches are not only the younger set's favorite food but are often called upon to fill the bill nutritionally in their speeded up and pressured world.

Here is a vast selection for the adventurous members of the new generation, male or female.

TIPS FOR TASTY SANDWICHES

1. Vary breads to suit the occasion and individual preferences. Choose white, whole wheat, pumpernickel, cheese bread, rye, cinnamon raisin, date-nut. Use rolls, muffins, French and Italian breads, biscuits, and crackers.
2. Leave the crusts on all but fancy sandwiches to keep them from drying out.
3. Spread both mayonnaise (or butter, mustard, etc.) and filling to the edges of the bread.
4. Use refrigerated 1-day-old bread.
   to use.
5. Wrap sandwiches in waxed paper and refrigerate until ready

SANDWICH FILLING

¼ cup mayonnaise
½ cup chopped celery
About 1 cup variation ingredient(s)

Combine all ingredients. Chill. (Makes about 1½ cups.)

Meat or Poultry

Add 1 cup diced cooked ham, chicken, turkey, leftover roast or luncheon meat, and if desired, ¼ cup chopped, drained pickle.

Seafood

Add 1 cup flaked tuna, salmon, crabmeat, or chopped shrimp, sprinkled with lemon juice.

Egg

Add 2 hard-cooked eggs, chopped, 2 tablespoons chopped dill pickle, ½ teaspoon each dry mustard, finely chopped onion, capers. Omit celery.

VARIATIONS ON THE THEME

SAN FRANCISCO CHICKEN SANDWICH

1 cup chopped cooked chicken
½ cup drained crushed pineapple
½ cup chopped walnuts

Moisten with mayonnaise or salad dressing. Combine ingredients. (Makes 2½ cups.)

CHICKEN LIVER AND BACON FILLING

½ pound cooked and chopped chicken livers (1 cup)
1 cup crumbled crisp bacon
¼ cup mayonnaise
¼ cup finely chopped hard-cooked egg

Combine ingredients. (Makes 2½ cups.)

CHEESE SALAD SPREAD

½ pound Swiss cheese, finely shredded (2 cups)
½ cup chopped tomato
3 tablespoons chopped pimiento-stuffed green olives
2 tablespoons chopped green pepper
½ cup mayonnaise
Salt to taste

Combine all ingredients. Chill. (Makes 2 cups.)

SALMON AND CUCUMBER FILLING

1 cup flaked salmon	¼ cup mayonnaise
½ cup chopped cucumber	1 teaspoon lemon juice

Combine ingredients. Sprinkle with freshly ground pepper. Chill. (Makes about 1½ cups.)

SUGAR AND SPICE HAM FILLING

1 cup ground ham	2 to 3 tablespoons orange
¼ cup mayonnaise	marmalade
	½ to 1 teaspoon dry mustard

Combine ingredients. (Makes 1½ cups.)

DATE-NUT FILLING

½ cup finely chopped dates
½ cup chopped nuts
¼ cup mayonnaise

Combine ingredients. (Makes 1 cup.)

PRUNE-NUT FILLING

Follow recipe for Date-Nut Filling, substituting finely chopped prunes for dates.

CHICKEN LIVER AND SHRIMP SPREAD

½ pound chicken livers, cooked and chopped (1 cup)	¼ cup mayonnaise
	¼ teaspoon grated onion
1 cup finely chopped cooked shrimp	

Combine ingredients. Chill. (Makes 2½ cups.)

CARROT-EGG FILLING

4 hard-cooked eggs, finely chopped
½ cup finely chopped carrot
¼ teaspoon curry powder

¼ teaspoon salt
Dash freshly ground pepper
¼ cup mayonnaise

Combine ingredients. Chill. (Makes 1½ cups.)

LIVERWURST FILLING

8 slices liverwurst
1 teaspoon grated onion

2 hard-cooked eggs, chopped
¼ cup mayonnaise

Mash liverwurst and onion with fork. Stir in egg and mayonnaise. (Makes about ¾ cup.)

ROQUEFORT FILLING

2 (3-ounce) packages cream cheese
½ cup mayonnaise

¼ pound Roquefort cheese, crumbled
¼ cup chopped nuts

Soften cream cheese, then blend in mayonnaise. Stir in Roquefort cheese and nuts. (Makes 2 cups.)

EGG AND BOLOGNA FILLING

2 hard-cooked eggs, chopped
8 slices bologna, chopped

¼ cup chopped celery
½ cup mayonnaise

Combine ingredients. Sprinkle lightly with freshly ground pepper. Chill. (Makes about 1½ cups.)

SIMPLE FAMILY FAVORITES—
LEFTOVERS ARE GREAT

Meat and Fish

Liverwurst, horseradish, lettuce on buttered white bread
Baked ham, turkey, Russian dressing on rye
Cold roast beef, American cheese, mayonnaise
Chicken salad, cranberry sauce on French toast
Bacon, Swiss cheese, mustard-mayonnaise on whole wheat toast
Turkey, pickle relish, lettuce, mayonnaise on toasted cheese bread
Cold lamb, pickled beet, catsup on rye
Bologna, American cheese, lettuce, mustard on seeded roll
Cold pot roast, sliced raw red onion, catsup
Liverwurst, Swiss cheese, red pepper relish
Meat loaf, green pepper, catsup on a bun
Open-face ham, pineapple ring, maraschino cherry on toasted English
  muffin
Bacon and peanut butter on white toast
Sardine, chopped hard-cooked egg, chopped onion, lemon juice, and
  pepper
Liverwurst, lettuce, sliced tomato, mayonnaise on whole wheat
Flaked tuna, chopped egg, chopped stuffed olives, mayonnaise
Crab meat salad, sliced hard-cooked egg
Chopped shrimp, chopped tomato, mayonnaise
Boiled ham, American cheese, corn relish
Bacon, lettuce, tomato, Russian dressing

Egg and Cheese

Many of the following are especially good for crust-trimmed, dainty
tea-time finger sandwiches, open or covered.

Chopped egg, chopped celery, chopped stuffed olives, mayonnaise
Chopped egg, chopped sweet pickle, mayonnaise
Sliced egg, canned salmon, chopped onion, lemon juice, mayonnaise
Chopped egg, mashed shad roe on buttered toast
Chopped egg, tartar sauce on whole wheat
Chopped egg, caviar, minced onion, lemon juice

Chopped egg, diced bacon, Russian dressing, pepper

Cream cheese, guava jelly on date-nut bread

Cream cheese with black raspberry jam, orange marmalade, or crushed pineapple

Cream cheese and chopped stuffed olive or finely chopped candied ginger

Cream cheese, caviar, grated onion

Cream cheese, cranberry jelly on date-nut bread

Cream cheese softened with mayonnaise, crumbled blue cheese, Worcestershire sauce

Cream cheese, cut raw prunes and apricots, sprinkling of mixed cinnamon and sugar

Cream cheese and chives, crumbled bacon

Cream cheese, bacon, honey spread

Cottage cheese, minced green pepper and onion, salt, paprika on whole wheat bread

HOT AND HEARTY— MEALS IN THEMSELVES

THE GREAT WESTERN

½ cup minced ham	¼ cup milk
¼ cup minced green pepper	4 eggs
½ cup minced onion	

Beat eggs with milk slightly, combine with other ingredients, pour into hot buttered skillet and cook until the mixture is firm. Serve on toast. (Makes 4 servings.)

BROILED LUNCHEON ROLLS

4 hard-cooked eggs, finely chopped	Dash pepper
¼ cup mayonnaise	4 frankfurter buns
1 tablespoon mustard with horseradish	¼ cup mayonnaise
½ teaspoon salt	½ cup finely shredded American cheese
¼ teaspoon grated onion	

Combine eggs, ¼ cup mayonnaise, mustard with horseradish, salt, onion, and pepper. Split buns lengthwise. Spread with remaining ¼ cup mayonnaise and sprinkle with ¼ cup cheese. Fill with salad mixture. Sprinkle with remaining ¼ cup cheese. Broil 4 inches from heat 3 to 4 minutes or until cheese is bubbly and rolls are toasted. (Makes 4 servings.)

DEVILED HAM BUNS

1 (4½-ounce) can deviled ham	2 tablespoons chopped sweet
2 chopped hard-cooked eggs	pickles
1 tablespoon prepared mustard	4 hamburger buns
1 tablespoon catsup	

Combine all ingredients and spread on buttered buns. Wrap each securely in foil. Place on cookie sheet and heat in 300° F. oven about 15 minutes. (Makes 4 servings.)

CORNED BEEF SANDWICH DELUXE

½ pound thin sliced cooked corned beef	½ cup Russian dressing
½ pound sliced Swiss cheese	1 cup drained sauerkraut

Spread pumpernickel bread with Russian dressing; add corned beef, Swiss cheese, and sauerkraut. Butter both top and bottom of each sandwich and grill on both sides till cheese begins to melt. (Makes 6 servings.)

BOSTON BEAN SPECIAL

Spread brown bread with prepared mustard and butter; top with baked beans, bacon slices, and shredded sharp processed cheese. Broil until cheese melts.

HOT CRAB BREAD

1 (7-½ ounce) can crab meat,
   flaked
⅓ cup mayonnaise
⅓ cup dairy sour cream
2 tablespoons chopped parsley
2 teaspoons lemon juice

¼ teaspoon garlic salt
1 loaf French or Italian bread,
   about 15 inches long
2 tablespoons margarine
¼ pound sliced Swiss cheese

Combine crab meat, mayonnaise, sour cream, parsley, lemon juice, and garlic salt. Chill. Slice bread in half lengthwise and arrange on baking sheet. Spread cut sides with margarine. Top with cheese slices, trimmed to fit bread. Cover cheese with crab mixture. Bake in 350° F. oven about 25 minutes or until lightly browned. Cut crosswise into serving pieces. (Makes 6 servings.)

HOT TUNA BREAD

Follow recipe for Hot Crab Bread, but substitute 1 (7-ounce) can tuna, drained and flaked, for crab meat. If desired, add 1 tablespoon chopped pimiento for color.

GRILLED HAM AND CHEDDAR CHEESE

1 cup shredded sharp Cheddar
   cheese
3 tablespoons mayonnaise

1 tablespoon chopped pimiento
12 slices boiled ham

Top 6 slices of lightly toasted bread with 2 slices each of ham. Combine pimiento and Cheddar cheese and mayonnaise and spread over ham. Broil 4 inches from heat until cheese melts. (Makes 6 open-face sandwiches.)

LEFT-OVER HOT MEATBALL SANDWICH

Add salted crisp green pepper rings to left-over meat balls re-heated in their own gravy and serve on lightly toasted buns.

HOT CHEESE SANDWICH TOPPING

1 cup mayonnaise
½ cup finely shredded American cheese

Combine mayonnaise and shredded cheese. Spoon mixture over desired open-face sandwich, covering filling completely so that it will remain moist. Broil 4 inches from heat until topping bubbles and browns. (Makes enough topping for about 6 sandwiches.)

TOMATO-CHEESE TOPPING

Add ¼ cup catsup and a generous dash oregano to Hot Cheese Topping.

ONION-CHEESE TOPPING

Add 2 tablespoons finely chopped onion to Hot Cheese Topping.

HERBED CHEESE TOPPING

Add 1 tablespoon each chopped parsley and chives to Hot Cheese Topping.

MUSTARD-CHEESE TOPPING

Add 1 teaspoon prepared mustard and ½ teaspoon Worcestershire sauce to Hot Cheese Topping.

PEANUT BUTTER-CHEESE TOPPING

Add 2 tablespoons creamy or chunk-style peanut butter to Hot Cheese Topping.

PARTY SPECIALS—A LITTLE MORE WORK, A LOT MORE FUN

SPREADS FOR PARTY SANDWICHES

Deviled Ham

Mix 1 (4½-ounce) can deviled ham spread, 2 tablespoons pickle relish, and 2 tablespoons mayonnaise together. (Makes ¾ cup.)

Chicken

Mix 1 cup minced or 1 (5½-ounce) can cooked, boned chicken, 2 tablespoons drained pickle relish, and 3 tablespoons mayonnaise. (Makes 1 cup.)

Caper Cheese

Mix 1 (3-ounce) package cream cheese, 2 tablespoons mayonnaise, 1 teaspoon capers, and ½ teaspoon caper liquid. (Makes ½ cup.)

Herb Margarine

Mix ½ cup margarine with 1 teaspoon each of crushed dry or snipped fresh tarragon and chervil leaves and ½ teaspoon celery seed. (Makes ½ cup.)

Olive Margarine

Mix ¼ cup margarine with 3 tablespoons finely chopped pimiento-stuffed green olives. (Makes about ⅓ cup.)

Note: Mince chicken and ham in a blender; mash capers.

SANDWICH LOAF

8 slices firm white bread	Grated carrot, sliced celery for
Mayonnaise	garnish
1 cup each of 3 desired fillings	
Frosting	

Trim crusts from bread. Spread 6 slices with mayonnaise, leaving 2 slices plain for top layer. Arrange 2 slices side by side on serving platter, ends touching. Cover with first filling. Top with 2 slices; cover with second filling. Top with 2 more slices; cover with last filling. Top with 2 plain bread slices. Press layers together firmly. Chill thoroughly. Spread top and sides evenly with about ¾ of frosting. Pipe remaining frosting around top and bottom of loaf, using decorating tube. Garnish with grated carrot, sliced celery. Chill well before cutting. (Makes 15 slices.)

Frosting

Blend 2 (8-ounce) packages cream cheese, softened, with ⅓ cup mayonnaise.

SALMON TREAT

4 slices pumpernickel	¼ cup mayonnaise
1 package cream cheese	½ teaspoon lemon juice
4 slices smoked salmon	¼ teaspoon dry dill weed
8 cucumber slices	

Spread 4 slices of bread with cream cheese. Arrange smoked salmon and 2 slices cucumber on each bread slice. Top with mixture of mayonnaise, lemon juice and dry dill weed.

SAUSAGE SPECIALTY

4 slices firm white bread	¼ cup mayonnaise
Cooked sausage	½ teaspoon caraway seed
Red cabbage	

Arrange cooked sausage and red cabbage on bread slices. Top with mixture of mayonnaise and caraway seed.

PINWHEEL SANDWICHES

Thinly sliced bread	Finely chopped olives, pickles, or
Mayonnaise	frankfurters
Selected fillings	

Trim crusts from bread. Spread with mayonnaise, then with selected filling. Arrange a lengthwise row of chopped olives, pickles, or frankfurters on one end of each slice. Roll up firmly but not tightly. Wrap in plastic film or waxed paper, twisting ends securely. Chill thoroughly. Cut into ¼- to ½-inch slices and arrange on platter just before serving.

RIBBON SANDWICHES

Using 3 slices whole wheat and 2 slices white bread, prepare a stack, alternating breads and using any colorful fillings. Press breads firmly together; wrap in plastic film. Chill several hours. Cut into ½-inch slices. Cut each slice into thirds, halves, or triangles.

CHECKERBOARD SANDWICHES

Stack alternately 2 slices whole wheat and 2 slices white bread, filling with spreads. Press each stack, trim crusts. Cut into ½-inch slices. Stack 4 slices together, alternating the whole wheat and white slices, filling with an herb mayonnaise. Wrap and chill in refrigerator several hours. Using a sharp knife, cut into ½-inch slices. For miniature Checkerboards, cut each slice in half. If desired, add one or two caper "checkers."

CORNUCOPIAS

Trim crusts from bread slices. Cut off ½ inch of bottom corner. Spread with filling. Overlap and press opposite corners; garnish.

ENVELOPES

Trim crusts from bread slices. Spread with Herb Margarine or other mixture. Fold 2 corners together and press firmly.

ROLL-UPS

Trim crusts from bread slices. Spread with filling. Lay a well-drained canned asparagus tip across one end of each slice. Roll up.

DIVAN SANDWICH

¼ cup milk
½ cup mayonnaise
½ cup finely shredded Cheddar cheese or grated Parmesan cheese
1 (ten-ounce) package frozen asparagus, cooked and drained

Cooked chicken or turkey slices
1 (3-ounce) can sliced mushrooms, drained
4 slices toast

Gradually stir milk into mayonnaise in saucepan. Place over low heat about 3 minutes or just until warm. Stir in cheese. Arrange asparagus spears, chicken or turkey slices, and mushrooms on toast. Spoon cheese sauce over all. Broil 4 to 5 inches from heat 3 to 5 minutes or until lightly browned. (Makes 4 servings.)

MONTE CRISTO SANDWICHES

12 slices fresh, firm bread	Pepper
Mayonnaise	2 eggs lightly beaten
12 slices Swiss cheese	½ cup light cream or milk
6 slices cooked ham	⅛ teaspoon salt
6 slices cooked chicken	¼ cup margarine
Nutmeg	

Spread bread with mayonnaise. Prepare 6 closed sandwiches, each using 2 slices cheese, 1 slice ham, 1 slice chicken, nutmeg, and pepper. Cut diagonally in half. Combine eggs, cream, and salt. Melt margarine in skillet or on griddle over low heat. Coat sandwich halves with egg mixture. Lightly brown on both sides in margarine. Place on ungreased cookie sheet. Bake in 400° F. oven 3 to 5 minutes or until cheese begins to melt. (Makes 6 servings.)

DAGWOODS—TRIPLE-DECKER FAVORITES

CLASSIC CLUB SANDWICH

1 slice buttered toast	2nd slice buttered toast
Lettuce	Sliced tomatoes
Cold sliced chicken	2 or 3 strips bacon, crisply cooked
Mayonnaise	3rd slice buttered toast

Peg with colored toothpicks, cut into small triangles, and serve, points up.

GOURMET'S DELIGHT

1 slice whole wheat bread
Tongue slices
Sliced hard-cooked eggs
Salt and pepper
2nd slice whole wheat bread

Sliced chicken
Watercress
Sprinkle with Worcestershire sauce
3rd slice sandwich rye bread

FOR ENERGY PLUS

1 slice whole wheat bread spread
    with mayonnaise
Lettuce
Sliced roast beef
Salt and pepper
2nd slice whole wheat bread spread
    with mustard

American cheese
Tomato slices
3rd slice whole wheat bread spread
    with mayonnaise

KNICKERBOCKER HOLIDAY

1 slice buttered toasted cheese
    bread
Sliced turkey
Lettuce
2nd slice buttered toasted cheese
    bread

Baked sliced ham
Russian dressing
3rd slice buttered toasted cheese
    bread

FISHERMAN'S PARADISE

1 slice white toast, buttered
Tuna salad
Russian dressing
2nd slice white toast, buttered

Egg salad
Chopped olive
Shrimp salad
3rd slice white toast, buttered

HERO SANDWICHES

SUBMARINE SPECIAL

Split a long French loaf lengthwise. Spread with mustard, garlic butter, and/or mayonnaise, and pile on an assortment of slices of any or all (are you game?) of the following:

Turkey	American cheese
Ham	Swiss cheese
Chicken	Lettuce
Bologna	Tomato slices
Salami	Cucumber slices
Corned beef	Green pepper slices
Pickled tongue	Onion rounds
Tuna	Ripe olive slices
Herring	Green olive slices
Hard cooked egg slices	Sliced dill pickles

HERO: ITALIAN STYLE

Split an Italian loaf lengthwise. Spread with garlic butter and fill with:

Lettuce	Mozzarella cheese
Sliced Genoa salami	Anchovies
Tomato slices	Chicory
Onion slices	Oregano

V

Salads and Dressings

Whether a dieter's entire lunch, a bit of lettuce and tomato with a hamburger, or a fancy tossed salad at dinner—salads can provide a splash of color and a variety of delicious flavors to enhance any meal, to say nothing of their well-known nutritional value. Here are the old reliables, with plenty of new twists.

TIPS

1. For simple tossed green salads use the many various types of greens. Besides iceberg lettuce, toss in Bibb and Boston lettuce, or tender young spinach leaves. Try escarole, endive, watercress, romaine, and dandelion greens.
2. Always handle greens gently, as they bruise easily.
3. Trim greens and rinse under cold running water. Shake off excess moisture, and turn upside-down to drain.
4. Do not separate until ready to use.
5. Store in refrigerator, in crisper or plastic bag.
6. Pat dry before using.
7. Greens are better torn or broken.
8. Sprinkle cut surfaces of avocado with fresh lemon or lime juice to keep them from turning dark.
9. To keep macaroni for macaroni salad from sticking together, add a little vegetable oil or bits of butter during the last few minutes of cooking. Allow about 2 or 3 tablespoons of oil, or the same of butter, to 6 quarts of water.
10. To unmold a jellied salad, invert the mold on a serving platter, and hold a hot cloth on the bottom—but not so hot or so long that the mold begins to melt. Or dip mold in hot water until the food "gives." In both cases it is a matter of judgment as to length of time and the amount of heat needed to break the seal without melting the food. Both ways, shake the mold gently sideways to help ease the salad out.
11. Start potatoes for potato salad in boiling salted water. Then cook covered, until they can be pierced easily with the point of a small sharp knife. Drain immediately, and shake the pan over a high heat to dry them quickly. Cover lightly with a clean, dry dish towel to keep them warm. Do not cover with lid, or the potatoes will get soggy.
12. To make onion juice, cut a slice off the onion, then squeeze on a reamer as you would an orange.

COLE SLAWS

QUICK AND EASY COLE SLAW

¾ cup mayonnaise
¼ cup vinegar
2 teaspoons sugar
1 teaspoon salt

Freshly ground pepper
3 quarts finely shredded cabbage
(about 3 pounds)

Combine mayonnaise, vinegar, sugar, salt, and pepper. Chill. Just before serving, add shredded cabbage and toss until coated. (Makes 2 quarts.)

CONFETTI SLAW

Follow recipe for Quick and Easy Cole Slaw.
Add 1 cup shredded carrot, ½ cup chopped green pepper, and ¼ cup thinly sliced radishes to cabbage before tossing with mayonnaise.

FRUIT SLAW

Follow recipe for Quick and Easy Cole Slaw.
Add 1 cup drained crushed pineapple, 1 cup drained mandarin orange sections, ½ cup raisins, and ½ cup miniature marshmallows to cabbage before tossing with mayonnaise.

BACON CURRY SLAW

Follow recipe for Quick and Easy Cole Slaw.
Blend ½ teaspoon curry powder into mayonnaise. Crumble ¼ pound bacon, cooked, over cabbage before tossing with mayonnaise.

CRANBERRY SLAW

Follow recipe for Quick and Easy Cole Slaw.
Add 1 chilled 1-pound can jellied cranberry sauce, cut in cubes,
just before serving.

PINK SLAW

Follow recipe for Quick and Easy Cole Slaw.
Blend ¼ cup catsup into mayonnaise.

NEW ENGLAND COLE SLAW

4 cups shredded cabbage (about
    1 pound)
⅔ cup coarsely shredded carrots
⅓ cup coarsely shredded green
    pepper

⅓ cup thinly sliced celery
⅔ cup light corn syrup
⅓ cup vinegar, white or cider
¾ teaspoon celery seed
½ teaspoon salt

Soak shredded cabbage in ice water for 1 hour. Meanwhile, prepare the other vegetables. Drain the cabbage well. Add to the
vegetables. Chill. Combine the syrup, vinegar, celery seed, and
salt. Just before serving, add the syrup mixture to the vegetables
and mix well. (Makes 4 to 6 servings.)

MOTHER'S COLE SLAW

¼ cup light corn syrup
¼ cup vinegar
2 tablespoons margarine
2 tablespoons sugar
½ teaspoon salt

⅛ teaspoon pepper
6 cups shredded cabbage
2 tablespoons dairy sour cream
Paprika

Combine syrup, vinegar, margarine, sugar, salt, and pepper in
saucepan. Bring to boil over medium heat, stirring constantly.
Pour over shredded cabbage; mix well. Chill at least 1 hour. Toss

with sour cream just before serving. Sprinkle with paprika. (Makes 6 servings.)

SUPER COLE SLAW

1 teaspoon salt	1 tablespoon chopped pimiento
¼ teaspoon pepper	½ teaspoon grated onion
½ teaspoon dry mustard	3 tablespoons corn oil
1 teaspoon celery seed	⅓ cup vinegar
2 tablespoons sugar	3 cups shredded cabbage
¼ cup chopped green pepper	

Combine all ingredients; mix well. Cover and chill thoroughly. (Makes 4 servings.)

CHINESE SLAW

Follow recipe for Super Cole Slaw, omitting celery seed, green pepper, and pimiento, and substituting diagonally cut Chinese celery cabbage for chopped cabbage.

SHRIMP COLE SLAW

Follow recipe for Super Cole Slaw, adding 1 cup chopped, cooked shrimp or 1 (4½-ounce) can tiny shrimp.

CALIFORNIA COLE SLAW

4 cups (about ½ medium head) chopped or shredded cabbage	1 (8-ounce) can crushed pineapple, drained
½ teaspoon salt	1 tablespoon pineapple juice
½ cup mayonnaise	
½ cup quartered or miniature marshmallows	

Combine cabbage, salt, marshmallows, pineapple, and juice. Chill. Toss with mayonnaise just before serving. (Makes 4 to 6 servings.)

COTTAGE CHEESE COLE SLAW

4 cups (about ½ medium head)
  chopped or shredded cabbage
½ teaspoon salt
½ cup mayonnaise

½ cup shredded carrot
¼ cup green pepper strips
¼ teaspoon celery seed
¼ cup cottage cheese

Combine all ingredients. Chill. (Makes 4 to 6 servings.)

SEA FOOD COLE SLAW

4 cups (about ½ medium head)
  chopped or shredded cabbage
½ teaspoon salt
½ cup mayonnaise
1 (6½- or 7-ounce) can tuna,
  drained and flaked or

1 (7-ounce) can salmon,
  drained and cleaned
3 tablespoons catsup
1 teaspoon sugar
1 teaspoon lemon juice

Combine all ingredients. Chill. (Makes 4 to 6 servings.)

RED AND WHITE COLE SLAW

2 cups (½ medium head) chopped
  or shredded cabbage
2 cups shredded red cabbage

½ teaspoon salt
½ cup mayonnaise

Combine cabbage and salt. Chill. Toss with mayonnaise just before serving. (Makes 4 to 6 servings.)

HOT MUSTARD SLAW

4 cups (about ½ medium head)
  shredded cabbage
½ cup mayonnaise
1 tablespoon mustard with

horseradish
1 teaspoon vinegar
½ teaspoon sugar
Salt

Put cabbage into skillet. Combine remaining ingredients and toss with cabbage. Cook over very low heat, stirring constantly, until hot. Good with frankfurters or cold sliced ham. (Makes 4 servings.)

VEGETABLE COLE SLAW

2 tablespoons cider vinegar
1 cup mayonnaise
1 teaspoon salt
½ teaspoon sugar
½ teaspoon pepper
½ teaspoon grated onion or onion juice

10 cups (1 medium head) shredded cabbage
2 carrots, shredded
¼ green pepper, shredded

Stir vinegar into mayonnaise, then blend in salt, sugar, pepper, and onion. Chill until just before serving. Combine cabbage, carrot, and green pepper; toss with mayonnaise mixture until well coated. (Makes 8 to 10 servings.)

POTATO SALADS

BASIC POTATO SALAD

Dressing

1 cup mayonnaise
1 teaspoon salt
¼ cup vinegar

Dash paprika
Dash pepper

Salad

5 cups (about 6 medium) cooked, pared, diced potatoes
½ cup diced celery

2 tablespoons finely chopped parsley sprigs
2 teaspoons chopped onion (optional)

Blend mayonnaise with vinegar, salt, paprika, and pepper. Toss the salad ingredients with the dressing until well mixed. Arrange in salad bowl; cover and chill. (Makes 6 servings.)

POTATO BACON SALAD

Add 4 hard-cooked eggs, chopped, and 8 cooked bacon slices, crumbled, to Basic Potato Salad before tossing.

TARRAGON VEGETABLE POTATO SALAD

Add ½ teaspoon dried tarragon to dressing; then add 1 (10-ounce) package frozen mixed vegetables, cooked, drained, and chilled to Basic Potato Salad before tossing with dressing.

TANGY POTATO SALAD

Follow recipe for Basic Potato Salad, omitting onion and adding a dash of thyme and 2 teaspoons mustard with horseradish to dressing before tossing.

HOT POTATO SALAD

Follow recipe for Basic Potato Salad, but heat the dressing in a saucepan over low heat, stirring constantly, for 1 minute. Pour over the diced potatoes while still warm. Then combine with all remaining salad ingredients and mix.

DEVILED POTATO SALAD

Follow recipe for Basic Potato Salad, but add ½ teaspoon celery salt, 1 (4½-ounce) can deviled ham, and ¼ cup India relish to dressing before tossing.

VEGETABLE POTATO SALAD

Follow recipe for Basic Potato Salad, but add ⅔ cup grated carrot and ⅔ cup frozen, French style green beans, cooked and drained, to salad before tossing with dressing.

MAIN DISH POTATO SALAD

Follow recipe for Basic Potato Salad, but add 2 tablespoons mustard with horseradish to dressing; add 6 sliced frankfurters, 1 cup diced Cheddar cheese, 2 hard-cooked eggs, chopped, and ¼ cup chopped pickle to salad before tossing with dressing.

MACARONI SALADS

BASIC MACARONI SALAD

1 (8-ounce) package elbow macaroni, cooked and drained
1 to 1½ cups mayonnaise
⅓ cup chopped celery
1 to 2 tablespoons chopped onion
1½ teaspoons salt
¼ teaspoon pepper

Rinse macaroni with cold water and drain. Stir in mayonnaise. Add celery, onion, salt, and pepper. Chill before serving. (Makes 6 servings.)

HAM MACARONI SALAD

Add ½ pound cooked ham, cubed (about 2 cups) and 1 tablespoon prepared mustard to Basic Macaroni Salad.

SEA FOOD MACARONI SALAD

Add 1 (7-ounce) can tuna or salmon, drained and flaked, and ¼ cup chopped green pepper to Basic Macaroni Salad.

CHEESE MACARONI SALAD

Add ½ pound Swiss cheese, cubed (about 2 cups) and 1 teaspoon Worcestershire sauce to Basic Macaroni Salad.

RAW VEGETABLE MACARONI SALAD

Add ¼ cup shredded carrot, ¼ cup chopped green pepper, ½ cup cauliflowerets, and 1 (4-ounce) can sliced mushrooms, drained, to Basic Macaroni Salad.

HOT MACARONI SALAD

8 ounces (2 cups) uncooked elbow macaroni	¾ cup diced American cheese
2 tablespoons Italian dressing	½ cup mayonnaise
2 cups cooked, cut green beans	2 teaspoons minced onion
2 cups cooked ham strips	1 teaspoon salt
	¼ teaspoon pepper

Cook macaroni in boiling, salted water according to directions on package. Drain well; then marinate in Italian dressing 5 minutes. Toss with beans, ham, cheese, mayonnaise, onion, salt, and pepper. If desired, serve on salad greens. (Makes 6 servings.)

COOKED VEGETABLE MACARONI SALAD

1 (8-ounce) package macaroni
   shells, cooked and drained
1 cup diced cooked carrots
1 cup cooked peas
½ cup chopped celery

2 teaspoons finely chopped onion
1 teaspoon salt
¼ teaspoon white pepper
1 cup mayonnaise

Combine all ingredients. Toss lightly. Chill. (Makes 8 servings.)

TUNA SALADS

BASIC TUNA SALAD

2 (6½- to 7-ounce) cans tuna,
   drained and flaked
1 cup diced celery
½ teaspoon lemon juice
1 teaspoon finely chopped onion

½ teaspoon salt
⅛ teaspoon pepper
½ cup mayonnaise
Lettuce

Lightly mix tuna, celery, lemon juice, onion, salt and pepper. Add mayonnaise and toss until evenly coated. Serve on lettuce. (Makes about 3 cups salad or 6 servings.)

TUNA-EGG SALAD

Follow recipe for Basic Tuna Salad, adding 3 diced hard-cooked eggs to tuna mixture before tossing with mayonnaise.

TUNA, VEGETABLE, AND EGG SALAD

Follow recipe for Basic Tuna Salad, adding 3 diced, hard-cooked eggs and 1 cup cooked peas to tuna mixture before tossing with mayonnaise.

TUNA RICE SALAD

Combine 1½ cups cooked rice, 1 tablespoon chopped pimiento, 2 tablespoons corn oil, and 2 tablespoons vinegar. Marinate in refrigerator at least one hour. Add to Basic Tuna Salad before tossing with mayonnaise.

LUAU TUNA SALAD

Follow recipe for Basic Tuna Salad, omitting lemon juice, onion, salt, and pepper. Blend 1 teaspoon curry powder with mayonnaise. Add 1 cup drained crushed pineapple and ½ cup chopped walnuts to tuna before tossing with mayonnaise.

CURRIED TUNA RICE SALAD

2 (6½- or 7-ounce) cans tuna, drained and flaked
1½ cups cold cooked rice
1 cup diced celery
1 teaspoon lemon juice
½ to 1 teaspoon curry powder
½ teaspoon salt
⅛ teaspoon pepper
½ cup mayonnaise
Lettuce

Condiments

Whole peanuts, chopped green pepper, toasted coconut, chopped scallion, raisins, mandarin orange segments.

Lightly mix tuna, rice, celery, lemon juice, curry powder, salt and pepper. Add mayonnaise and toss until evenly coated. Serve on lettuce, accompanied by 2 or 3 of the condiments, each in a separate bowl. (Makes 8 ½-cup servings.)

HOT TUNA SALAD

Salad

2 (6½- to 7-ounce) cans tuna, drained and flaked
3 cups (about 4 medium) cooked, pared, and diced potatoes
2½ cups diced celery
3 hard-cooked eggs, chopped
2 tablespoons chopped parsley
2 teaspoons finely chopped onion
½ teaspoon salt
1 cup mayonnaise

Line 1 (8-inch) square pan *or* 1 (9-inch) layer-cake pan *or* 9 (5-ounce) custard cups with waxed paper. Combine ingredients for salad. Firmly pack into prepared molds. Chill about 2 hours. Unmold onto ovenproof platter. Remove waxed paper. Broil 5 inches from source of heat 5 minutes or bake in 375° F. oven 10 minutes.

Topping

1 egg white
¼ cup mayonnaise

While salad is heating, beat egg white until stiff but not dry, then fold in remaining ¼ cup mayonnaise. Remove salad from broiler or oven. Spread top with egg-white mixture. Broil 3 to 5 minutes or bake in 425° F. oven 10 minutes or until topping is lightly browned. Serve immediately. (Serves 6 to 8.)

SEAFOOD SALADS

TROPICAL CRAB SALAD

1 cup uncooked rice (not precooked variety)

Unsweetened pineapple juice

2 (6-ounce) packages frozen crab meat, thawed and drained, or 2 (7¾-ounce cans crab meat, drained, cleaned, and flaked

1 (1-pound) can mixed Chinese vegetables

1 (5-ounce) can water chestnuts, drained and sliced

1 cup thin, diagonally sliced celery

¼ cup light cream or unsweetened pineapple juice

2 cups mayonnaise

⅓ cup chopped scallions

2 tablespoons curry powder

Salad greens

Cook rice according to directions on package, substituting unsweetened pineapple juice for water. Toss with crab meat, Chinese vegetables, water chestnuts, and celery. Gradually blend cream or pineapple juice into mayonnaise. Mix in scallions and curry powder. Toss with rice mixture, mixing well. Chill. Serve on salad greens. (Makes 6 servings.)

To Serve Hot

Reduce scallions to 3 tablespoons. Spoon mixture into shallow 2-quart baking dish; cover and heat in 350° F. oven about 30 minutes.

HEARTY SALMON SALAD

1 red apple, unpared, cored, and diced

1 tablespoon lemon juice

1 (7¾-ounce) can salmon, drained, cleaned, and flaked

1 cup cooked peas

½ cup chopped cooked carrot

1 tablespoon chopped pickle

⅛ teaspoon salt

⅔ cup mayonnaise

Salad greens

Sprinkle apple with lemon juice. Combine all ingredients. Chill. Serve on salad greens. (Makes 4 to 6 servings.)

SAILOR'S SALAD

1 (10-ounce) package frozen halibut	¼ cup mayonnaise
3 tablespoons Italian dressing	2 tablespoons capers, drained
2 tomatoes	¼ teaspoon salt
½ cup diced, pared cucumber	Dash pepper
	Salad greens

Cook fish according to directions on package; flake. Pour Italian dressing over fish. Let marinate in refrigerator until chilled. Meanwhile, cut tomatoes in half. Spoon out pulp, leaving shell intact. Turn upside-down to drain. If desired, sprinkle with salt. Combine cucumber, mayonnaise, capers, salt, pepper, and fish, mixing lightly. Spoon into tomato shells. Arrange on greens. (Makes 4 servings.)

LOBSTER AND AVOCADO SALAD

2 avocados	1 cup cooked diced lobster meat, fresh or canned
Lemon juice	½ cup diced celery
½ cup mayonnaise	Salad greens
½ teaspoon salt	
¼ teaspoon curry powder	

Cut avocados in half lengthwise and remove seeds; sprinkle with lemon juice. Combine remaining ingredients. Fill centers of avocados. Serve on greens with additional mayonnaise on the side. (Makes 4 servings.)

SHRIMP AND APPLE SALAD

1 cup cooked or canned shrimp,
  cleaned
2 medium apples, diced
1 medium green pepper, cut into
  narrow strips
8 pimiento-stuffed green olives,
  sliced

¼ cup mayonnaise
1 tablespoon lime or lemon juice
Salad greens
1 grapefruit, sectioned

Combine shrimp, apples, pepper, and olives in large bowl. Blend mayonnaise with lime or lemon juice. Add to shrimp mixture; toss. Chill. Serve on salad greens. Garnish with grapefruit sections. (Makes 4 servings.)

SHRIMP AND VEGETABLE SALAD

Follow recipe for Shrimp and Apple Salad, but substitute 1 (10-ounce) package frozen mixed vegetables, cooked and drained, for diced apple.

CRAB MEAT LOUIS

½ medium head lettuce, shredded
1 to 1½ cups cooked or canned
  lump crab meat, chilled
1 large tomato, cut into wedges

2 hard-cooked eggs, sliced
8 ripe olives
Pimiento strips

Arrange lettuce in individual serving bowls. Mound crab meat on top. Garnish with tomato wedges, egg slices, olives, and pimiento strips. Chill until ready to serve. Serve with Louis dressing. (Serves 4.)

Louis Dressing

1 cup mayonnaise	1 teaspoon lemon juice
½ cup chili sauce	¼ teaspoon tarragon
1½ teaspoons grated onion	Salt
1 teaspoon horseradish	Pepper

Blend ingredients. Chill. (Makes 1½ cups.)

Note: This dressing is equally delicious served on chilled lobster and shrimp.

CHICKEN SALADS

BASIC CHICKEN SALAD

4 cups diced cooked chicken	1 teaspoon salt
1½ cups diced celery	⅛ teaspoon pepper
1 cup mayonnaise	Salad greens
2 tablespoons lemon juice	

Combine chicken and celery in large bowl. Blend mayonnaise, lemon juice, salt, and pepper. Toss lightly with chicken and celery. Chill. Serve on salad greens, garnished with additional mayonnaise, if desired. (Makes 6 to 8 servings.)

HEARTY CHICKEN SALAD

Add 1 cup cooked peas, ¾ cup chopped walnuts, and 1 teaspoon grated onion to Basic Chicken Salad before tossing with dressing.

RICH CHICKEN SALAD

Follow recipe for Basic Chicken Salad, but add ¾ cup sliced pimiento-stuffed green olives, halved. Omit lemon juice. Blend

¼ cup milk and a dash of Tabasco sauce into 1 (3-ounce) package cream cheese, softened; add to dressing.

ORIENTAL CHICKEN SALAD

Follow recipe for Basic Chicken Salad, but omit celery. Add ½ cup toasted cashew nuts, coarsely chopped, and ¼ cup raisins to salad; add ½ teaspoon curry powder to dressing.

CRANBERRY CHICKEN SALAD

Toss 1 cup well-chilled cubes of jellied cranberry sauce with Basic Chicken Salad just before serving.

CHICKEN CURRY SALAD WITH FRUIT GARNISH

⅔ cup mayonnaise
2 tablespoons lemon juice
1 teaspoon salt
1 teaspoon curry powder

2½ cups diced cooked chicken
1 cup diced celery
¼ cup slivered blanched almonds
Salad greens

Garnish

1 avocado, cut into wedges
½ cantaloupe, cut into wedges

1 cup canned pineapple chunks, drained
1 cup seedless grapes

Blend mayonnaise, lemon juice, salt, and curry powder. Pour over the combined chicken and celery and mix lightly. Chill. Just before serving, mound salad in center of a serving platter. Sprinkle with almonds and garland with greens. Arrange small mounds of fruit on greens. (Serves 6.)

MEAL-IN-ONE, VEGETABLE, AND TOSSED SALADS

EGG SALAD SUPREME

Salad greens
9 hard-cooked eggs, cut into quarters
⅔ cup mayonnaise
3 tablespoons diced green pepper
3 tablespoons chopped celery

2 tablespoons chili sauce
1½ tablespoons finely chopped onion
¼ teaspoon salt
Pepper

Arrange salad greens in bowl with the eggs in center. Combine remaining ingredients. Pour over eggs. Chill. If desired, garnish with celery tops. (Makes 6 servings.)

SPICY MEAT-POTATO SALAD

1 medium apple, unpared and diced
1 tablespoon lemon juice
1 cup leftover cooked meat, cubed (such as beef, steak, chicken, veal, lamb, pork, ham)
1 cup coarsely chopped celery

1 cup cubed cooked potato
1 hard-cooked egg, diced
½ tablespoon chopped onion
1 cup cooked peas and carrots
1 medium tomato, cut into wedges
1 hard-cooked egg, sliced

Dressing

½ cup mayonnaise
¼ cup commercial sour cream
1½ tablespoons prepared mustard

1 teaspoon salt
¼ teaspoon pepper

Sprinkle apple with lemon juice. Toss with cubed meat, celery, potato, diced egg, onion and cooked peas and carrots. Blend mayonnaise, sour cream, prepared mustard, salt, and pepper.

132

Pour over salad and toss until well coated. Garnish with tomato and sliced egg. (Serves 6.)

CHEF'S SALAD

1 medium head romaine or lettuce, torn into bite-size pieces
1 avocado, peeled and sliced
2 tomatoes, cut into wedges
1 cup julienne cheese strips (about ¼ pound)
1 cup julienne ham strips (about ¼ pound)

4 hard-cooked eggs, sliced
⅓ cup corn oil
2 tablespoons lemon juice
⅛ teaspoon herb seasoning
¼ teaspoon salt
Dash freshly ground pepper

Place greens in salad bowl. Arrange avocado, tomatoes, cheese, ham, and eggs on greens. Combine corn oil, lemon juice, herb seasoning, salt, and pepper. Just before serving toss with salad. (Makes 4 servings.)

CAESAR SALAD

2 tablespoons lemon juice
2 tablespoons cider vinegar
1 tablespoon Worcestershire sauce
¼ teaspoon dry mustard
½ teaspoon salt
¼ teaspoon pepper
⅓ cup corn oil

1 clove garlic
1 small can anchovies
3 quarts salad greens
¼ cup grated Parmesan cheese or crumbled blue cheese
1 egg
2 cups croutons

Combine first 8 ingredients in a small bowl. Cut anchovies into small pieces and add to dressing. Tear crisp, well-drained salad greens into pieces, and place in large salad bowl. When ready to mix salad, remove garlic from dressing, pour over greens; add cheese and toss lightly until all greens glisten and are coated. Break egg into salad and toss until well mixed. Sprinkle croutons over salad; mix lightly. Serve immediately. (Makes 8 servings.)

HEARTY SUPPER SALAD

½ pound thinly sliced frankfurters
1 tablespoon corn oil
1 green pepper, cut in narrow
   strips
½ cup thinly sliced celery
2 cooked potatoes, diced
½ cup finely chopped onion
½ cup Zesty French Dressing (see
   p. 145)

1 teaspoon salt
¼ teaspoon pepper
1 head lettuce, shredded
¼ cup Swiss cheese, cut in thin
   strips
2 tomatoes, cut in thin wedges

Sauté frankfurters in corn oil until lightly browned. Combine frankfurters, green pepper, celery, potatoes, onion, French dressing, salt, and pepper. Cover and chill. Just before serving, add lettuce, cheese, and tomato wedges. Toss gently and mix thoroughly. (Makes 8 to 10 servings.)

ANY BEAN SALAD

1 (1-pound, 13-ounce) can beans
   (green beans, red or white
   kidney beans, or chick peas)
1 tablespoon chopped scallions
1 tablespoon chopped green
   pepper
1 tablespoon chopped pimiento

½ cup corn oil
¼ cup vinegar
1 tablespoon sugar
1 teaspoon salt
¼ teaspoon pepper
2 radishes, sliced

Drain beans; reserve liquid for marinade. Add water to liquid, if necessary, to make ⅓ cup. Combine beans, scallions, green pepper, and pimiento in medium-size bowl. Mix corn oil, vinegar, sugar, salt, pepper, and bean liquid together. Pour over vegetables and marinate in refrigerator at least 3 hours. Add radishes just before serving. Serve plain or on lettuce leaves. (Makes 4 salad servings or 8 appetizer servings.)

134

SUMMER BEAN SALAD

Follow recipe for Any Bean Salad, substituting one pound fresh beans or 2 (9 ounce) packages frozen beans, cooked and drained, for canned beans and using ⅓ cup cooking liquid in marinade.

COLOMBIAN RELISH

¼ cup corn oil
½ cup cider vinegar
1 tablespoon sugar
¼ cup finely chopped onion
¼ cup finely chopped green
   pepper
¼ cup finely chopped cooked
   green beans
1 tablespoon finely chopped
   pimiento
¼ cup finely chopped cucumber

Combine corn oil, vinegar, and sugar. Add remaining ingredients and blend. Refrigerate several hours. Drain slightly to serve as a relish or spoon over hearts of lettuce. (Makes 1¾ cups.)

SHRIMP COLOMBIAN

Follow recipe for Colombian Relish, adding 2 cups cooked shrimp to relish before chilling. (Serves as appetizer salad.)

GREEN GODDESS SALAD

1 head iceberg lettuce, broken into
   pieces
2 tomatoes, cut into wedges
1 bunch watercress, cut into small
   sprigs
1 medium onion, sliced and
   broken into rings
Loster or crab meat

Dressing

½ clove garlic, minced
½ cup mayonnaise
¼ cup commercial sour cream
1½ tablespoons anchovy paste

1½ tablespoons tarragon vinegar
1½ teaspoons lemon juice
3 tablespoons chopped parsley

Arrange lettuce, watercress, tomatoes, and onion in large bowl. Chill. Blend minced garlic, mayonnaise, sour cream, and anchovy paste. Slowly stir in vinegar and lemon juice. Add parsley. Chill. To serve, pour dressing over salad, and garnish with lobster or crab meat. (Makes 6 servings.)

HAM AND VEGETABLE SALAD

1 cup chopped, cooked ham
1 cup (8-ounce can) small peas, drained
½ cup cooked, chopped carrots
¼ cup chopped raw apple

⅓ cup mayonnaise
1 tablespoon chopped cucumber pickle
1 teaspoon lemon juice

Combine all ingredients. Marinate in refrigerator at least 2 hours. (Serves 4.)

MEDITERRANEAN SALAD

1 (10-ounce) package frozen Italian green beans
2 tablespoons margarine
2 cups bread cubes
1 (12-ounce) can corn, drained
¼ cup cashew nuts

2 tablespoons chopped pimiento
¼ cup mayonnaise
1 tablespoon grated Parmesan cheese
1 teaspoon basil
1 teaspoon salt

Cook beans as directed on package, drain, and cool. Melt margarine in skillet. Add bread cubes; sauté until crisp, turning as needed. Combine all ingredients. (Makes 4 to 6 servings.)

VEGETABLE SALAD

1 (10-ounce) package frozen peas and carrots
1 (10-ounce) package frozen Italian green beans
1 (9-ounce) package frozen artichoke hearts
1 cup sliced cooked potatoes
¼ cup lemon juice
½ teaspoon salt
¼ teaspoon tarragon
½ cup mayonnaise
2 teaspoons mustard with horseradish
1 teaspoon tarragon
Mayonnaise
Red and green pepper strips
Ripe olives

Cook each frozen vegetable separately, according to directions on package. Drain. Mix cooked vegetables and potatoes with lemon juice, salt and ¼ teaspoon tarragon in shallow dish. Marinate in refrigerator several hours. Blend the ½ cup mayonnaise, mustard with horseradish, and 1 teaspoon tarragon. Gently mix with marinated vegetables. Arrange in serving bowl. Spread top with mayonnaise. Garnish with pepper strips and olives. (Serves 6.)

BEAN SPROUT SALAD

1 (1-pound) can bean sprouts, drained and crisped in ice water
1 cup drained pineapple chunks
1 (11-ounce) can mandarin orange segments, drained
1 (5-ounce) can water chestnuts, sliced
¼ cup diagonally sliced celery
1 cup mayonnaise
1 teaspoon soy sauce
1 teaspoon chopped, candied ginger
¾ teaspoon curry powder
Crisp spinach leaves

Combine drained bean sprouts, pineapple, orange segments, water chestnuts, and celery. Chill. Blend mayonnaise, soy sauce, candied ginger, and curry powder in small bowl; chill. Just before serving, mix salad with dressing. Serve on spinach leaves. (Makes about 6 servings.)

HUNTER'S SALAD

2 cups cooked lima beans or 1
(10-ounce) package frozen
lima beans, cooked and drained
1 cup chopped celery
1 cup diced American cheese
3 hard-cooked eggs, cut into
wedges

1 medium onion, thinly sliced and
separated into rings
½ cup sliced radishes
½ cup mayonnaise
Salad greens

Gently mix all ingredients except salad greens together until well mixed. Arrange on salad greens in bowl. (Makes 6 servings.)

COTTAGE CHEESE AND VEGETABLE SALAD

1½ cups cottage cheese
½ cup mayonnaise
1½ teaspoons salt
2 cups diced carrots
2 cups thinly sliced celery

1 cup diced cucumber
½ cup chopped green pepper
½ cup sliced radishes
¼ cup chopped onion
Lettuce leaves

Combine cottage cheese, mayonnaise, and salt. Toss with cut vegetables. Chill. Mound on lettuce leaves. (Makes 8 servings.)

Note: If preferred, salad may be packed into custard cups, chilled and unmolded on lettuce leaves.

SUMMER SALAD

1½ cups shredded lettuce
4 cups sliced fresh or frozen fruit
1 (3-ounce) package cream cheese

2 tablespoons lemon juice
¼ cup corn syrup
1 tablespoon finely chopped nuts

Arrange lettuce and fruit on serving platter or individual plates. Soften cream cheese in a bowl, blend in lemon juice, then stir in syrup a little at a time until the mixture is smooth. Sprinkle with nuts. Serve with salad. (Makes 6 servings.)

TOSSED RED AND GREEN SALAD

1 clove garlic
⅔ cup French dressing
⅓ cup mayonnaise
¼ cup Roquefort cheese,
    crumbled
1 head Boston lettuce, torn into
    pieces

1 bunch watercress, cut into small
    sprigs
3 scallions, sliced
3 radishes, sliced
½ cup canned artichoke hearts,
    quartered
1 avocado, pared and sliced

Cut garlic clove, rub cut sides on small mixing bowl; discard. Then blend French dressing and mayonnaise in bowl. Lightly stir in crumbled Roquefort cheese. Add vegetables and avocado and mix lightly. (Makes 6 servings.)

SPINACH SALAD WITH BACON DRESSING

6 slices bacon
1 tablespoon sugar
2 teaspoons cornstarch
½ teaspoon salt
⅛ teaspoon pepper
1 tablespoon reserved bacon
    drippings

¼ cup mayonnaise
½ cup water
¼ cup vinegar
2 tablespoons minced onion
1 (10-ounce) bag fresh spinach,
    washed and cleaned

Cook bacon until crisp and reserve drippings. Blend sugar, cornstarch, salt, and pepper into reserved drippings in skillet, then blend in mayonnaise. Combine water and vinegar. Slowly stir into mixture in skillet. Cook over medium heat, stirring constantly, 3 to 5 minutes or just until bubbly. Sprinkle onion and bacon over spinach. Add sauce and toss until spinach is well coated. (Serves 5.)

BASIC SOUFFLE SALAD

1 cup boiling water	Dash pepper (omit for fruit salads)
1 (3-ounce) package lemon- or lime-flavored gelatin	1 to 1½ cups diced vegetables, fruit, meat, fish, poultry, eggs, or cheese
½ cup cold water	
1 to 2 tablespoons vinegar or lemon juice	½ to 1 tablespoon chopped onion, optional
½ cup mayonnaise	Salad greens
¼ teaspoon salt	

Pour boiling water over gelatin in bowl; stir until gelatin is completely dissolved. Add cold water, vinegar or lemon juice, mayonnaise, salt, and pepper; blend with rotary beater. Pour into freezing tray or metal loaf pan. Chill in freezing unit 20 to 25 minutes or until firm about 1 inch from edge of pan but still soft in center. Then turn mixture into bowl and whip with rotary beater until fluffy and thick. Fold in selected ingredients and onion. Pour into 1-quart mold or individual molds. Chill in refrigerator (not freezing unit) 45 to 60 minutes or until firm. Unmold. Garnish with greens and serve extra mayonnaise on the side. (Makes 5 to 6 servings.)

Suggested Combinations

Ham, pineapple, and celery
Tuna, cucumber, and olives
Peaches, almonds, and cream cheese
Oranges, cottage cheese, and nuts

KIDNEY BEAN AND ONION SALAD

1 (1-pound, 4-ounce) can kidney beans, drained	2 hard-cooked eggs, diced
¼ to ½ cup chopped onion	½ teaspoon salt
¼ cup pickle relish	⅛ teaspoon pepper
	¼ cup mayonnaise

Combine all ingredients. Chill. If desired, garnish with parsley and hard-cooked egg slices. (Makes 6 servings.)

ORIENTAL RICE SALAD

1 (6-ounce) can mushroom caps
¾ cup uncooked rice (not pre-cooked variety)
1 bay leaf
½ teaspoon curry powder
¼ teaspoon salt
Dash ginger
⅓ cup chopped celery

3 tablespoons chopped chives
¾ cup mayonnaise
1 (6½- to 7½-ounce) can crab meat, drained, cleaned, and flaked
1 small apple, cored and cubed
Salad greens
Tomato slices

Drain mushroom caps, adding water to liquid to make 1½ cups. Combine rice, mushroom liquid and water, bay leaf, curry powder, salt, and ginger in saucepan. Bring to boil; cover and simmer 15 to 20 minutes or until rice is tender. Discard bay leaf. Fluff rice with fork; cool in large bowl. Meanwhile, halve mushroom caps, then combine with celery, chives, and ½ cup mayonnaise. Add to rice. Mix well and pack into 1-quart ring mold. Chill. Combine crab meat and apple with remaining ¼ cup mayonnaise. Chill. To serve, unmold rice ring on salad greens. Fill center with crab mixture. Garnish with tomato slices. (Makes 4 servings.)

FRUIT SALADS

BANANA SALAD WITH FLUFFY DRESSING

¾ cup mayonnaise
¼ cup light corn syrup
¼ cup light cream
1½ teaspoons prepared mustard

1 medium head lettuce
1 large banana
2 tablespoons chopped walnuts
Dash paprika

Blend mayonnaise, light corn syrup, cream, and mustard. Break lettuce into bite-size pieces in bowl. Slice banana. Combine lettuce, banana, and walnuts. Toss with mayonnaise mixture. Sprinkle with paprika. Serve immediately. (Makes 6 servings.)

PEAR BLUSH SALAD

1 cup red cinnamon candies	1 (3-ounce) package cream cheese
1 cup light corn syrup	⅓ cup coarsely chopped nuts
1½ cups water	Crisp salad greens
6 large fresh pears	

Cook and stir cinnamon candies, syrup, and water in saucepan over low heat to dissolve candies. Boil 5 minutes, stirring occasionally. Meanwhile, peel and core pears cut in halves. Simmer pear halves in syrup until tender. Remove from syrup, drain, and chill. Soften cream cheese, adding a few drops of cream if needed. Stir in nuts. Spread flat sides of pear halves with mixture, and put them together sandwich fashion. Stand on bed of greens. Serve with a fruit salad dressing. (Makes 6 servings.)

GRANDMA'S ROSY CHEEK APPLE SALAD

Follow recipe for Pear Blush Salad, using small peeled and cored apples instead of pear halves. Turn in syrup during cooking to color apples evenly.

Note: Leftover cinnamon syrup can be used again or used to sweeten fresh applesauce, or served on pancakes, waffles, or French toast.

PEAR AND COTTAGE CHEESE SALAD

1 (1-pound, 13-ounce) can pear halves	1 cup mayonnaise
	1 (8-ounce) carton cottage cheese
1 teaspoon grated orange or lemon rind	Grapes (optional)
	Salad greens
½ teaspoon lemon juice	

Drain pears; reserve ¼ cup juice. Blend reserved juice, grated rind, and lemon juice into mayonnaise. Arrange pear halves, cottage cheese, and grapes on salad greens. Serve dressing on the side. (Makes 6 servings.)

WALDORF SALAD

3 red apples, cored and diced	⅔ cup mayonnaise
1 tablespoon lemon juice	1 cup diced celery
1 tablespoon sugar	⅓ cup chopped pecans or walnuts
⅛ teaspoon salt	Salad greens

Toss apples with lemon juice, sugar, salt, and 2 tablespoons mayonnaise. Cover and chill. Add remaining mayonnaise, celery, and chopped nuts just before serving. Toss until well mixed. Serve on salad greens. (Makes 4 or 5 servings.)

CHEESE WALDORF SALAD

Add 1½ cups coarsely shredded Cheddar cheese to Waldorf Salad just before serving.

FRUIT WALDORF SALAD

Add 2 cups drained pineapple tidbits to Waldorf Salad just before serving

MANDARIN SALAD

1 (11-ounce) can mandarin orange segments, drained	1 cup flaked coconut
	1 cup miniature marshmallows
1 (8¾-ounce) can pineapple tidbits, drained	½ cup commercial sour cream
	½ cup mayonnaise
1 cup fresh or canned seedless grapes	Lettuce
	Watercress

Combine mandarin orange segments, pineapple tidbits, grapes, coconut, marshmallows, sour cream, and mayonnaise. Chill. Serve on lettuce leaves, garnished with watercress. (Makes 5 servings.)

FROZEN FRUIT SALAD

1 orange, sectioned and cut into small pieces
1 medium banana, diced
½ cup crushed pineapple, drained
¼ cup diced maraschino cherries, drained
¼ cup toasted slivered almonds
2 tablespoons chopped celery
½ cup mayonnaise
½ cup heavy cream, whipped
Lettuce

Combine orange, banana, pineapple, cherries, almonds, and celery. Fold mayonnaise into whipped cream. Fold carefully into fruit mixture. Turn into freezing tray or metal loaf pan. Freeze about 1½ hours or until firm. Cut into squares and serve on lettuce. (Makes about 6 servings.)

LEMON-LIME SALAD

1 cup boiling water
1 (3-ounce) package lemon-flavored gelatin
1 (3-ounce) package lime-flavored gelatin
1 cup mayonnaise
1 cup commercial sour cream
1 cup cottage cheese
1 (8½-ounce) can crushed pineapple
2 teaspoons prepared horseradish
½ cup chopped pecans

Pour boiling water over gelatin. Stir until gelatin is *completely* dissolved. Combine mayonnaise, sour cream, cottage cheese, pineapple, horseradish, and pecans. Stir in hot gelatin, mixing well. Pour into 1½-quart mold. Chill until set. Unmold. (Makes 6 servings.)

MOLDED CRANBERRY RELISH SALAD

2 envelopes unflavored gelatin
¼ cup cold water
1 cup boiling water
2 (1-pound) cans whole-berry cranberry sauce
½ cup light corn syrup
¼ cup orange juice
⅛ teaspoon salt
½ cup sliced apple
½ cup drained orange sections
Salad greens
½ cup mayonnaise

Sprinkle gelatin over cold water in large bowl; let soften 5 minutes. Add boiling water and stir until gelatin is *completely* dissolved. Break up cranberry sauce with fork; reserve ¼ cup. Stir remainder into gelatin; then mix in corn syrup, orange juice, and salt. Chill until mixture reaches consistency of unbeaten egg white. Fold in apple and orange sections. Turn into 6-cup mold. Chill until firm. Unmold onto serving plate; garnish with salad greens. Meanwhile, blend reserved cranberry sauce with mayonnaise. Serve with molded salad. (Makes 8 to 12 servings.)

DUNKING SALAD

½ cup mayonnaise
¼ cup French dressing
½ to 1 teaspoon grated onion
6 bread and butter pickles, finely chopped
Assorted vegetables for dunking (raw cauliflowerets, celery sticks, cucumber slices, tomato wedges, carrot sticks, radishes, scallions, etc.

Combine mayonnaise and French dressing. Stir in onion and pickles. Chill. Serve with vegetables for dunking.

DRESSINGS

BASIC FRENCH DRESSING

1 cup corn oil
⅓ to ½ cup vinegar
1 to 3 tablespoons sugar
1½ teaspoons salt

½ teaspoon paprika
½ teaspoon dry mustard
1 clove garlic

Measure all ingredients into a bottle or jar. Cover tightly and shake well. Chill several hours; then remove garlic. Shake thoroughly before serving. (Makes about 1½ cups.)

Note: Lemon juice may be substituted for all or part of the vinegar.

ZESTY DRESSING

Follow recipe for Basic French Dressing, adding 2 tablespoons catsup, 1 tablespoon lemon juice, and 1 teaspoon Worcestershire sauce.

LEMON HERB DRESSING

Follow recipe for Basic French Dressing, using lemon juice instead of vinegar, reduce sugar to 2 tablespoons, and substitute ½ teaspoon salad herbs for dry mustard.

CREAMY DRESSING

Follow recipe for Basic French Dressing, increasing sugar to ¼ cup, omit dry mustard and garlic, and add ½ cup sour cream and ¼ cup catsup. (Makes 2 cups.)

VINAIGRETTE DRESSING

Follow recipe for Basic French Dressing, omitting paprika, dry mustard, and garlic, and adding 1 hard-cooked egg (chopped), 1 tablespoon chopped pimiento, 1 tablespoon chopped chives, and 1 tablespoon chopped green pepper. (Makes 1⅔ cups.)

SWEET AND SPICY FRENCH DRESSING

1½ cups corn oil
¾ cup tarragon vinegar
½ cup light corn syrup
1 teaspoon salt
½ teaspoon curry powder

¼ teaspoon pepper
Dash cayenne
1 teaspoon finely chopped onion
1 clove garlic

Combine all ingredients. Beat with rotary beater until well blended and thick. Chill in covered container several hours; then remove garlic. Shake thoroughly before serving. (Makes 2 cups.)

TOMATO FRENCH DRESSING

1 cup tomato juice
¼ cup vinegar
½ cup corn oil
2 tablespoons sugar
1 teaspoon dry mustard

1 teaspoon paprika
1 teaspoon salt
1 teaspoon Worcestershire sauce
1 clove garlic

Measure all ingredients into a bottle or jar. Cover tightly and shake well. Chill several hours; then remove garlic. Shake thoroughly before serving. (Makes about 2 cups.)

FRUIT FRENCH DRESSING

½ teaspoon dry mustard
¼ teaspoon salt
¾ cup corn oil

2 tablespoons tarragon vinegar
1 (10-ounce) package frozen strawberries, partially thawed

Measure all ingredients into a bottle or jar. Cover tightly and shake well. Chill several hours. Shake thoroughly before serving. (Makes about 1½ cups.)

CREAMY FRENCH DRESSING

1 teaspoon salt	¼ cup undiluted evaporated milk
½ teaspoon dry mustard	½ cup corn oil
3 to 4 tablespoons sugar	3 tablespoons vinegar
3 tablespoons catsup	

Measure all ingredients except vinegar into measuring bowl. Beat with rotary beater until smooth and well blended. Add vinegar all at once, beating until thoroughly mixed. Dressing will be creamy thick. (Makes about 1¼ cups.)

CELERY SEED DRESSING

1 teaspoon salt	½ cup light corn syrup
1 teaspoon dry mustard	¼ to ⅓ cup vinegar
1 teaspoon paprika	1 cup corn oil
1 teaspoon celery seed	1 tablespoon grated onion

Combine all ingredients. Beat with rotary beater until well blended and thick. Place in covered container. Chill several hours. Shake thoroughly before serving. (Makes about 1¾ cups.)

QUICK BLUE CHEESE DRESSING

¾ cup corn oil	Dash pepper
¼ cup vinegar	¼ cup crumbled blue or Roque-
1 clove garlic	fort cheese
¼ teaspoon salt	

Combine corn oil, vinegar, garlic, salt, and pepper. Chill. Remove garlic. Add cheese and toss with salad just before serving. (Makes 1¼ cups dressing.)

JIFFY FRUIT SALAD DRESSING

½ cup light corn syrup
½ cup corn oil
⅔ cup lemon juice, fresh, frozen,
    or bottled

½ teaspoon salt
¼ teaspoon pepper

Beat syrup and corn oil together with rotary beater; then beat in fruit juice, salt, and pepper. Chill. Serve with any desired combination of fruit. (Makes 1½ cups.)

APPLE SALAD DRESSING

½ cup apple sauce
½ cup corn syrup
⅓ cup lemon juice
½ teaspoon grated lemon rind

½ teaspoon paprika
¼ teaspoon salt
¼ teaspoon dry mustard
½ cup corn oil

Combine all ingredients except corn oil in bowl. Beat oil in gradually until it is all blended in. Chill. Shake or beat before serving. Serve with fruit salad. (Makes 1½ cups.)

CUMBERLAND DRESSING

2 tablespoons currant jelly
½ cup mayonnaise

¼ teaspoon grated lemon rind
¼ cup heavy cream, whipped

Beat jelly with fork until smooth. Stir in mayonnaise and grated lemon rind. Fold in whipped cream. Chill. Serve on orange and grapefruit sections arranged on a bed of salad greens. (Makes about 1 cup.)

CLASSIC BLUE CHEESE DRESSING

1 cup mayonnaise
½ cup commercial sour cream
½ cup (3-ounce package)
    crumbled blue cheese
2 tablespoons tarragon vinegar
1 teaspoon Worcestershire sauce

1 tablespoon sugar
½ teaspoon salt
⅛ teaspoon pepper
1 clove garlic, finely chopped
    (optional)

Blend mayonnaise, sour cream, and blue cheese. Gradually stir in vinegar, Worcestershire sauce, sugar, salt, pepper, and garlic. Chill. Excellent on sliced tomato and lettuce. (Makes about 1¾ cups.)

BASIC CREAM FRUIT DRESSING

½ cup mayonnaise
¼ cup light corn syrup
½ cup commercial sour cream or heavy whipped cream

Combine mayonnaise and corn syrup; blend until smooth. Fold in cream. Serve with fresh pineapple, blueberries, or strawberries. (Makes about 1¼ cups.)

Raspberry Cream Dressing

To the Basic Cream Fruit dressing, add ¾ cup fresh or thawed, frozen red raspberries, drained. (Makes 2 cups.)

Celery Seed Dressing

To the Basic Cream Fruit Dressing, add 1 tablespoon lemon juice and 1 teaspoon celery seed. (Makes 1¼ cups.)

Spicy Salad Dressing

To the Basic Cream Fruit Dressing, add 1 teaspoon lime juice, ¼ teaspoon ground ginger, and ¼ teaspoon nutmeg. (Makes about 1¼ cups.)

QUICK CREAMY DRESSINGS

Blend 1 cup mayonnaise with ¼ cup of any of the following: fruit juice (canned, fresh, or frozen), maraschino cherry juice, tomato juice, milk, light cream, pickle juice, French dressing, or prepared mustard. (Makes about 1¼ cups.)

THOUSAND ISLAND DRESSING

1 cup mayonnaise
¼ cup chili sauce
2 tablespoons chopped green pepper
1 tablespoon finely chopped pimiento
1 tablespoon chopped onion

Combine all ingredients. Chill before serving. If it seems a little thick, stir in 2 tablespoons or so of cream or milk. Serve on wedges of lettuce. (Makes 1½ cups.)

SWEET MALTAISE DRESSING

¾ cup mayonnaise
1 teaspoon orange rind
¼ cup orange juice
1½ teaspoons confectioners' sugar
1 egg white

Blend mayonnaise, orange juice, rind, and sugar. Beat egg white until soft peaks form when beater is raised. Fold in mayonnaise mixture. Serve with fresh fruit, such as pineapple, strawberries, or sliced orange. (Makes about 1 cup.)

FRUIT SALAD DRESSING

½ cup mayonnaise
½ cup commercial sour cream

2½ tablespoons confectioners' sugar
1½ tablespoons lemon juice

Blend all ingredients. Chill about 1 hour. Serve with fruit salads. (Makes about 1¼ cups.)

Almond Dressing

Add 2 tablespoons toasted slivered almonds and ½ teaspoon almond extract to Fruit Salad Dressing.

Ginger Dressing

Add 1 tablespoon chopped candied ginger or ½ teaspoon powdered ginger to Fruit Salad Dressing.

Peppermint Dressing

Add 1 teaspoon peppermint flavoring to Fruit Salad Dressing.

Avocado Dressing

Follow recipe for Fruit Salad Dressing, increasing lemon juice to 2 tablespoons and blending in 1 medium avocado, mashed.

Curry Dressing

Add ½ teaspoon curry powder to Fruit Salad Dressing.

GREEN MAYONNAISE

12 spinach leaves	9 sprigs fresh tarragon *or* 1
12 watercress leaves	teaspoon dried tarragon leaves
8 sprigs parsley	1 tablespoon chopped green onion
9 sprigs fresh chervil *or* 1 teaspoon	1 cup mayonnaise
dried chervil leaves	

Blanch fresh greens in boiling water 2 minutes. Drain, reserving 2 tablespoons liquid. Purée blanched greens, onion, and liquid in blender 30 seconds at high speed. Stir into mayonnaise. (If dried chervil and tarragon are used, stir into mayonnaise with blanched greens.) Chill. Serve on chilled fish or vegetable salads. (Makes 1⅓ cups.)

Note: If desired, omit liquid and press drained blanched greens through sieve. Stir into mayonnaise.

TARRAGON WINE DRESSING

½ teaspoon dried tarragon
2 tablespoons dry white wine *or* 1 teaspoon lemon juice
½ cup mayonnaise

Soak tarragon in wine or lemon juice 20 to 30 minutes. Combine with mayonnaise. Chill. Serve on shredded lettuce and cooked asparagus, or with chilled, cooked shrimp. (Makes about ½ cup.)

COTTAGE CHEESE DRESSING

½ cup French dressing
½ cup mayonnaise
¼ cup cottage cheese

Fold French dressing into mayonnaise. Lightly fold in cottage cheese. Chill. Serve with fruit, vegetable, or mixed green salad. (Makes 1¼ cups.)

HERB DRESSING

¾ cup mayonnaise
1 hard-cooked egg, finely chopped
2 tablespoons finely chopped
  parsley

1½ teaspoons tarragon vinegar
½ teaspoon prepared mustard
½ teaspoon finely chopped chives

Blend all ingredients. Chill. Serve with mixed green, vegetable, or meat salads. (Makes 1 cup.)

CHEESE DRESSING

¼ cup milk
¼ cup grated Parmesan, crumbled blue or finely shredded Cheddar cheese
¼ teaspoon Worcestershire sauce

Blend milk into mayonnaise. Mix in cheese and Worcestershire sauce. Chill. Serve with mixed greens, citrus, egg, or fish salads. (Makes ¾ cup.)

PIQUANT DRESSING

1 cup mayonnaise
½ cup hot catsup
1 teaspoon Worcestershire sauce

½ teaspoon chili powder
½ teaspoon soy sauce

Blend mayonnaise and catsup. Mix in Worcestershire sauce, chili powder, and soy sauce. Serve with cold meat, hearts of lettuce, or tossed green salad. (Makes about 1½ cups.)

MOCK HOLLANDAISE SAUCE

¾ cup mayonnaise
⅓ cup milk
¼ teaspoon salt

Dash white pepper
1 tablespoon lemon juice
1 teaspoon grated lemon rind

Blend mayonnaise, milk, salt, and pepper in saucepan. Heat very slowly, stirring constantly, about 3 minutes or until warm. Stir in lemon juice and rind. Serve with cooked artichokes, asparagus, broccoli, or poached fish. (Makes 1¼ cups.)

MUSTARD SAUCE

Stir into Mock Hollandaise Sauce 2 teaspoons mustard with horseradish.

MOCK MOUSSELINE

Fold into Mock Hollandaise Sauce ¼ cup heavy cream, whipped.

CUCUMBER DRESSING

To 1 cup mayonnaise, add 1 cup finely chopped cucumber. Delicious on tomato slices. (Makes 1¾ cups.)

CELERY DRESSING

To 1 cup mayonnaise, add ¼ cup diced celery and 2 tablespoons diced green pepper. Serve with wedges of lettuce. (Makes about 1¼ cups.)

HORSERADISH DRESSING

To 1 cup mayonnaise, add ½ cup prepared horseradish. Excellent with cold cuts. (Makes about 1½ cups.)

MUSTARD DRESSING

To 1 cup mayonnaise, add ⅓ cup mustard with horseradish. Serve with ham or use in making ham sandwiches. (Makes about 1¼ cups.)

TOMATO DRESSING

To 1 cup mayonnaise, add 1 cup finely chopped fresh tomato. Pleasant with cottage cheese salad. (Makes about 2 cups.)

AVOCADO DRESSING

To 1 cup mayonnaise, add 1 mashed ripe avocado and 1 teaspoon lemon juice. Perfect with fruit salads. (Makes about 1¾ cups.)

CHIVE DRESSING

To 1 cup mayonnaise, add 2 tablespoons finely chopped chives. Serve with sliced hard-cooked eggs. (Makes 1 cup.)

PARMESAN DRESSING

To 1 cup mayonnaise, blend in ½ cup milk gradually. Add ½ cup grated Parmesan cheese and ½ teaspoon Worcestershire sauce. Splendid with hot vegetables. (Makes 1½ cups.)

LEMON DRESSING

To 1 cup mayonnaise, add 2 teaspoons lemon juice and ½ teaspoon grated lemon rind. Delicious on hot or cold asparagus. (Makes about 1 cup.)

HERBED DRESSING

Soak 1 teaspoon dried basil, mint, tarragon or dill weed in 2 or 3 tablespoons milk, 10 to 20 minutes. Add to 1 cup mayonnaise. Chill. Serve basil dressing with tomatoes; mint dressing with pear salad; tarragon dressing with artichokes or chicken salad; and dill dressing with sliced cucumber. (Makes 1 cup.)

VI

Casseroles and Other One-Dish Meals

There is no need for even the most inexperienced young cook to depend solely on TV dinners when called on to prepare a meal for herself, family, or guests. Apart from the many and varied frozen and canned foods currently on the market which require very little know-how, the following substantial, flavorful and interesting one-dish meals can be prepared quickly, easily, and economically by all nervous neophytes.

THE BASIC CASSEROLE

Prepare 2 cups cooked, cut-up meat, fish, poultry, or vegetables (leftovers are great), or leave food pieces in serving size if desired. Prepare 2 cups sauce—select from list below. In an attractive 1½-quart heatproof casserole, mix sauce with cut-up food, or arrange alternate layers of sauce and cut-up food. Top with fine crumbs mixed with melted butter or margarine. Bake in 375°F. oven 20 minutes or until sauce bubbles. If you start with hot, freshly cooked food, just brown crumbs lightly under broiler. Serve in same casserole. (Makes 4 servings.)

BASIC WHITE SAUCES

Medium

Melt 2 tablespoons margarine in saucepan; blend in 1 tablespoon cornstarch, ½ teaspoon salt, and ⅛ teaspoon pepper. Remove from heat; slowly stir in 1 cup milk. Stir and cook over medium heat until sauce thickens, then boil 1 minute. (Makes 1 cup sauce. Ingredients may be doubled or tripled for more cups of sauce as needed for different uses.)

Thick

Follow directions for Medium White Sauce, but use 3 tablespoons margarine, 2 tablespoons cornstarch, ½ teaspoon salt, and ⅛ teaspoon pepper for each cup of milk.

Velouté Sauce

Follow directions for Medium White Sauce, but replace milk with stock or bouillon (chicken, fish, or beef).

A La King Sauce

Follow directions for Medium White Sauce, but sauté ½ cup sliced mushrooms, 2 tablespoons green pepper slivers, and 2 tablespoons chopped pimiento in margarine before adding cornstarch. Substitute ½ cup light cream for milk.

Amandine Sauce

Just before serving, stir ⅓ cup toasted, slivered almonds into Medium White or Velouté Sauce.

Curry Sauce

Heat 1 tablespoon curry powder in margarine before adding cornstarch in Medium White or Velouté Sauce.

Herb Sauce

Stir 1 tablespoon chopped fresh herbs such as parsley or dill into Medium White or Velouté Sauce.

Mornay Sauce

Stir ¼ cup grated cheese, either Cheddar or half and half Gruyère and Parmesan, and ⅓ cup light cream into Medium White or Velouté Sauce.

Newburg Sauce

Replace ¼ cup milk in Medium White or Velouté Sauce with light cream. Stir 2 tablespoons sherry into the cooked sauce.

Soubise Sauce

Sauté 1 minced small onion in margarine before adding corn-starch in Velouté Sauce. Replace ¼ cup stock with light cream.

Try:
1. Crabmeat, lobster, or shrimp with Newburg Sauce.
2. Chicken, turkey, ham, or veal with A La King Sauce.
3. Small, browned beef balls (about 1 pound chopped beef) or slices of leftover beef with Soubise Sauce.
4. Lamb balls or slices with Curry Sauce.
5. Fish steaks or fillets (about 1 pound sole, salmon, or halibut) baked in casserole, brushed with margarine, until fish flakes easily. Top with Mornay Sauce and brown lightly under broiler.

GRAVIES

For Pan Fried or Roasted Meats or Poultry

Remove meat from pan; pour off fat, and measure back into pan 1 tablespoon fat for each cup of gravy desired. For each table-spoon fat, add 1 cup liquid: water, stock, or milk. Stir and cook over medium heat, scraping pan to loosen browned meat juices. Remove from heat. For each cup of liquid you added, blend 1 tablespoon cornstarch (or 2 for thicker gravy) with ¼ cup cold water and stir in. Stir and cook until thickened. Add seasonings. For an extra flavor touch, try herbs or spices: a touch of mint for lamb, curry for pork, mustard for beef, or rosemary for chicken. Add gravy coloring if browner gravy is desired. Simmer 5 minutes. Serve hot.

For Braised Meats or Poultry or Stews

Remove cooked meat and vegetables from pan. Measure liquid. For each cup, stir in 1 tablespoon cornstarch with ¼ cup cold water. Stir and cook until thickened. Add seasonings, and color if desired. Add meat and vegetables. Serve gravy hot.

FOR THE ADVENTUROUS

CLAM AND RICE CASSEROLE

3 cups hot cooked rice	Milk
¼ cup mayonnaise	1 teaspoon lemon juice
¼ cup chopped parsley	¼ teaspoon grated onion
3 tablespoons margarine	½ teaspoon salt
3 tablespoons flour	Dash pepper
2 (10½-ounce) cans minced clams	

Mix rice, mayonnaise, and parsley together. Melt margarine; blend in flour. Drain liquid from clams; add milk to make 1½ cups. Stir into flour mixture; cook over low heat, stirring constantly, until thickened. Mix in lemon juice, clams, onion, salt, and pepper. Alternate layers of rice mixture and sauce in greased 1½-quart casserole. Bake in 350° F. oven 30 minutes. (Makes 4 servings.)

CHICKEN POT PIE

1 (3-pound) chicken, cooked and cubed	1 cup water
4 carrots, pared, sliced, and cooked	2 cups chicken broth
1½ to 2 cups cooked peas	2 tablespoons flour
1 envelope cream of leek soup	¼ cup water
	1 package refrigerator biscuits

Combine chicken, carrots, and peas in 2-quart casserole. Mix soup with 1 cup water; then stir into chicken broth. Bring to a boil; simmer 5 minutes. Blend flour with ¼ cup water. Stir into soup mixture; cook until smooth and thickened. Pour over chicken and vegetables. Mix lightly. Bake in 450° F. oven until hot and bubbly. Place biscuits on top of hot chicken mixture. Continue baking until biscuits are done, 10 to 15 minutes (Makes 4 to 6 servings.)

FINNISH BEEF CASSEROLE

1 medium onion, chopped	3 cups cooked rice
½ cup margarine, melted	¾ cup dark corn syrup
2 eggs	½ cup raisins
3 cups milk	1 tablespoon salt
1½ pounds ground beef	

Cook onion in 2 tablespoons melted margarine in skillet over low heat, until transparent. Beat eggs foamy in large bowl; blend in milk. Stir in onions, beef, rice, syrup, margarine, raisins, salt. Bake in 3-quart ovenproof casserole in 400° F. oven about 1½ hours or until firm. Serve with cranberry or lingonberry sauce. (Makes 6 to 8 servings.)

BLANCHE'S TURKEY CASSEROLE

2 to 3 cups leftover turkey cut in bite-size pieces	1 can cream of mushroom soup (undiluted)
1 large onion sliced in thin rings	2 cups mashed potatoes
1 box frozen or 1 can mixed green peas and carrots	

Grease large, deep, round casserole thoroughly with butter. Spread one layer of turkey, one layer of onions, one layer of green peas and carrots, one layer of cream of mushroom soup, one layer of mashed potatoes, and repeat each layer again in order. Season with salt, pepper and a dash of paprika. Preheat oven to 350° F. and bake about 45 minutes or until potatoes begin to gently brown. (Makes 6 servings.)

COUNTRY STYLE MEAT CASSEROLE

1 pound ground beef
1 recipe Spicy Barbecue Sauce
  (see below)
1 (1-pound) can stewed tomatoes

¼ teaspoon oregano
8 ounces wide noodles, cooked and
  drained
1 cup grated Cheddar cheese

Brown ground beef in skillet over medium heat, stirring occasionally. Drain off fat. Mix in Barbecue Sauce, tomatoes, and oregano. Bring to boil, stirring occasionally. Combine with drained noodles. Pour half into 2-quart casserole. Sprinkle with half the cheese. Repeat layers. Bake in 350° F. oven 30 minutes or until casserole bubbles and cheese is melted. (Makes 4 servings.)

Spicy Barbecue Sauce

¼ cup syrup
¼ cup tarragon vinegar
2 tablespoons corn oil
1 teaspoon salt
⅛ teaspoon pepper

¼ cup chopped onion
⅓ cup catsup
2 teaspoons dry mustard
1 teaspoon Worcestershire sauce

Blend first 5 ingredients; add those remaining and bring to boil over medium heat, stirring occasionally. Simmer 5 minutes, uncovered. (Makes 1 cup.)

PASTA AND PIZZA

PERFECT SPAGHETTI

Use *large* kettle and a lot of water—at least 3 quarts to 8 ounces
spaghetti. Add 1 teaspoon salt for each quart water. Allow water
to boil briskly before adding spaghetti. Do not break. Hold sheaf
firmly at one end, dip other end in pot, and as it softens swirl it
around until it is completely submerged in the water. Cook uncovered with water still boiling until tender but firm. Be sure
not to overcook or spaghetti will be mushy. Drain immediately.

There are many delightful varieties of bottled or canned spaghetti
sauces available—*e.g.*, marinara, mushroom, meat sauce—and it
is a good idea to keep these as a staple on your pantry shelf. For
a quick home-made sauce, however, the following is unbeatable:

Quick-as-a-Flash Spaghetti Sauce

1 pound chopped beef
2 (8-ounce) cans (or 2 cups)
  seasoned tomato sauce
2 large onions, chopped
2 tablespoons salad oil
2 cloves garlic, minced

2 teaspoons chili powder
1 (6-ounce) can tomato paste
1 teaspoon salt
1 teaspoon sugar
Dash cayenne pepper

In pressure cooker, mix all ingredients and allow to cook 10 or
11 minutes at about 14 or 15 pounds pressure. Carefully and
quickly reduce pressure under cold water and serve over cooked
spaghetti. Sprinkle with pepper and Parmesan cheese. (Makes 6
servings.)

LASAGNE

1 pound Italian sausage or
    chopped beef
1 teaspoon basil
1 teaspoon salt
1 clove garlic, minced
2 cups canned tomatoes
2 (6-ounce) cans Italian tomato
    paste
10 ounces lasagne or wide noodles

3 cups ricotta cheese or creamy
    small-curd cottage cheese
½ cup grated Parmesan cheese
2 tablespoons dehydrated parsley
    flakes
2 eggs, beaten
2 teaspoons salt
½ teaspoon pepper
16 ounces mozzarella cheese,
    thinly sliced

Brown meat over low heat and drain off fat. Add basil, salt, garlic, tomatoes, and tomato paste and simmer 20 to 25 minutes, stirring occasionally. Cook noodles in several quarts of boiling salted water; drain. Combine ricotta or cottage cheese, Parmesan cheese, parsley flakes, eggs, salt, and pepper. Place half the noodles in 13 x 9 x 2-inch baking dish, cover with half the ricotta or cottage cheese filling, then spread with layer of half the mozzarella cheese and top with half the meat sauce. Repeat these four layers. Bake in 375° F. oven. Cool for 5 to 10 minutes and cut into squares. (Makes 12 servings.)

PIZZA

¼ cup salad oil
⅔ cup water
1 package biscuit mix (2 cups)
2 cups canned tomatoes
1 medium onion, chopped

¼ teaspoon garlic powder
1 teaspoon oregano
½ cup grated Parmesan cheese
Salt
Pepper

Grease 2 cake pans. Add water to biscuit mix and roll out to cover the cake pans. Brush dough with half the oil. Bake 10 minutes in 450° F. oven. Spread remaining oil, onion, garlic, oregano, and tomatoes on crust, and sprinkle with cheese. Season with salt

+ Bake another 10 min at 450°

166

and pepper and bake another 10 minutes at 450° F. (Makes 8 servings.)

AROUND THE WORLD ONE-DISH SUPPERS FOR THE STAY-AT-HOME BUDGET

All the following are shortcut adaptations of classic dishes:

PAELLA
(Spanish casserole of rice, seafood, and vegetables)

1 small onion, chopped
2 tablespoons margarine
3 cups liquid
1 envelope beef or chunk chicken
    noodle soup mix
1 (14½-ounce) can tomatoes
1 (10½-ounce) can minced clams
1 (8½-ounce) can green peas
1 (4½-ounce) can shrimp
1 (4-ounce) jar pimientos

1 cup uncooked rice (not pre-cooked variety
Saffron threads

Drain and reserve liquid

Add enough water to the reserved liquid to make the three cups liquid called for in the recipe. Chop pimientos. Cook onion in margarine in large skillet or electric fry-pan. Add liquid and soup mix. Stir in ½ teaspoon saffron threads and rice. Bring to a boil. Cover and simmer over low heat 20 minutes. Stir in tomatoes, clams, peas, shrimp, and pimientos. Recover and continue cooking 10 minutes or until rice is tender and liquid is absorbed. (Makes 4 to 6 servings.)

CHOUCROUTE GARNIE
(Garnished Sauerkraut)

2 (1-pound) cans sauerkraut
2 tablespoons margarine
1 (2½-ounce) jar junior food
    franks
1 (4-ounce) can Vienna sausage

1 pound cooked ham steak or
    Canadian bacon, cut in thin
    strips
½ envelope onion soup mix
2 cups water

Soak sauerkraut in cold water 20 minutes; drain. Meanwhile, melt margarine in electric fry-pan at 300° F. Add franks and sausage with can juices and ham or bacon. Add soup mix, water, and sauerkraut. Stir lightly. Reduce heat; cover and simmer about 30 minutes or until liquid is absorbed. (Makes 4 to 6 servings.)

VEAL PARMIGIANA

¼ cup corn oil
1½ pounds thinly sliced lean veal
¼ cup chopped onion
2 (8-ounce) cans tomato sauce

¾ teaspoon Italian seasoning
½ pound mozzarella cheese, sliced
½ cup grated Parmesan cheese

Heat 2 tablespoons of the corn oil in electric fry-pan set at 350° F. or in skillet over medium heat. Add veal, several pieces at a time; brown lightly. Repeat until all meat is browned, adding more oil as necessary. Set veal aside. Add remaining corn oil to skillet. Add onion; cook, stirring occasionally, until tender but not brown. Stir in tomato sauce and seasoning. Add veal, turning to coat with sauce. Arrange cheese slices on top. Sprinkle with Parmesan cheese. Reduce heat to simmer; cover and cook 30 minutes. (Makes 6 servings.)

VII

Peanut Butter—
Morning, Noon, and Night

Did you know that 4 tablespoons of peanut butter—
that food dearest to the heart of a child—give the same
amount of protein as 2 eggs or 2 to 3 ounces of lean
meat? With these new ideas for an old stand-by, young
cooks and nibblers can follow the little kids' lead and
enjoy a truly amazing variety.

BREAKFAST

QUICK BREAKFAST ROLLS

Open 1 can refrigerator biscuits. Spread half of each biscuit with mixture of peanut butter and tangy orange marmalade. Fold over and bake according to directions on package.

PEANUT-BACON TOAST

Spread generous amounts of peanut butter on hot toast (whole wheat is especially good here), and top with crumbled crisp bacon.

PEANUT-CORN MUFFINS

Cut ½ cup peanut butter into 1 (12-ounce) package corn muffin mix with pastry blender or 2 knives until coarse crumbs form. Prepare and bake muffins according to directions on package. (Makes 12 medium muffins.)

HEARTY PEANUT BUTTER PANCAKES

> ¼ cup creamy peanut butter
> ¼ cup light corn syrup
> Pancake recipe using 1 cup mix

Blend peanut butter and syrup. Prepare pancakes as directed on package for 1 cup mix, adding peanut butter-syrup mixture with melted shortening or corn oil. (Makes 7 or 8 [4-inch] pancakes.)

PEANUT PANCAKE SYRUP—FOR PLAIN PANCAKES

¼ cup margarine
⅓ cup chunk-style peanut butter

1 cup pancake and waffle syrup
½ cup water

Melt margarine in saucepan. Blend in peanut butter, then add syrup and water. Bring to boil, stirring constantly. (Makes about 2 cups.)

PEANUT BUTTER COFFEE RING

½ cup milk	½ teaspoon salt
2 tablespoons margarine	1 package active dry yeast
2 tablespoons creamy or chunk-style peanut butter	¼ cup very warm water
	1 egg, beaten
2 tablespoons sugar	1½ cups flour

Scald milk in small saucepan. Add margarine, peanut butter, sugar, and salt. Cook over low heat, stirring constantly, until margarine and peanut butter melt and mixture is well blended. Cool to lukewarm. Sprinkle yeast over water, stir until dissolved. Combine peanut butter mixture, yeast, egg, and flour in mixing bowl. Beat with wooden spoon until smooth, about 1 minute. Cover; let rise in a warm place, free from draft, until doubled in bulk, about one hour. Stir batter down. Turn into greased 1-quart ring mold; spread evenly. Cover; let rise as directed before until doubled in bulk, about 20 minutes. Bake in 375° F. oven about 30 minutes or until done. Remove from pan immediately; cool. Cover top with Glaze, letting some run down the sides. Sprinkle with Topping. (Makes 6 to 8 servings.)

Glaze

Combine 1 cup confectioners' sugar with 2 tablespoons water, mixing well.

Topping

Combine 3 tablespoons fine dry bread crumbs, 2 tablespoons flour, 1 tablespoon creamy or chunk-style peanut butter, and 1 tablespoon margarine, mixing with fork until crumbs form.

PEANUT BUTTER MUFFINS

2 cups sifted flour	2 eggs
2 tablespoons sugar	¼ cup margarine
1 tablespoon baking powder	¼ cup chunk-style peanut butter
½ teaspoon salt	1 cup milk

Sift flour, sugar, baking powder, and salt together into mixing bowl; make well in center. Beat eggs until foamy. Melt margarine and peanut butter in small saucepan; add to eggs, stir in milk. Pour into well in dry ingredients; stir, lightly and quickly, just until flour mixture is moistened. (Batter should be lumpy.) Pour into greased muffin pans, filling cups ⅔ full. Bake in 425° F. oven 25 minutes. Serve warm. (Makes 10 to 12 medium-size muffins.)

PEANUT BUTTER BREAD

¾ cup creamy or chunk-style peanut butter	1 teaspoon salt
	½ teaspoon baking soda
¼ cup margarine	1 tablespoon grated orange rind
2 cups sifted flour	1 egg
½ cup sugar	1 cup milk
1½ teaspoons baking powder	

Cream peanut butter and margarine until light and fluffy. Sift flour, sugar, baking powder, salt, and baking soda together over creamed mixture; then work in with spoon or fork until fine crumbs form. Add orange rind. Beat egg slightly; mix in milk. Add to crumbs and stir until dry ingredients are moistened. Pour batter into greased 9½ x 5¼ x 2¾-inch loaf pan. Bake in 350° F. oven about 55 minutes or until bread tests done.

FLAKY BISCUITS

2 cups sifted flour	⅓ cup corn oil
3 teaspoons baking powder	⅓ cup creamy peanut butter
1 teaspoon salt	⅔ cup milk

Sift flour, baking powder, and salt together into mixing bowl. Blend in corn oil with fork or pastry blender; then blend in peanut butter. Add milk; mix until dough forms. Gently knead on lightly floured board, 15 to 20 times. Roll out or pat to ½-inch thickness. Cut with floured biscuit cutter. Place on ungreased cookie sheet. Bake in 450° F. oven 12 to 15 minutes or until lightly browned. (Makes 12 [2-inch] biscuits.)

LUNCH

TASTY PEANUT BUTTER SANDWICH FILLINGS

Just mix creamy peanut butter with:

Grated raw carrot	Grated Cheddar cheese
Deviled ham	Marshmallow creme
Applesauce	Tomato catsup

NEW IDEAS FOR PEANUT BUTTER SANDWICHES

Spread bread with peanut butter and top with:

Crumbled bacon	Sliced pickle or pickle relish
Sliced bananas	Jelly, jam, or orange marmalade
Raisins	

FRENCH-TOASTED PEANUT BUTTER SANDWICH

1 egg, beaten	Creamy or chunk-style peanut
½ cup milk	butter
8 slices white bread	

Combine egg and milk. Spread 4 slices of bread generously with peanut butter; top with remaining 4 slices. Dip sandwiches into egg-milk mixture. Bake on a well-greased griddle or skillet. Brown one side, turn and brown other side. Serve hot with syrup. (Makes 4 servings.)

PEANUT BUTTER-APPLE SANDWICH

1 cup creamy or chunk-style
   peanut butter
¼ cup margarine
½ cup sugar

½ teaspoon cinnamon
8 bread slices
8 apple slices
½ cup firmly packed brown sugar

Cream peanut butter, margarine, sugar, and cinnamon. Toast bread one side under broiler, 3 inches from source of heat. Turn slices and spread with peanut butter mixture. Top each with apple slice. Sprinkle with brown sugar. Broil about 3 minutes or until mixture bubbles. (Makes 8.)

DATE-PEANUT BUTTER SANDWICH SPREAD

1 cup cut-up dates
¾ cup creamy peanut butter
⅓ cup pancake syrup

¼ cup warm water
⅛ teaspoon cinnamon

Cut up dates, using warm scissors or knife, into mixing bowl. Add remaining ingredients. Cream together until smooth and light. (Makes about 1½ cups spread, enough for 12 large slices toast or bread.)

BROILED PEANUT BUTTER-CHEESE SANDWICH

½ cup creamy peanut butter
1½ cups grated American cheese
½ cup mayonnaise
2 teaspoons Worcestershire sauce

¼ teaspoon salt
8 slices white bread
2 medium tomatoes, sliced thin

Combine peanut butter, cheese, mayonnaise, Worcestershire sauce, and salt. Toast one side of bread under broiler. Spread untoasted side of bread with peanut butter-cheese mixture. Arrange tomato slices on top. Broil sandwiches until tomato is hot and cheese is melted. Serve immediately. (Makes 8 generous servings.)

PEANUT BUTTER-BANANA SANDWICH SPREAD

¾ cup creamy peanut butter
⅓ cup light corn syrup
¼ cup warm water

⅛ teaspoon cinnamon
½ cup mashed banana
1 teaspoon lemon juice

Cream together peanut butter, syrup, warm water, and cinnamon until smooth and light. Mash banana; add lemon juice and mix well. Add banana to creamed mixture and blend well. (Makes about 1½ cups sandwich spread, enough to spread 12 sandwiches.)

CREAMY PEANUT BUTTER AND APPLE SPREAD

Follow above recipe; but omit water and lemon juice, substitute ½ cup applesauce for mashed banana, and increase cinnamon to ½ teaspoon.

HEARTY PEANUT BUTTER SANDWICH

1 slice toast
Margarine
¼ cup creamy or chunk-style
    peanut butter
2 slices bacon, cooked and
    crumbled

2 slices tomato
1 hard-cooked egg, quartered
2 tablespoons mayonnaise

Spread toast with margarine and peanut butter. Top with crumbled bacon, then tomato slices, then hard-cooked-egg quarters. Garnish with mayonnaise. (Makes 1 serving.)

PEANUT BUTTER AND BANANA SALAD

4 small bananas
1 tablespoon lemon juice
Creamy or chunk-style peanut
    butter

Salad greens
½ cup mayonnaise
¼ teaspoon grated lemon rind

Peel bananas and cut in half lengthwise. Dip in lemon juice.
Spread half of each banana with peanut butter and press other
half on top. Arrange on salad greens. Blend mayonnaise and
lemon rind. Serve with salad. (Makes 4 servings.)

PEANUT BUTTER–SOUR CREAM DRESSING

¼ cup dairy sour cream
2 tablespoons creamy or chunk-
style peanut butter

½ teaspoon lemon juice
¼ teaspoon salt

Combine all ingredients, blending well. Chill. Serve as dressing
for fruit salad or dip for chilled apples or pineapple wedges.
(Makes about ⅓ cup.)

PEANUT BUTTER SALAD DRESSING

1 tablespoon sugar
½ teaspoon salt
½ teaspoon dry mustard
Dash cayenne
1 egg

⅔ cup (6-ounce can) undiluted
evaporated milk
2 tablespoons creamy peanut
butter
3 tablespoons lemon juice

Mix sugar, salt, dry mustard, and cayenne in double boiler top.
Add egg; beat with spoon until blended. Stir in milk. Cook over
boiling water, stirring constantly, until mixture begins to thicken.
Remove from boiling water. Beat in peanut butter. Gradually add
lemon juice, beating after each addition. Chill several hours.
(Makes 1 cup.)

PEANUT BUTTER COOKIES

1⅔ cups sifted flour
Dash salt
1½ teaspoons baking powder
½ cup margarine
½ cup firmly packed brown sugar

1 cup creamy or chunk-style
peanut butter
⅓ cup light or dark corn syrup
1 egg, beaten
½ teaspoon vanilla

Sift flour, baking powder, and salt together. Cream margarine, and gradually add sugar; cream until light and fluffy. Beat in ½ cup of the peanut butter and syrup until smooth and well blended. Add beaten egg and vanilla, then sifted dry ingredients, a little at a time, mixing well after each addition. Shape dough into 1-inch balls. Place on ungreased cookie sheet; flatten with fork. Place about ½ teaspoon peanut butter on top of each. Bake in 350° F. oven 12 to 15 minutes. (Makes about 3½ dozen cookies.)

SNOW MOUNDS

½ cup margarine
¼ cup creamy or chunk-style
   peanut butter
2 tablespoons sugar

1 teaspoon vanilla
1 cup sifted flour
Confectioners' sugar

Cream margarine with peanut butter. Add sugar and vanilla; beat until fluffy. Mix in flour, beating until smooth. Shape into 1-inch balls and place on ungreased cookie sheet. Bake in 300° F. oven about 45 minutes or until lightly browned. Roll in confectioners' sugar while still warm. Roll in sugar again before serving. (Makes about 1½ dozen.)

Note: Cookies should be stored in covered container.

VANILLA WAFER SANDWICHES

½ cup creamy peanut butter
¼ cup light cream
36 vanilla wafers

Put peanut butter into small bowl. Gradually blend in cream. For each sandwich, spread mixture on bottom of one wafer and cover with second, placing bottom sides together. (Makes 18 sandwiches.)

CHEWY CRISPS

1 cup creamy peanut butter ½ cup undiluted evaporated milk
1 cup sugar 4 teaspoons cornstarch

Blend all ingredients together. Drop by teaspoonfuls onto ungreased cookie sheet. Flatten each cookie with fork dipped in water. Bake in 350° F. oven about 15 minutes or until light golden brown. Cool 1 to 2 minutes; remove from cookie sheet. (Makes 3 dozen cookies.)

BUTTERSCOTCH-PEANUT BUTTER CRUNCHIES

1 (6-ounce) package butterscotch 2 cups ready-to-eat high protein
chips cereal
¼ cup creamy or chunk-style
peanut butter

Melt butterscotch chips in double boiler top over boiling water. Blend in peanut butter; then stir in cereal. Drop by small teaspoonfuls onto waxed paper. Let stand until set, about 1 hour. (Makes about 3 dozen.)

FRUIT AND NUT COOKIES

½ cup creamy or chunk-style 1 cup chopped dates or chopped
peanut butter figs or raisins
1 cup sugar 1 cup chopped nuts
½ cup undiluted evaporated milk

Mix peanut butter and sugar thoroughly. Blend in evaporated milk. Mix in fruit and nuts. Drop by teaspoonfuls onto greased cookie sheet. Bake in 325° F. oven 18 to 20 minutes or until lightly browned. Cool 1 to 2 minutes; remove from cookie sheet. (Makes about 3 dozen.)

COCONUT MACAROONS

3 eggs whites
1 cup sugar
1 tablespoon flour

½ cup creamy or chunk-style
    peanut butter
1 cup shredded coconut

Beat egg whites until foamy. Gradually add sugar and continue to beat until egg whites are stiff and thick. Fold in flour. Fold egg whites into creamed peanut butter. Fold in coconut. Drop by tablespoonfuls onto ungreased cookie sheet covered with brown paper. Bake in 325° F. oven 20 to 25 minutes. Remove from paper when cool. (Makes approximately 3 dozen macaroons.)

ONE-EYED JACKS

¾ cup creamy or chunk-style
    peanut butter
¾ cup firmly packed brown sugar
⅔ cup (6-ounce can) undiluted
    evaporated milk

½ cup unsifted flour
¼ teaspoon baking soda
Raisins

Blend peanut butter and brown sugar. Add evaporated milk flour, and baking soda; mix well. Drop by tablespoonfuls onto greased cookie sheet. Gently press a cluster of 3 to 4 raisins on top of each cookie. Bake in a 325° F. oven 20 to 25 minutes. (Makes 1½ dozen cookies.)

CHOCO-NUT BROWNIES

½ cup sifted flour
½ teaspoon baking powder
¼ teaspoon salt
¼ cup margarine
2 (1-ounce) squares unsweetened
    chocolate

¼ cup creamy or chunk-style
    peanut butter
1 egg, well beaten
1 cup firmly packed brown sugar
1 teaspoon vanilla
½ cup chopped peanuts

Sift flour, baking powder, and salt together. Melt margarine, chocolate, and peanut butter in saucepan over low heat. Add sugar to egg; beat well. Stir in peanut butter mixture and vanilla. Mix in sifted dry ingredients, then nuts. Turn into greased 8 x 8 x 2-inch baking pan. Bake in 350° F. oven about 30 minutes or until brownies test done. Cut as desired. (Makes 16 [2-inch] squares.)

Note: If salted peanuts are used, omit salt.

PEANUT BUTTER STICKS

6 slices day-old white bread
¼ cup margarine

⅓ cup creamy or chunk-style peanut butter
⅓ cup cinnamon sugar

Cut each bread slice into 3 strips. Melt margarine in saucepan; stir in peanut butter. Coat stick with peanut butter mixture; then roll in cinnamon sugar. Place on ungreased cookie sheet. Bake in 350° F. oven 8 minutes; then turn sticks and bake 2 minutes longer. Store in covered cookie container. (Makes 18 sticks.)

PEANUT BUTTER ICE CREAM BALLS

1 cup graham cracker crumbs
¼ cup creamy or chunk-style peanut butter
2 tablespoons sugar

¼ teaspoon cinnamon
1 quart vanilla ice cream
Fortified chocolate-flavored syrup

Blend graham cracker crumbs, peanut butter, sugar, and cinnamon. Scoop ice cream into large balls and roll in crumb mixture until well coated. Freeze until serving time. Serve with chocolate syrup. (Makes 6 to 8 servings.)

PEANUTTY CHOCOLATE SAUCE

¼ cup creamy or chunk-style peanut butter
¼ cup chocolate-flavored syrup
3 tablespoons milk

Combine peanut butter and chocolate syrup. Gradually blend in milk. Beat until creamy and thickened. (Makes about ¾ cup sauce.)

MAPLEY PEANUT BUTTER SAUCE

⅓ cup chunk-style peanut butter
⅔ cup pancake and waffle syrup

Combine peanut butter and syrup, stirring until well blended. (Makes 1 cup.)

PEANUT BUTTER FUDGE TOPPING

½ cup fortified chocolate-flavored syrup
½ cup creamy or chunk-style peanut butter
½ cup light corn syrup

Thoroughly combine chocolate syrup and peanut butter. Add corn syrup, stirring until well blended. Spoon generously on ice cream or plain cake. (Makes 1½ cups.)

PEANUT BUTTER FUDGE FROSTING

Follow recipe for Fudge Topping above, reducing syrup to ¼ cup. (Makes enough to frost top and sides of 1 [8-inch] layer.)

BEST-EVER FROSTED

¼ cup creamy peanut butter
2 tablespoons light corn syrup
   or pancake syrup

¼ teaspoon vanilla
2 cups cold milk
Ice cream

Blend peanut butter, syrup, and vanilla. Mix in enough milk to make a smooth paste; then gradually mix in remaining milk. Beat with rotary beater until foamy. Pour into 2 tall glasses. Top each with scoop of ice cream. (Makes 2 servings.)

PEANUT BUTTER MILK SHAKE

1 tablespoon creamy or chunk-
style peanut butter

1 cup milk
1 large scoop vanilla ice cream

Blend peanut butter and ¼ cup milk in small bowl. Beat in remaining milk. Pour into large jar with lid. Add ice cream. Shake until ice cream is almost melted. (Makes 1 serving.)

HAPPY HOUR DIPS AND CANAPES

QUICK HORS D'OEUVRES

Celery stuffed with creamy peanut butter blended with cottage cheese

Crackers spread with peanut butter mixed with chopped chicken

Chilled cucumber slices topped with creamy peanut butter

Toast strips spread with peanut butter and topped with stuffed olive slices

PEANUT BUTTER NIBBLERS

3 slices white bread
2 tablespoons margarine
3 tablespoons creamy or chunk-
style peanut butter

Salt
Pepper

Cut bread into ½-inch cubes. Melt margarine in saucepan; stir in peanut butter. Toss bread cubes in mixture; spread out on ungreased cookie sheet. Bake in 375° F. oven 10 minutes. Season with salt and pepper. (Makes 1 cup.)

SAVORY DIP

½ cup creamy peanut butter
2 (3-ounce) packages cream
    cheese, softened
2 teaspoons finely chopped onion

½ teaspoon celery salt
¼ cup catsup
2 drops Tabasco sauce

Blend peanut butter with cream cheese. Add remaining ingredients and beat until smooth. Milk may be added for a thinner consistency. (Makes about 1½ cups.)

FANCY STUFFED CELERY

1 (3-ounce) package cream cheese
¼ cup creamy or chunk-style
    peanut butter

1 tablespoon milk
2 teaspoons soy sauce
Celery stalks

Blend cream cheese and peanut butter; then blend in milk and soy sauce. Stuff into celery stalks and cut to desired size. (Makes about ½ cup mixture.)

SPICY STUFFED CELERY

Follow recipe for Fancy Stuffed Celery, substituting 3 tablespoons catsup for 2 teaspoons soy sauce.

ORIENTAL DIP

½ cup chunk-style peanut butter
1 cup cottage cheese
2 teaspoons soy sauce

½ teaspoon lemon juice
½ teaspoon ginger
⅓ cup milk

Combine peanut butter and cottage cheese. Add remaining ingredients and beat until well blended. (Makes about 1½ cups.)

PEANUT BUTTER CANAPES

Rounds or squares of bread   Cocktail onions
Creamy peanut butter   Mayonnaise

Arrange bread slices on ungreased cookie sheet and broil until toasted on one side. Spread untoasted side of each with peanut butter and place 1 cocktail onion in center. Top with mayonnaise. Broil about 2 minutes or until mayonnaise puffs and has browned slightly. Serve warm.

CURRY CANAPES

2 tablespoons creamy or chunk-   6 cooked shrimp, halved
   style peanut butter   lengthwise
2 tablespoons margarine   1 tablespoon chopped chives
1 teaspoon curry powder
6 slices bread

Cream peanut butter and margarine together. Mix in curry powder. Cut each bread slice into 2 (2-inch) rounds; spread each with curry mixture, top with one shrimp half, and garnish with chives. (Makes 12 canapés.)

RELISH DIP

½ cup creamy peanut butter
1 cup sour cream
¼ cup India pickle relish

Combine ingredients and blend well. (Makes about 1½ cups.)

DINNER

HAITIAN PEANUT BUTTER SOUP

2 tablespoons margarine
⅔ cup finely chopped celery
¼ cup finely chopped onion
¼ cup flour
1 cup creamy peanut butter

2 cups milk
4 cups chicken stock or bouillon
¼ teaspoon salt
Dash pepper

Melt margarine in skillet. Add celery and onion; cook over low heat, stirring frequently until tender. Stir in flour, mixing until smooth. Blend peanut butter with 1 cup milk. Stir into mixture in skillet with remaining milk, stock, salt, and pepper. Cook over medium heat, stirring constantly, until slightly thickened. Serve hot. (Makes about 7 cups.)

BAKED HAM ROLLS

2 cups mashed sweet potatoes
2 tablespoons margarine
8 large thin slices cooked ham
1 cup dark corn syrup

½ cup creamy peanut butter
¼ cup orange juice
1 tablespoon margarine, melted
1 teaspoon grated orange rind

Combine sweet potatoes and 2 tablespoons margarine. Place about ¼ cup mixture on each ham slice. Roll up and fasten with wooden picks. Place in shallow dish. Combine remaining ingredients. Pour over ham rolls. Bake in 350° F. oven about 30 minutes or until heated, basting and turning occasionally. (Makes 4 servings.)

NUTTY SPAGHETTI SAUCE

2 tablespoons corn oil
¼ cup finely chopped onion
¼ cup finely chopped green
    pepper
2½ cups water
1 (4-ounce) can tomato paste

½ teaspoon salt
¼ teaspoon oregano
2 bay leaves
½ cup creamy or chunk-style
    peanut butter

Heat corn oil in skillet. Add onion and green pepper; sauté until tender. Add water, tomato paste, salt, oregano and bay leaves. Bring to boil. Mix in peanut butter. Cover and simmer about 30 minutes to blend flavors. (Makes 3 cups.)

DELUXE PEANUT BUTTER PIE

1 unbaked 9-inch pastry shell
2 eggs, beaten
1 cup dark corn syrup
⅛ teaspoon salt

1 teaspoon vanilla
1 cup sugar
½ cup creamy or chunk-style
    peanut butter

Mix filling ingredients together, adding peanut butter last. Pour into unbaked pastry shell. Bake in 400° F. oven 15 minutes. Reduce heat to 350° F. and bake 30 to 35 minutes longer. Filling should appear slightly less set in center than around edge.

CHUNKY CHOCOLATE PUDDING

1 package chocolate pudding
2⅔ cups milk
⅓ cup chunk-style peanut butter

Cook pudding according to package directions, using 2⅔ cups milk. Remove from heat. Blend a small amount into peanut butter; then mix with remaining hot pudding. Pour into serving dishes. Chill. (Makes 4 servings.)

SOPHISTICATED BEDTIME SNACKS

GINGER-PEANUT SPREAD

¼ cup creamy peanut butter
1 (3-ounce) package cream cheese
2 tablespoons milk
1 teaspoon soy sauce

½ teaspoon lemon juice
¼ teaspoon ginger
Crackers

Combine peanut butter and cream cheese; then beat in remaining ingredients, blending well. Chill. Spread on crackers. (Makes about ¾ cup.)

SWEET TEA TREATS

½ cup creamy or chunk-style
    peanut butter
3 tablespoons margarine
⅓ cup chopped raisins

¼ cup pineapple juice
1 can refrigerated pan-ready
    biscuits
Melted margarine

Cream peanut butter with margarine. Mix in raisins and pineapple juice. Blend until mixture is thick. Separate biscuits; roll each up and down with rolling pin to make an oval about 5 inches long. Spread about 1 heaping tablespoon mixture on half of each biscuit. Fold over unspread half and pinch sides together to seal. Brush with melted margarine. Place on ungreased cookie sheet. Bake in 350° F. oven about 15 minutes or until biscuits are golden brown. Cut each into 3 wedges. Serve warm. (Makes 30 wedges.)

PEANUT BUTTER-BACON SPREAD

⅓ cup creamy peanut butter
½ teaspoon Worcestershire sauce
2 to 3 tablespoons chili sauce

4 slices bacon, cooked and
    crumbled

Blend first three ingredients; add bacon. Spread on crackers. (Makes about ½ cup spread.)

EASY CHUTNEY SPREAD

½ cup creamy or chunk-style peanut butter	½ cup margarine
	¼ cup chopped chutney

Blend peanut butter and margarine. Mix in chopped chutney. Chill. Use as spread for melba toast or crackers. (Makes 1 cup spread.)

CANDY

Candy-making is not passé! Making fudge is still the best diversion for young ladies with "problems of the heart," especially when the result is presented for the young man's consumption. And nothing breaks the ice at a party like an old-fashioned taffy pull. So try these old favorites with a new peanut butter twist.

SURPRISE FUDGE

½ cup milk	2 teaspoons vanilla
⅓ cup margarine	⅛ teaspoon salt
3 (1-ounce) squares unsweetened chocolate	1 pound confectioners' sugar, sifted
½ cup creamy peanut butter	

Heat milk, margarine, and chocolate in saucepan over low heat, stirring constantly, until margarine and chocolate melt. Remove from heat. Add peanut butter, vanilla, salt, and about ½ the sugar; stir until smooth. Blend in remaining sugar. Turn into greased 8 x 8 x 2-inch pan. Chill until firm. (Makes 64 [1-inch] pieces.)

MARY JANE TAFFY

1 cup dark corn syrup	½ cup creamy or chunk-style
1 cup sugar	peanut butter
2 tablespoons vinegar	

Combine syrup, sugar, and vinegar in saucepan. Cook over medium heat, stirring occasionally, until temperature reaches 248° F. or until a small amount of mixture dropped into very cold water forms a firm ball which does not flatten on removal from water. Add peanut butter. Cook, stirring constantly, to 260° F. or until a small amount of mixture dropped into very cold water forms a ball which is hard enough to hold its shape, yet plastic. Remove from heat. Pour into greased pan and let stand until cool enough to handle. Pull with fingers until candy is elastic, light in color, and has satinlike finish. Pull into long strips, ½ inch in diameter. Cut into 1-inch pieces. Wrap in waxed paper. (Makes about 1 pound.)

COCONUT CANDY

1 cup flaked coconut	1 tablespoon light corn syrup or
¼ cup creamy or chunk-style	pancake and waffle syrup
peanut butter	1 teaspoon vanilla
	Confectioners' sugar

Mix coconut, peanut butter, syrup, and vanilla together thoroughly. Shape into 1-inch balls. Chill until firm. Roll in confectioners' sugar. (Makes 12.)

PEANUT BUTTER KISSES

2 egg whites	½ cup creamy or chunk-style
⅛ teaspoon cream of tartar	peanut butter
⅔ cup sugar	

Beat egg whites and cream of tartar until mixture holds stiff peaks when beater is raised. Add sugar, 1 tablespoon at a time, beating well after each addition. Continue beating until mixture holds very stiff peaks when beater is raised. Lightly fold in peanut butter just until mixed. Drop by teaspoonfuls onto greased cookie sheet. Bake in 300° F. oven about 25 minutes or until lightly browned. Remove from cookie sheet immediately. (Makes 2 dozen.)

QUICK NO-COOK PEANUT BUTTER FUDGE

⅓ cup margarine
½ cup light corn syrup
¾ cup creamy or chunk-style
    peanut butter
½ teaspoon salt

1 teaspoon vanilla
4½ cups sifted confectioners'
    sugar
¾ cup chopped nuts

Blend margarine, corn syrup, peanut butter, salt, and vanilla in large mixing bowl. Stir in sifted confectioners' sugar gradually. Turn onto board and knead until well blended and smooth. Add nuts gradually, pressing and kneading into candy. Press out with hands or rolling pin into ½-inch squares. Cut into serving pieces. (Makes about 2 pounds fudge.)

PEANUT BUTTER FUDGE

Follow recipe for Peanut Butter Fudge Topping (see p. 181), gradually adding 1 pound sifted confectioners' sugar, first blending in with spoon, then kneading with hands. Spread in 8 x 8 x 2-inch pan. Chill until firm enough to cut. (Makes about 1½ pounds.)

JELLY BEAN FUDGE

½ cup milk
⅓ cup margarine
3 (1-ounce) squares unsweetened
    chocolate
½ cup creamy peanut butter

2 teaspoons vanilla
⅛ teaspoon salt
1 pound confectioners' sugar,
    sifted
64 jelly beans

Heat milk, margarine, and chocolate in saucepan over low heat, stirring constantly, until margarine and chocolate melt. Remove from heat. Add peanut butter, vanilla, salt, and about ½ of the sugar; stir until smooth. Blend in remaining sugar. Spread mixture in bottom of 8-inch-square pan. Mark into 1-inch squares; press 1 jelly bean into top of each. Cover; refrigerate. (Makes 64 pieces.)

PEANUT BUTTER DELIGHTS

1½ cups vanilla wafer or graham cracker crumbs
½ cup sugar
¼ cup creamy or chunk-style peanut butter

2 egg whites
¼ cup finely chopped nuts (optional)
Confectioners' sugar

Combine crumbs and sugar; blend in peanut butter thoroughly. Beat egg whites until stiff, but not dry. Fold in crumb mixture and nuts. Shape into firm ½-inch balls and place on ungreased cookie sheet. Bake in 350° F. oven 10 to 12 minutes or until done. Cool slightly before removing from sheet. Roll in confectioners' sugar. (Makes about 3 dozen.)

CHOCOLATE PEANUT BUTTER ROLL

½ cup creamy peanut butter
¼ cup confectioners' sugar

¼ cup fortified chocolate syrup
2 tablespoons cornflake crumbs

Blend peanut butter, confectioners' sugar, and chocolate syrup. Form into a roll 1 inch in diameter. Roll in cornflake crumbs to coat sides completely. Chill until firm. Store in refrigerator. (Makes about ½ pound candy.)

VIII

The Fountain of Youth
—Beverages

Here are nifty non-alcoholic beverages with enough zing to inspire a party for any age group or to supplement the daily intake of coffee, tea, or milk with an emphasis on fruit juices. They are simple and quick to prepare, relying mainly on bottled or frozen ingredients.

ADES, ALES, PUNCHES, AND COOLERS

BRAD'S ADE

Equal parts { diluted grape juice
diluted orange juice
Grated orange and lemon rind
Add sugar to taste

CRANBERRY COOLER

1 quart cranberry juice (bottled)
1 quart club soda

1 (6-ounce) can lime or lemon juice concentrate
Add sugar to taste

Pour over shaved ice. For punch bowl, float sliced fresh pineapple rings on surface. (Makes 15-20 small servings.)

FANCY ALE

7 ounces ginger ale poured over shaved ice
Freshly squeezed wedge of lime

2 teaspoons maraschino cherry juice
Garnish: 1 sprig mint leaf and maraschino cherries

(Makes 1 [8-ounce] tumbler.)

SIMPLE PARTY PUNCH

Equal parts { pineapple juice (canned or frozen)
pink lemonade (canned or frozen)
club soda

Float on surface: slices of fresh peach, blueberries, and crushed strawberries.

THANKSGIVING CINNAMON APPLE CIDER

1 quart apple cider
2 cinnamon sticks
¼ teaspoon powdered cloves

Simmer 5 minutes, strain, and pour into mugs. (Makes about 4 servings.)

LEMONADE SPECIAL

2 ounces lemon juice
4 ounces water
Light corn syrup

Add light corn syrup to taste. Garnish with crushed raspberries and a sprig of mint leaf. Serve chilled. (Makes 1 portion.)

PLEASING PUNCH

1 quart water
⅓ cup unsweetened instant tea or
   12 tea bags
1 (1-pint) bottle light corn syrup
1 quart cold water

2 (6-ounce) cans frozen lemonade
1 (8-ounce) bottle grenadine syrup
2 (1-pint, 12-ounce) bottles club
   soda

Bring 1 quart water to boil in saucepan. Remove from heat; immediately add tea. If tea bags are used, let stand 4 minutes; remove bags. Stir corn syrup into hot tea. Pour cold water into punch bowl. Pour in tea mixture, lemonade, and grenadine syrup. Just before serving, add soda and ice. (Makes about 4¾ quarts or 25 [¾-cup] servings.)

QUICKIE QUENCHER

3 (6-ounce) cans frozen pink
    lemonade
1 (1-pint) bottle light corn syrup
2 (1-pint, 12-ounce) bottles

raspberry or cherry carbonated
    beverage
1 (1-pint, 12-ounce) bottle ginger
    ale

Mix lemonade and corn syrup in a punch bowl or suitable container. Just before serving, add carbonated beverage, ginger ale, and ice. (Makes about 3½ quarts or 19 [¾-cup] servings.)

ORANGE BLOSSOM PUNCH

1 (½-ounce) envelope orange soft
    drink mix
1 quart cold water
1 (1-quart) can or bottle unsweet-
    ened grapefruit juice

1 (1-pint) bottle light corn syrup
1 (1-pint, 12-ounce) bottle or 2
    (1-pint) bottles orange
    carbonated beverage

Mix soft drink mix and water in punch bowl. Stir in grapefruit juice and corn syrup. Just before serving, add carbonated beverage and ice. (Makes about 3 quarts or 18 [¾-cup] servings.)

POPSICLE PUNCH

1 (7-ounce) jar orange breakfast
    drink
1½ quarts cold water
1 (1-pint) bottle light corn syrup

1 (1-pint, 12-ounce) bottle club
    soda
Vanilla ice cream, pineapple or
    orange sherbet

Mix breakfast drink and water in a punch bowl. Stir in corn syrup. Just before serving add club soda and sherbet or ice cream. (Makes 3 quarts or 16 [¾-cup] servings.)

PARTY EGGNOG PUNCH

6 eggs
½ cup light corn syrup
¼ teaspoon ground ginger
¼ teaspoon ground cloves
¼ teaspoon ground cinnamon
¼ teaspoon ground nutmeg

2 quarts orange juice, chilled
½ cup lemon juice, chilled
1 quart vanilla ice cream
1 quart ginger ale, chilled
Nutmeg

Beat eggs well. Mix in corn syrup, ginger, cloves, cinnamon, and nutmeg. Stir in orange juice and lemon juice. Cut ice cream into chunks the size of small eggs; put into large punch bowl. Pour ginger ale over ice cream. Stir in egg mixture. Sprinkle with nutmeg. (Makes 6 quarts.)

BLACK COW

Stir a double scoop of vanilla ice cream into chilled root beer and serve in tall tumbler.

SPEEDY TALL SUMMER COOLER

Blend or beat a scoop of vanilla ice cream and some dark corn syrup with chilled milk. Sprinkle with cinnamon or nutmeg before serving.

WINTER NIGHT WARMERS

TEA PARTY TEA

Pre-heat teapot by filling with scalding water which is poured out just before pot is filled. Fully boil cold water from tap. Put tea (1 teabag or 1 teaspoon loose tea) per cup into pot. Pour boiling water over tea and allow to steep for 3 or 4 minutes. Sweeten with sugar and a sprinkle of cinnamon, and serve with milk or lemon.

HOT MARSHMALLOW COCOA

Mix 2 or 3 heaping teaspoons prepared cocoa mix per cup with hot (not boiling) milk. Stir in 1 tablespoon marshmallow syrup or float a marshmallow on surface.

CAFE-AU-LAIT

Mix exactly equal parts of strong hot coffee and scalded milk. Optional: a sprinkle of cinnamon and sugar.

CAPUCCINO IN AN INSTANT

Blend to taste:
- Instant coffee
- Chocolate-flavored syrup
- Cinnamon sticks
- Nutmeg
- Non-dairy cream (instant)
- Dried grated orange peel

ICE CREAM SODAS

BASIC RECIPE

Flavoring(s)
Ice cream, whipped cream, or light cream
Carbonated water (from soda or seltzer bottle or bottled carbonated or sparkling water)
Ice cream
Whipped cream (optional)

Mix together the flavoring(s), ice cream, whipped cream, or light cream in a 14-ounce glass. Fill the glass ¾ full with carbonated water and stir slightly. Add ice cream. If glass is not full, finish filling with carbonated water. Top with whipped cream, if desired.

CHOCOLATE ICE CREAM SODA

3 tablespoons chocolate syrup
1 tablespoon whipped cream or
    light cream

Carbonated water
2⅓ cups chocolate or vanilla ice
    cream

Follow Basic Recipe.

COFFEE ICE CREAM SODA

¼ cup warm water
3 teaspoons instant coffee
1 teaspoon light corn syrup or
    sugar

1 tablespoon whipped cream or
    light cream
Carbonated water
2⅓ cups coffee or vanilla ice cream

Follow Basic Recipe.

CHERRY ICE CREAM SODA

3 tablespoons minced maraschino
    cherries
1½ tablespoons cherry juice
1 tablespoon whipped cream or

light cream
Carbonated water
2⅓ cups vanilla ice cream

Follow Basic Recipe.

PINEAPPLE ICE CREAM SODA

3 tablespoons crushed, well-
    sweetened fresh, frozen, or
    canned pineapple

1 tablespoon whipped cream or
    light cream
Carbonated water
2⅓ cups vanilla ice cream

Follow Basic Recipe.

BLUEBERRY ICE CREAM SODA

3 tablespoons crushed fresh
   blueberries
1 tablespoon whipped cream or
   light cream

Carbonated water
2⅓ cups vanilla ice cream

Follow Basic Recipe.

STRAWBERRY ICE CREAM SODA

4 tablespoons crushed, well-
   sweetened fresh or frozen
   strawberries

1 tablespoon whipped cream or
   light cream
Carbonated water
2⅓ cups vanilla ice cream

Follow Basic Recipe.

MALTS

BASIC COLD MALT

Add 3 heaping teaspoons of chocolate malted milk mix to 1 glass of cold milk. Stir and serve. (Instant malted mix is available in both chocolate and vanilla flavors.)

FOUNTAIN MALT

Blend ¾ cup milk, 2 scoops ice cream, 3 heaping teaspoons instant malted milk mix in an electric mixer or blender.

HIGH-PROTEIN EGGNOG MALTS

Add an egg to regular cold malt

LANCE'S MINT-MALT

Blend milk, chocolate ice cream, instant chocolate malt mix, and a handful of white after-dinner mints in an electric mixer or blender.

BANANA-STRAWBERRY MALT

Blend milk, vanilla ice cream, instant vanilla malt mix, 1 banana, and about 12 strawberries.

FOR WASP WAISTS AND CLEAR COMPLEXIONS

For those young people who are inclined (to their ultimate despair) to consume "gross" quantities of soft drinks to the detriment of skin, teeth, and figures, here are some suggestions for low-calorie thirst quenchers. All of them are appealing to eye and palate. And because they are prepared with a base of non-fat dry milk, they have about half the calories of fresh whole milk. Served "as is," in a tall glass, each drink contains about 60 to 80 calories. A dollop of whipped non-fat dry milk will add about 10 calories more per glass.

† BLACK CHERRY MILK FIZZ

⅓ cup instant non-fat dry milk
¼ cup cold water

½ cup low-calorie black cherry carbonated soda, chilled

In a tall 10-ounce glass, combine non-fat dry milk and water. Gradually add chilled soda and ice, if necessary. Stir until well blended. Serve immediately. If desired, garnish with whipped non-fat dry milk, frosted maraschino cherries, and fresh mint.

† dagger is explained in acknowledgments at end of book.

† ORANGE MILK FIZZ

⅓ cup instant non-fat dry milk ½ cup low-calorie orange carbon-
¼ cup cold water ated soda, chilled

In a tall 10-ounce glass, combine non-fat dry milk and water.
Gradually add chilled soda and ice, if necessary. Stir until well
blended. Serve immediately. If desired, garnish with whipped non-
fat dry milk and an orange slice speared with maraschino cherries.

† GRAPE MILK FIZZ

¼ cup instant non-fat dry milk ½ cup low-calorie grape carbon-
¼ cup cold water ated soda, chilled

Follow above recipe. If desired, garnish with whipped non-fat dry
milk and grape halves.

† COFFEE MILK FIZZ

⅓ cup instant non-fat dry milk ¼ teaspoon calorie-free sweetening
¼ cup cold water solution
1½ teaspoons instant coffee ½ cup low-calorie club soda,
 chilled

In a tall 10-ounce glass, combine non-fat dry milk, water, coffee,
and sweetening solution. Gradually add chilled soda and ice, if
necessary. Stir until well blended. Serve immediately. If desired,
garnish with whipped non-fat dry milk.

† LIME OR LEMON MILK FIZZ

¼ cup instant non-fat dry milk ½ cup low-calorie ginger ale
¼ cup cold water carbonated beverage, chilled
Few drops green or yellow food 1½ teaspoons reconstituted lime
 coloring or lemon juice

In a tall 10-ounce glass, combine non-fat dry milk, water, and food coloring. In a measuring cup mix ginger ale and lime or lemon juice. Gradually add to milk. Add ice, if necessary. Stir until well blended. Serve immediately. Garnish with lemon or lime rind and whipped non-fat dry milk.

IX

Goodies à Go Go—
Cakes, Cookies,
and Frostings

Here is a group of recipes for the young crowd's favorite cakes that are a snap to prepare. They're as
delicious as their fancy, time-consuming counterparts,
and the ease with which they can be put together
should convince you that baking really can be just "a
piece of cake."

TIPS

1. Read the recipe through before starting, to be sure you have all the proper ingredients.
2. Turn oven on and set at the correct temperature before starting to mix your cake.
3. Bake only in size pans recommended in the recipe.
4. Prepare pans as directed in the recipe before measuring ingredients.
5. Have all ingredients at room temperature unless otherwise stated.
6. Sift flour before measuring, unless otherwise stated.
7. Use level measures.
8. Use shortening called for in recipe; do not substitute.
9. Test cake after suggested time. Test as recipe suggests.
10. When baked, remove from oven and place on wire rack. Cool cake in pan for 10 minutes, remove from pan, and continue to cool on rack. (Exceptions: Angel, Sponge, or Chiffon. They must "hang" upside-down while cooling.)
11. Almost all cakes should be thoroughly cooled before frosting or cutting.
12. Cool bar-type cookies in pan; then cut.
13. Cookies should be removed from cookie sheet immediately unless otherwise directed.

MEASUREMENT CHART

Pinch or dash	less than ⅛ teaspoon
1 tablespoon	3 teaspoons; ½ fluid ounce
¼ cup	4 tablespoons; 2 fluid ounces
⅓ cup	5 tablespoons plus 1 teaspoon
½ cup	8 tablespoons; 4 fluid ounces
1 cup	16 tablespoons; 8 fluid ounces
1 pint	2 cups; 16 fluid ounces
1 pound	16 ounces

NOTE:

1. When a recipe calls for cake flour, an equal measure of self-rising cake flour may be substituted, and baking powder and salt omitted.
2. When a recipe calls for all-purpose flour, an equal measure of self-rising cake flour may be substituted, plus 2 extra tablespoons for each cup of all-purpose flour, and baking powder and salt omitted.
3. When a recipe calls for soda or sour milk, buttermilk, or sour cream, sweet milk may be substituted, and soda and salt omitted.

CAKES

QUICK CHOCOLATE CAKE

2¼ cups sifted self-rising cake flour
1¼ cups sugar
½ cup cocoa
½ teaspoon baking soda

⅔ cup margarine
1 cup milk
1½ teaspoons vanilla
2 eggs

Grease 2 (8-inch) layer-cake pans and line bottoms with waxed paper. Sift self-rising cake flour, sugar, cocoa, and baking soda together. Stir margarine to soften. Sift dry ingredients over margarine. Add milk and vanilla. Stir until dry ingredients are completely moistened; then beat 1 minute with medium speed of electric mixer or about 150 vigorous strokes by hand, scraping bowl and beaters often. Add eggs. Beat 1½ minutes with medium speed of electric mixer or 225 vigorous strokes by hand. Pour into prepared pans. Bake in 350° F. oven 40 to 45 minutes or until cake springs back when touched lightly with finger.

QUICK MIX LAYER CAKE

½ cup margarine
2½ cups sifted self-rising cake
    flour
1½ cups sugar

¾ cup milk
2 eggs
2 tablespoons milk
1 teaspoon vanilla

Grease 2 (9-inch) layer-cake pans. Line bottoms with waxed paper. Stir margarine to soften. Sift self-rising cake flour and sugar together over margarine. Add ¾ cup milk; mix until all flour mixture is dampened. Beat 2 minutes with medium speed of electric mixer or 300 strokes by hand. Add eggs, 2 tablespoons milk, and vanilla. Beat 1 minute with medium speed of electric mixer or 150 strokes by hand. Pour into prepared pans. Bake in 350° F. oven 30 to 35 minutes or until cake springs back when touched lightly with finger.

Note: Cake may also be baked in 1 greased 13 x 9 x 2-inch pan 40 to 45 minutes.

QUICK SPONGE CAKE

3 eggs, separated
1 cup sugar
⅓ cup cold water

1 teaspoon vanilla or grated lemon
    rind
1 cup sifted self-rising cake flour

Beat egg whites until foamy. Gradually add ½ cup sugar, beating until mixture forms soft peaks when beater is raised. Set aside. Beat egg yolks, gradually adding remaining ½ cup sugar; continue beating until mixture is thick and lemon colored. Add water and flavoring, then self-rising cake flour, stirring until batter is smooth. Fold in egg white mixture. Pour into ungreased 9 x 3½-inch tube pan. Bake in 300° F. oven about 60 minutes or until cake springs back when touched lightly with finger. Immediately invert pan over funnel or bottle. When cake is cool, remove from pan, loosening sides of cake with spatula.

BOSTON CREAM PIE

2 eggs
½ cup sugar
½ teaspoon vanilla
1 cup sifted self-rising cake flour

⅓ cup heavy cream
1 recipe Creamy Filling
1 recipe Thin Chocolate Frosting

Grease 1 (8-inch) layer-cake pan; line bottom with waxed paper. Beat eggs with rotary beater or electric mixer until thick and lemon colored. Add sugar and vanilla; beat until light and fluffy. Stir in sifted self-rising cake flour alternately with cream, adding flour about ½ cup at a time and mixing batter until smooth after each addition. Pour into prepared pan. Bake in 325° F. oven 25 to 30 minutes or until cake springs back when touched lightly with finger. Cool *completely*. Then beat chilled Creamy Filling just until smooth. Split cake layer in half horizontally. Spread one half with Creamy Filling. Top with second half. Pour Thin Chocolate Frosting over top of cake, letting some drip down sides.

Creamy Filling

¼ cup sugar
1½ tablespoons cornstarch
¼ teaspoon salt

1 cup milk
1 egg, beaten
1 teaspoon vanilla

Combine sugar, cornstarch, and salt in double boiler top. Gradually add milk, stirring until smooth. Cook over boiling water, stirring constantly, until mixture thickens. Cover and continue cooking 10 minutes, stirring occasionally. Blend a little hot mixture into beaten egg, then stir all into remaining hot mixture in double boiler top. Cook over boiling water 2 minutes, stirring constantly. Remove from heat. Stir in vanilla. Chill.

Thin Chocolate Frosting

1 tablespoon margarine	2 tablespoons hot water
1 ounce unsweetened chocolate	¾ cup sifted confectioners' sugar

Melt margarine and chocolate in double boiler top over boiling water. Stir in hot water. Remove from boiling water. Stir in confectioners' sugar. Place over boiling water and beat 1 to 2 minutes or until smooth and glossy. Cool slightly before pouring on cake.

QUEEN ELIZABETH CAKE

1 cup boiling water	1 teaspoon vanilla
1 cup chopped dates	1¾ cups sifted self-rising cake
¼ cup margarine	flour
1 cup sugar	½ cup chopped walnuts
1 egg, beaten	

Grease 1 (13 x 9 x 2-inch) cake pan. Pour boiling water over chopped dates. Set aside; cool to lukewarm. Blend margarine and sugar. Add beaten egg and vanilla; stir until smooth. Pour liquid off dates and reserve. Add self-rising cake flour and reserved liquid alternately to the margarine mixture, stirring until smooth after each addition. Stir in walnuts and dates. Pour into prepared pan. Bake in 350° F. oven about 35 minutes or until cake springs back when touched lightly with finger. Cool. Spread with topping.

Topping

½ cup brown sugar, firmly packed	½ cup coconut
2 tablespoons margarine	½ cup chopped walnuts
¼ cup heavy cream	

Combine brown sugar, margarine, and heavy cream together in a small saucepan. Stirring constantly, bring to a boil over medium heat and boil for 3 minutes. Spread on cooled cake. Sprinkle with coconut and walnuts.

DEVIL'S FOOD CAKE

2½ cups sifted flour	2 cups buttermilk
2 cups sugar	¾ cup corn oil
½ cup cocoa	2 eggs
2 teaspoons baking soda	2 teaspoons vanilla
1 teaspoon salt	

Sift flour, sugar, cocoa, baking soda, and salt together into mixing bowl. Combine buttermilk and corn oil, eggs, and vanilla. Blend half the mixture into dry ingredients. Beat 2 minutes with medium speed of electric mixer. Add half the remaining mixture. Beat 1 minute. Add remaining mixture. Beat 1 minute. Pour into greased baking pan. Bake in 350° F. oven until cake tests done. See below for pan sizes and times.

PAN SIZE	BAKING TIME
1 (13 x 2-inch) baking pan	45 to 50 minutes
1 (10 x 4-inch) tube pan	50 to 55 minutes
2 (9 x 1½-inch) layer-cake pans	30 to 35 minutes
30 (2½ x 1¼-inch) cupcake cups	20 to 25 minutes

CHEESECAKE

Graham cracker crumbs	¼ cup cornstarch
1 pound cream-style cottage cheese	2 tablespoons lemon juice
2 (8-ounce) packages cream cheese, softened	1 teaspoon vanilla
1½ cups sugar	½ cup margarine, melted
4 eggs, slightly beaten	1 pint dairy sour cream

Grease 1 (9-inch) spring-form pan; dust with graham cracker crumbs. Sieve cottage cheese into large mixing bowl. Beat in cream cheese at high speed of electric mixer until well blended and creamy. Beating at high speed, blend in sugar, then eggs. Reduce speed to low. Add cornstarch, lemon juice, and vanilla. Beat until well blended. Blend in margarine and sour cream at low speed. Pour into prepared pan. Bake in 325° F. oven about 1 hour and 10 minutes or until firm around edges. Turn off oven. Let cake stand in oven 2 hours. Remove and cool completely on wire rack. Chill. Remove sides of pan. Top, if desired, with either of the following fruit glazes. (Makes about 12 servings.)

Strawberry Glaze

1 pint whole strawberries	⅓ cup light corn syrup
1 tablespoon cornstarch	1 teaspoon lemon juice
Dash salt	Red food coloring
¼ cup water	

Crush enough strawberries to make ¼ cup; leave remainder whole. Combine cornstarch and salt in small saucepan. Gradually blend in water and corn syrup. Add crushed berries. Cook over medium heat, stirring constantly, until mixture comes to a boil and boils one minute. Remove from heat. Strain. Stir in lemon juice and food coloring. Cool slightly. Dip whole berries into glaze one at a time, coating each evenly. Arrange upside-down on top of cheesecake. (Or arrange berries on cake and evenly pour glaze over all.) Chill until set.

Peach Glaze

Slice 1 pound peaches, mashing about 1 small peach to make ¼ cup. Follow recipe for Strawberry Glaze, substituting peaches for strawberries, arranging sliced peaches on top of cheesecake, and pouring glaze over peaches.

6-EGG CHIFFON CAKE

2¼ cups sifted cake flour
1½ cups sugar
3 teaspoons baking powder
1 teaspoon salt
½ cup corn oil
6 egg yolks

¾ cup water
1 teaspoon grated lemon rind
2 teaspoons vanilla
½ teaspoon cream of tartar
6 egg whites

Sift flour, sugar, baking powder, and salt together into mixing bowl. (Omit baking powder and salt if self-rising cake flour is used.) Make a well in center and add in order: corn oil, egg yolks, water, lemon rind, and vanilla. Beat with a spoon until smooth. Beat cream of tartar with egg whites until mixture forms very stiff peaks when beater is raised. Gently *fold* (do not stir) first mixture into egg whites, blending well. Turn batter into an ungreased 10 x 4-inch tube pan. Bake in 325° F. oven 70 to 75 minutes or until cake springs back when touched lightly with finger. Immediately invert pan over funnel or bottle and allow to cool. When cold, remove from pan, loosening sides of cake with a spatula.

Note: Cake may also be baked in a 13 x 9½ x 2-inch cake pan in 350° F. oven 40 to 45 minutes.

MOCHA CHIFFON CAKE

Follow recipe for Chiffon Cake, sifting 2 tablespoons instant coffee powder with dry ingredients, omitting lemon rind, decreasing vanilla to 1 teaspoon, and stirring ½ cup semi-sweet chocolate pieces, melted, into batter before folding it into beaten egg whites.

ORANGE CHIFFON CAKE

Follow recipe for Chiffon Cake, substituting ¾ cup orange juice for water and 1 teaspoon grated orange rind for lemon rind.

BANANA CHIFFON CAKE

Follow recipe for Chiffon Cake, substituting 1 cup mashed ripe banana and 1 tablespoon lemon juice for water, lemon rind, and vanilla.

CHOCOLATE BANANA CHIFFON CAKE

Follow recipe for Chiffon Cake, substituting 1 cup mashed banana and 1 ounce unsweetened chocolate (coarsely grated) for water, lemon rind, and vanilla.

WINE CHIFFON CAKE

Follow recipe for Chiffon Cake, substituting ¾ cup white wine for water and omitting lemon rind if desired.

CHIFFON PINEAPPLE UPSIDE-DOWN CAKE

Topping

1 tablespoon margarine	5 to 6 small pineapple rings
2 tablespoons light brown sugar	(3-inch diameter)
2 tablespoons dark corn syrup	

Cake

¾ cup sifted self-rising cake flour	2 eggs, separated
⅓ cup sugar	¼ cup water
3 tablespoons corn oil	½ teaspoon vanilla
	¼ teaspoon cream of tartar

Blend margarine, brown sugar, and dark corn syrup. Spread in bottom of 1 (8 x 8 x 2-inch) cake pan. Arrange pineapple slices over mixture. Bake in 325° F. oven 15 minutes. Remove from oven. Meanwhile, sift self-rising cake flour and sugar into mixing bowl. Make well in center and add corn oil, egg yolks, water, and vanilla in order given. Beat with spoon until smooth. Beat egg whites and cream of tartar until mixture forms very stiff peaks when beater is raised. Gently *fold* (do not stir) batter mixture into egg whites, blending well. Carefully pour over pineapple mixture. Bake in 325° F. oven about 45 minutes or until cake springs back when touched lightly with finger. Immediately invert cake onto serving plate.

JELLY ROLL

3 eggs	1 cup sifted cake flour
1 teaspoon baking powder	1 teaspoon vanilla
¼ teaspoon salt	1½ cups tart jelly, softened or
½ cup sugar	whipped
½ cup light corn syrup	

Grease 1 (15½ x 10½ x 1-inch) jelly roll pan. Line bottom with waxed paper and grease paper. Beat eggs, baking powder, and salt with rotary or electric beater. Gradually beat in sugar, then syrup, 1 tablespoon at a time. Beat until mixture is thick and light colored. Fold in flour and vanilla. Bake in prepared pan in 375° F. oven 15 minutes, or until cake is delicately browned and springs back when touched lightly with finger. Turn at once onto cloth covered with confectioners' sugar, paper-side-up, and remove paper. Roll cake and towel together. Cool on rack. Unroll, spread cake with jelly, spreading almost to edge. Roll up cake. (Makes about 8 servings.)

PINEAPPLE UPSIDE-DOWN CAKE

¼ cup margarine
¼ cup light brown sugar
½ cup light or dark corn syrup
12 slices well-drained pineapple *or*
   2 (1-pound, 4-ounce) cans
   well-drained, crushed
   pineapple
1 package white or yellow cake
   mix

Pre-heat oven to temperature cake-mix package directs. Blend margarine, sugar, and syrup in 13 x 9 x 2-inch pan; arrange pineapple on mixture. Heat in oven 15 minutes. Meanwhile, mix cake batter as package directs. Remove pan from oven; pour batter carefully over fruit. Bake 45 to 55 minutes or until cake tests done. Invert onto cake rack set on waxed paper. Let stand 1 minute; remove pan. Serve cake warm, with whipped cream if desired. (Makes 20 servings.)

APRICOT-PRUNE UPSIDE-DOWN CAKE

Follow above recipe, substituting 12 stewed, drained apricot halves and 24 stewed, pitted, and drained prunes for the pineapple.

CRANBERRY-ORANGE UPSIDE-DOWN CAKE

Follow above recipe, substituting 2 cups whole cranberry sauce mixed with ⅔ cup well drained, ground, or finely chopped whole orange for the pineapple.

YELLOW CAKE

3 cups sifted flour	3 eggs
3½ teaspoons baking powder	1 teaspoon vanilla
1 teaspoon salt	½ teaspoon almond extract
¾ cup margarine	1 cup milk
1⅓ cups sugar	

Sift flour, baking powder, and salt together; set aside. (Omit baking powder and salt if self-rising cake flour is used.) Blend margarine and sugar in mixing bowl. Add eggs, one at a time, blending until smooth. Add vanilla and almond extracts. Add sifted flour mixture in 4 additions alternately with milk, beginning and ending with flour and mixing just until smooth. (If electric mixer is used, use low speed.) Pour into greased and lightly floured pans. Bake in 350° F. oven until cake tests done. See below for pan sizes and times.

PAN SIZE	BAKING TIME
2 (9-inch) layer-cake pans	30 to 35 minutes
1 (13 x 9 x 2-inch) cake pans	35 to 40 minutes
30 (2½ x 1¼-inch) cupcake cups	25 to 30 minutes

MOCK POUND CAKE

3 cups sifted flour	1½ cups sugar
3½ teaspoons baking powder	3 eggs, beaten
½ teaspoon salt	⅓ cup milk
½ cup margarine	1 teaspoon vanilla
1 (8-ounce) package cream cheese	

Sift cake flour, baking powder, and salt together; set aside. Cream margarine and cream cheese. Gradually add sugar; beat until fluffy. Blend in beaten eggs. Add sifted dry ingredients alternately with milk, blending well after each addition. Stir in vanilla. Pour into lightly greased and floured cake pan. Bake in 350° F. oven until cake tests done. (See below for pan sizes and baking times.)

PAN SIZE	BAKING TIME
1 (10 x 4-inch) tube pan	about 1 hour
1 (13 x 9 x 2-inch) cake pan	about 50 minutes
2 (9 x 5 x 3-inch) loaf pans	about 1 hour

NUT CAKE

Follow recipe for Mock Pound Cake, sifting ¼ teaspoon mace with dry ingredients and adding 1 cup chopped nuts with vanilla.

RUM RAISIN CAKE

Follow recipe for Mock Pound Cake, substituting ¼ cup rum for vanilla and adding 1 cup cut-up raisins with rum.

MINCEMEAT CAKE

½ cup margarine	¼ cup water
½ cup sugar	2¼ cups sifted self-rising cake
2 eggs, slightly beaten	flour
1 cup ready-to-use mincemeat	⅓ cup chopped nuts (optional)

Grease 1 (8 x 8 x 2-inch) cake pan; line bottom with waxed paper. Blend margarine and sugar. Add eggs, blending until smooth. Combine mincemeat and water. Stir sifted self-rising cake flour into margarine mixture alternately with mincemeat, beginning and ending with flour and mixing until smooth after each addition. Stir in nuts, if desired. Pour into prepared pan. Bake in 350° F. oven about 50 minutes or until cake springs back when touched lightly with finger. Serve with fruit sauce, if desired.

APRICOT ORANGE COBBLER

1 (1-pound, 14-ounce) can apricot halves	2 tablespoons cornstarch
¾ cup orange sections (2 oranges)	1 cup self-rising cake flour
½ teaspoon grated orange rind	⅓ cup light cream *or* milk
¼ cup sugar	2 tablespoons margarine, melted
	2 teaspoons sugar

Drain apricot halves, reserving syrup. Arrange apricot halves and orange sections in bottom of 8 x 8 x 2-inch baking dish. Sprinkle with orange rind. Combine ¼ cup sugar and cornstarch in medium saucepan. Stir in reserved syrup. Cook over medium heat, stirring constantly, until mixture comes to a boil and boils 1 minute. Pour cornstarch mixture over fruit. Heat in 400° F. oven while preparing biscuit topping. Combine self-rising cake flour, light cream (or milk) and margarine. Stir just until moistened. Drop by tablespoons onto hot fruit. Sprinkle with 2 teaspoons sugar. Continue baking 20 to 25 minutes or until biscuits are golden brown. Serve warm with ice cream. (Makes 5 to 6 servings.)

ORANGE NUT CAKE

½ cup margarine	2¼ cups self-rising cake flour
1 cup light brown sugar, firmly packed	1 cup milk
1 egg, beaten	½ cup chopped raisins
	½ cup walnuts

Grease 1 (13 x 9 x 2-inch) cake pan. Blend margarine and sugar. Add beaten egg; stir until smooth. Add in self-rising cake flour and milk alternately, mixing until smooth after each addition. Stir in chopped raisins and walnuts. Pour into prepared pan. Bake in 350° F. oven about 40 minutes or until cake springs back when touched lightly with finger. Meanwhile, prepare topping and let stand while cake is baking. Spread over hot cake. Cool and serve with whipped cream.

220

Topping

> ¾ cup whole ground orange
> ¾ cup sugar

Grind whole orange in food chopper or blender. Mix ground orange and sugar together. Spread over hot cake.

SHAKER LOAF CAKE

2 eggs	1 cup heavy cream
¾ cup sugar	1½ cups unsifted self-rising cake
½ teaspoon vanilla	flour

Grease and flour 1 (9½ x 5¼ x 2¾-inch) loaf pan. Put eggs and sugar into a 2-quart juice shaker. Cover tightly; shake vigorously 50 times, holding top and bottom of shaker securely. Add vanilla and heavy cream. Cover; shake 20 times. Add self-rising cake flour. Cover; shake 20 times. Pour into prepared pan. Bake in 350° F. oven about 50 minutes or until cake springs back when touched lightly with finger. Cool. Remove from pan.

SHAKER SPICE CAKE

Follow recipe for Shaker Loaf Cake, adding ½ teaspoon nutmeg, ½ teaspoon cinnamon, and ¼ teaspoon ground cloves with eggs and sugar.

VELVETY CUPCAKES

¼ cup margarine	½ cup sugar
½ teaspoon lemon juice	6 tablespoons milk
1 cup sifted self-rising cake flour	1 egg

Grease and flour 9 (2½-inch) or 7 (3-inch) cupcake cups. Blend margarine and lemon juice. Sift self-rising cake flour and sugar together over margarine mixture. Add 3 tablespoons milk and egg; stir until blended. Beat 2 minutes with medium speed of electric mixer or 300 strokes by hand. Add remaining 3 table-spoons milk. Beat 1 minute with medium speed of mixer or 150 strokes by hand. Pour into prepared pans, filling cups ½ full. Bake in 375° F. oven 20 to 25 minutes or until tops spring back when touched lightly with finger.

To decorate: Cool cupcakes. Brush tops with light corn syrup in desired pattern using small brush. Dip into colored sugar, or sprinkle sugar over tops and shake off excess.

DATE-NUT BREAD

3 cups sifted flour	1 egg
3½ teaspoons baking powder	⅔ cup milk
1 teaspoon salt	⅔ cup orange juice
¾ cup sugar	1¼ cups chopped dates
3 tablespoons corn oil	½ cup chopped nuts

Sift flour, baking powder, and salt together; set aside. Blend sugar, corn oil, and egg in mixing bowl. Blend in milk and orange juice. Gradually mix in sifted dry ingredients. Fold in dates and nuts. Pour into well-greased, lightly floured 9 x 5 x 3-inch loaf pan. Let stand 20 minutes. Bake in 350° F. oven about 1 hour and 15 minutes or until a cake tester inserted in center of loaf comes out clean. Cool completely before slicing.

APRICOT-NUT BREAD

Follow recipe for Date-Nut Bread, increasing sugar to 1 cup and substituting 1 cup finely chopped dried apricots for dates. Bake about 1½ hours.

BANANA-NUT BREAD

Follow recipe for Date Nut Bread, increasing sugar to 1 cup and milk to ¾ cup, substituting 1 cup mashed very ripe banana, and

½ teaspoon lemon juice for orange juice, and omitting dates. Bake
1½ hours.

MOCHA FLUFF TORTE

3 ounces unsweetened chocolate
¾ cup hot, strong coffee
½ cup light corn syrup
1¾ cups sifted cake flour
3 teaspoons baking powder

¼ teaspoon salt
½ cup margarine
1 cup sugar
3 eggs
1 teaspoon vanilla

Grease 2 (9-inch) layer-cake pans; line bottoms with waxed paper.
Melt chocolate with hot coffee. Add corn syrup. Stir until mixture thickens. Cool. Sift cake flour, baking powder and salt together; set aside. Blend margarine and sugar in mixing bowl. Add eggs, one at a time, blending until smooth. Add vanilla. Stir in sifted flour mixture alternately with cold chocolate mixture, beginning and ending with flour and mixing until smooth after each addition. Pour into prepared cake pans. Bake in 350° F. oven about 35 minutes or until cake tests done. Meanwhile, prepare Mocha Fluff Frosting. Chill. Cool cake. Split each layer in two. Stack, spreading frosting between each layer. Frost completely.

Mocha Fluff Frosting

1 (6-ounce) package semi-sweet
   chocolate pieces
¼ cup water
1 teaspoon instant coffee powder

¾ cup light corn syrup
3 egg yolks, well beaten
1 cup margarine
2 teaspoons vanilla

Melt chocolate chips in ¼ cup water over boiling water. Remove from boiling water. Stir in instant coffee powder, until smooth. Cool. Cook syrup over medium heat until temperature reaches 230° F. or syrup spins a thread when dropped from fork or spoon. Beating constantly, slowly add to beaten egg yolks. Continue beating until thick and creamy. Blend in margarine, vanilla, and cooled chocolate mixture. Beat until fluffy. Chill while cake cools.

MISTY MOISTY ORANGE CAKE

2 cups sifted flour
1 teaspoon baking soda
½ teaspoon baking powder
½ teaspoon salt
½ cup margarine
1 cup sugar
2 eggs

1 cup sour milk (to make sour milk, add 1 tablespoon vinegar to 1 cup regular milk)
1 cup golden raisins
3 tablespoons grated orange rind
½ cup orange juice
½ cup light corn syrup

Sift flour, baking soda, baking powder, and salt together; set aside. Blend margarine and sugar in mixing bowl. Add eggs, blending until smooth. Stir in sifted flour mixture alternately with sour milk, beginning and ending with flour and mixing until smooth after each addition. Fold in raisins and grated orange rind. Pour into 1 greased (13 x 9½ x 2-inch) baking pan. Bake in 350° F. oven 30 to 35 minutes or until cake tests done. Meanwhile, combine orange juice and syrup. As soon as cake is removed from oven, pour mixture over cake in pan. Serve warm or cold, with ice cream or custard sauce.

GRATED-APPLE CAKE

2 cups sifted flour
1 teaspoon baking powder
1 teaspoon baking soda
1 teaspoon salt
½ teaspoon nutmeg
½ cup margarine

¾ cup firmly packed brown sugar
½ cup dark brown corn syrup
2 eggs
1½ cups coarsely grated pared cooking apple

Sift flour, baking powder, baking soda, salt, and nutmeg together; set aside. Blend margarine and brown sugar in mixing bowl. Add syrup, then egg; blend until smooth. Add sifted dry ingredients, a small amount at a time, beating until blended. Fold in grated apple. Pour into greased and lightly floured 13 x 9½ x 2-inch baking pan. Bake in 350° F. oven about 35 minutes or until cake tests done. Cut into squares and serve warm or cold with lemon sauce or sour cream.

SHORTCUT COFFEE CAKE

¼ cup margarine
⅓ cup sugar
1 cup plus 2 tablespoons unsifted
   self-rising cake flour
1 egg

Milk
1 tablespoon margarine
Cinnamon sugar
Chopped nuts (optional)
1 tablespoon milk

Melt ¼ cup margarine in 1 (8-inch) layer-cake pan. Stir in sugar thoroughly with fork. Put flour on top of sugar mixture. Break egg into measuring cup; stir in enough milk to make ¾ cup. Pour into cake pan. Stir until flour disappears. Bake in 350° F. oven 25 minutes. Spread hot cake with 1 tablespoon margarine. Sprinkle with cinnamon sugar and nuts; then 1 tablespoon milk. Bake 5 minutes longer. Serve warm.

ORANGE COFFEE CAKE

2½ cups sifted self-rising cake
   flour
¾ cup sugar
⅓ cup margarine
2 eggs, beaten
¾ cup orange juice

½ cup brown sugar, firmly packed
1½ teaspoons cinnamon
1½ tablespoons grated orange
   rind
⅓ cup chopped nuts
2 tablespoons margarine

Grease and flour 1 (9 x 9 x 2-inch) pan; sift cake flour and sugar together. Cut in ⅓ cup margarine until mixture resembles coarse crumbs. Combine beaten eggs and orange juice; add to flour mixture; stir just enough to blend. Pour batter into prepared pan. Combine brown sugar, cinnamon, orange rind, and nuts. Sprinkle on cake batter; dot with 2 tablespoons margarine. Bake in 350° F. oven 30 to 35 minutes or until cake tester comes out clean when inserted in center of cake. Serve warm.

SOUR CREAM COFFEE CAKE

⅓ cup sugar
⅓ cup brown sugar, firmly packed
½ cup chopped nuts
1 teaspoon cinnamon
½ teaspoon baking soda

1 cup dairy sour cream
1 cup margarine
1 cup sugar
3 eggs
3½ cups sifted self-rising cake flour

Grease 1 (10 x 4-inch) tube pan. Combine ⅓ cup sugar, brown sugar, nuts, and cinnamon. Stir baking soda into sour cream. Set aside both mixtures. Blend margarine and 1 cup sugar. Add eggs, one at a time, blending until smooth. Stir in cake flour alternately with sour cream mixture, beginning and ending with flour and mixing until smooth after each addition. Pour half the batter into prepared pan, spreading batter evenly. Sprinkle with half the sugar mixture. Repeat with remaining batter and sugar mixture. Bake in 350° F. oven about 50 minutes or until cake springs back when touched lightly with finger.

FROSTINGS

CHOCOLATE FROSTING

½ cup margarine
⅓ cup light or dark corn syrup
¼ teaspoon salt
½ teaspoon vanilla

½ cup cocoa
1 to 2 tablespoons milk
4½ cups (1 pound) sifted confectioners' sugar

Blend margarine, corn syrup, vanilla, and salt. Stir in cocoa. Alternately add milk and confectioners' sugar, beating until smooth and creamy after each addition. Add enough milk to make good spreading consistency. (Makes 2½ cups, enough to frost tops and sides of 2 [9-inch] cake layers.)

RICH CHOCOLATE FROSTING

Follow recipe for Chocolate Frosting, increasing cocoa to 1 cup and milk to ⅓ cup.

MOCHA FROSTING

Follow recipe for Chocolate Frosting, substituting cold, strong coffee for milk.

CARAMEL FROSTING

Follow recipe for Chocolate Frosting, using dark corn syrup and omitting cocoa.

VANILLA FROSTING

Follow recipe for Chocolate Frosting, using light corn syrup, increasing vanilla to 1 teaspoon, and omitting cocoa.

CREAMY FROSTING

¼ cup margarine
¼ teaspoon salt
2½ cups sifted confectioners' sugar

2 to 2½ tablespoons hot milk
1 teaspoon vanilla

Blend margarine and salt. Gradually add 1 cup sugar, blending well. Add remaining sugar alternately with milk, beating until smooth and creamy. (Add only enough milk to make a good spreading consistency.) Add vanilla. (Makes enough to cover top and sides of 1 [8-inch] square cake, tops of 18 large cupcakes, or tops of 2 [8-inch] layers.)

MOCHA CREAMY FROSTING

Follow recipe for Creamy Frosting, sifting 2 tablespoons cocoa with the sugar and omitting vanilla. Dissolve 1 teaspoon powdered coffee in the hot milk.

ORANGE CREAMY FROSTING

Follow recipe for Creamy Frosting, omitting vanilla and adding 2 teaspoons grated orange rind. If desired, use 1 teaspoon grated lemon rind and 1 teaspoon grated orange rind.

COFFEE CREAMY FROSTING

Follow recipe for Creamy Frosting, omitting vanilla and dissolving 2 teaspoons powdered coffee in the hot milk.

FLUFFY WHITE FROSTING

2 egg whites
⅛ teaspoon salt
1 cup light corn syrup

¼ cup sugar
1½ teaspoons vanilla

Beat egg whites and salt until soft peaks form when beater is raised. Combine light corn syrup and sugar in small saucepan. Cook over low heat, stirring constantly, until sugar is completely dissolved and mixture just reaches full boil. Beat hot syrup into egg whites, a little at a time. Beat in vanilla. Continue beating until mixture holds stiff peaks. (Makes 4⅓ cups, enough to cover tops and sides of 2 [8- or 9-inch] layers.)

Note: To tint frosting, add a few drops of food coloring.

PECAN FROSTING

Follow recipe for Fluffy White Frosting, folding in 1 cup chopped pecans.

SUPER CREAMY FROSTING

1 cup margarine	2 unbeaten egg whites
4½ cups (1 pound) sifted confec-	Dash salt
tioners' sugar	1 teaspoon vanilla

Stir margarine slightly to soften. Gradually add half the sugar, beating until smooth. Add egg whites and salt; beating until light and fluffy. Gradually add remaining sugar, beating well. Fold in vanilla. (Makes about 3 cups or enough to cover tops and sides of 2 [9-inch] cake layers.)

SUPER CREAMY CITRUS FROSTING

Follow recipe for Super Creamy Frosting, folding in 1 or 2 tablespoons grated lemon or orange rind and ½ teaspoon lemon extract instead of vanilla.

SUPER CREAMY MOCHA FROSTING

Follow recipe for Super Creamy Frosting, sifting ¼ cup cocoa and 1 teaspoon instant coffee with sugar before adding to margarine, and omitting vanilla.

MARSHMALLOW NO-COOK FROSTING

2 egg whites	¾ cup dark or light corn syrup
¼ teaspoon salt	1¼ teaspoons vanilla
¼ cup sugar	

Beat egg whites and salt with electric mixer or rotary beater until foamy. Gradually beat in sugar, beating until mixture is smooth and glossy. Beat in syrup, a little at a time. Beat until frosting holds firm peaks when beater is raised. Fold in vanilla. Tint with food coloring, if desired. (Makes enough to frost 2 [9-inch] layers or 1 [10-inch] tube cake.)

ORANGE NO-COOK FROSTING

Follow recipe for Marshmallow No-Cook Frosting, omitting vanilla and substituting 1 tablespoon grated orange rind and ½ teaspoon orange extract.

LEMON NO-COOK FROSTING

Follow recipe for Marshmallow No-Cook Frosting, substituting 2 teaspoons grated lemon rind for vanilla.

COFFEE NO-COOK FROSTING

Follow recipe for Marshmallow No-Cook Frosting, omitting vanilla and adding 1 tablespoon instant coffee powder with syrup.

SPICE NO-COOK FROSTING

Follow recipe for Marshmallow No-Cook Frosting, using dark corn syrup, omitting vanilla, and adding ½ teaspoon ginger, ¼ teaspoon cinnamon, and dash ground cloves with syrup.

COCONUT NO-COOK FROSTING

Follow recipe for Marshmallow No-Cook Frosting, folding in 1 cup flaked coconut with vanilla.

CHOCOLATE MARBLE NO-COOK FROSTING

Prepare Marshmallow No-Cook Frosting. Swirl 1 envelope no-melt chocolate (1 ounce chocolate equivalent) into frosting, cutting down with spatula to give marbled effect.

TUTTI-FRUTTI NO-COOK FROSTING

Prepare Marshmallow No-Cook Frosting. Fold in ¼ cup each chopped nuts, raisins, and chopped candied cherries.

MINT CANDY NO-COOK FROSTING

Prepare Marshmallow No-Cook Frosting, omitting vanilla and folding in ¼ teaspoon peppermint extract and 1 to 2 drops red food coloring. Sprinkle frosted cake with crushed peppermint candy.

DOUBLE BOILER FROSTING

2 egg whites
½ cup light corn syrup
½ cup sugar
⅛ teaspoon salt
1 teaspoon vanilla

With rotary beater or electric mixer, beat egg whites, syrup, sugar, and salt in top of double boiler set over rapidly boiling water until frosting stands in firm peaks. This should take from 3 to 4 minutes. Remove from heat, beat in vanilla, and beat 1 minute longer. (Makes frosting for 2 [9-inch] cake layers.)

BUTTERSCOTCH FROSTING

Follow recipe for Double Boiler Frosting, using dark corn syrup and brown sugar. Very good on spice cake.

CARAMEL TOPPING

½ cup brown sugar, firmly packed   ¼ cup margarine, melted
¼ cup flour   ½ cup chopped nuts
½ cup waffle and pancake syrup

Prepare cake from cake mix or recipe and bake in 1 (13 x 9 x 2-inch) pan for time and at temperature recipe directs. Prepare topping while cake is baking. Blend sugar and flour, stir in syrup, then margarine and nuts. Remove baked cake from oven and reset oven to 400° F. Spread topping carefully over hot cake, a small amount at a time. Return to oven; bake 7 to 10 minutes or until entire topping surface is bubbly. To serve, cut cake in pan while warm.

COCONUT TOPPING

Follow recipe for Caramel Topping, substituting 1 cup flaked coconut for nuts. For 8-inch-square cake prepare topping recipe using ½ of all ingredients. Bake topping 5 to 7 minutes.

DESSERT PASTRIES AND COOKIES

CREAM PUFFS

1 cup water   1¼ cups flour
½ cup corn oil   4 eggs
½ teaspoon salt

Bring water to a full boil in medium saucepan. Add corn oil and salt, then flour all at once. Beat rapidly with spoon over low heat until mixture leaves sides of pan and forms a smooth, compact ball. Remove from heat. Add eggs, one at a time, beating until shiny and smooth after each addition. (Mixture should be thick when last egg has been added.) Drop by tablespoonfuls onto un-greased cookie sheet, about 2 inches apart. Bake in 450° F. oven 20 minutes; reduce oven to 350° F. and continue baking about 15 minutes longer. Cool. To serve, cut slit in side of each puff and fill with sweetened whipped cream, vanilla pudding, or ice cream. (Makes 12 large puffs.)

Note: For drier puffs, leave in oven for about 10 minutes after oven has been turned off.

CHOCOLATE DROPS

1 cup sifted flour	2 eggs
1 teaspoon baking powder	1 teaspoon vanilla
½ teaspoon salt	½ cup sifted confectioners' (or
⅓ cup margarine	granulated) sugar
1 cup sugar	
2 ounces unsweetened chocolate, melted	

Sift flour, baking powder, and salt together; set aside. Blend margarine and sugar in mixing bowl. Mix in melted chocolate. Add eggs, one at a time, beating well. Add vanilla. Stir in sifted dry ingredients; mix well. Cover and chill several hours or over-night. Shape into 1-inch balls. Roll in confectioners' sugar until well coated. (Do not flatten.) Place on ungreased cookie sheet, 2 inches apart. Bake in 350° F. oven 15 minutes. (Cookies will be soft.) Store in tightly covered container. (Makes 3 dozen.)

DATE AND NUT BARS

¾ cup sifted flour	½ teaspoon vanilla
1 cup sugar	1 cup (8-ounce package) dates, finely cut
¼ teaspoon baking powder	
⅛ teaspoon salt	1 cup chopped nuts
½ cup corn oil	Confectioners' sugar
2 eggs	

Sift flour, sugar, baking powder, and salt into mixing bowl. Make a well in center and add in order corn oil, eggs, and vanilla. Beat with spoon until smooth. Add dates and nuts; mix well. Turn into greased 9 x 9 x 2-inch baking pan. Bake in 350° F. oven 30 to 35 minutes. Cut into bars while still warm. Dust with confectioners' sugar. (Makes 24.)

SUGAR COOKIES

2 cups sifted flour	1 egg plus milk to make ⅓ cup
1¼ teaspoons baking powder	¾ cup sugar
¼ teaspoon salt	1 teaspoon vanilla
⅓ cup corn oil	

Sift flour, baking powder, and salt together into mixing bowl. Add corn oil; blend well with fork or pastry blender. (Mixture will appear dry.) Combine egg-milk mixture, sugar, and vanilla in a bowl. Beat until very light and fluffy. Stir into flour mixture. Chill about 1 hour. Roll out on floured board or cloth until ⅛ to ¼ inch thick. Cut out into desired shapes. Place on ungreased cookie sheet. Bake in 400° F. oven about 9 minutes or until delicately browned. (Makes 3 dozen [2-inch] cookies.)

SHORTBREAD

2 cups sifted flour	1 cup butter
1 cup cornstarch	½ cup sugar
Pinch salt	Sugar

Sift flour, cornstarch and salt together. Cream butter and ½ cup sugar until light and fluffy. Add dry ingredients gradually until dough is stiff enough to work with hands. Knead on lightly floured cloth or board until well blended and smooth. Press into 12 x 8-inch rectangle on baking sheet. Smooth over top. Score almost through with knife into 1 x 2-inch rectangles; prick with fork. Bake in 325° F. oven for 30 to 40 minutes or until golden brown. Recut rectangles and sprinkle with sugar while still hot. Cool completely; remove from baking sheet. Store in airtight container. (Makes 4 dozen [1 x 2-inch] rectangles.)

Note: For triangles divide 12 x 8-inch rectangle into 24 2-inch squares. Cut each square in half diagonally. (Makes 4 dozen triangles.)

REFRIGERATOR COOKIES

3 cups sifted flour
1 teaspoon baking powder
¼ teaspoon salt
¾ cup margarine
½ cup dark corn syrup

⅔ cup firmly packed brown sugar
1 egg, beaten
1 teaspoon vanilla
1 cup chopped nuts

Sift flour, baking powder, and salt together. Cream margarine; then beat in corn syrup and sugar until well blended. Add egg; beat until thoroughly combined. Mix in vanilla and nuts; then sifted dry ingredients. Chill dough about 1 hour. Shape into 2 rolls, about 2 inches thick. Wrap in waxed paper and chill at least 4 hours. Cut into ⅛-inch slices with sharp knife. Place on ungreased cookie sheet. Bake in 350° F. oven 10 to 12 minutes. (Makes about 6 dozen.)

CHOCOLATE COOKIES

Follow recipe for Refrigerator Cookies, omitting baking powder, sifting ¼ teaspoon baking soda with dry ingredients, and blending 2 ounces unsweetened chocolate, melted, into batter before mixing in dry ingredients.

ORANGE-COCONUT COOKIES

Follow recipe for Refrigerator Cookies, using light corn syrup instead of dark corn syrup, granulated sugar instead of brown sugar, and 1 cup flaked coconut instead of nuts. Add 2 table-spoons grated orange rind and ¼ teaspoon nutmeg with vanilla.

OATMEAL DROP COOKIES

2 cups sifted flour
1 teaspoon baking powder
1 teaspoon salt
1 teaspoon cinnamon
½ teaspoon baking soda
3 cups oatmeal

1 cup raisins
1¼ cups margarine
1¼ cups sugar
2 eggs, slightly beaten
¼ cup milk

Sift flour, baking powder, salt, cinnamon, and baking soda to-gether in a bowl. Mix in oatmeal and raisins. Blend margarine and sugar in mixing bowl. Add eggs; beat until fluffy. Stir in half the dry ingredients, then milk, then remaining dry ingredients. Drop by teaspoonfuls, 2 inches apart, onto an ungreased cookie sheet. Bake in 400° F. oven 10 to 12 minutes or until edges are lightly browned. Remove from cookie sheet immediately. (Makes about 6 dozen.)

CHOCOLATE CHIP OATMEAL COOKIES

Follow recipe for Oatmeal Drop Cookies, substituting 1 cup chocolate chips for raisins.

DATE OATMEAL COOKIES

Follow recipe for Oatmeal Drop Cookies, substituting 1 cup cut-up dates for raisins.

NUT OATMEAL COOKIES

Follow recipe for Oatmeal Drop Cookies, substituting one cup chopped nuts for raisins.

NUTMEG OATMEAL COOKIES

Follow recipe for Oatmeal Drop Cookies, substituting ½ teaspoon nutmeg for 1 teaspoon cinnamon.

CITRUS OATMEAL COOKIES

Follow recipe for Oatmeal Drop Cookies, substituting 1 teaspoon grated lemon or orange rind for cinnamon.

FUDGE BROWNIES

2 eggs	1 teaspoon vanilla
1 cup sugar	⅔ cup sifted self-rising cake flour
¼ cup corn oil	½ cup coarsely chopped nuts
2 ounces unsweetened chocolate, melted	

Grease 1 (8 x 8 x 2-inch) pan. Beat eggs well. Gradually add sugar; beat well. Mix in corn oil, melted chocolate, and vanilla. Stir in sifted self-rising cake flour and nuts, mixing well. Pour into prepared pan. Bake in 350° F. oven about 30 minutes. Cool; cut into squares. (Makes 16 [2-inch] brownies.)

BUTTERSCOTCH BROWNIES

⅓ cup margarine	½ cup chopped nuts
1 cup brown sugar, firmly packed	1 teaspoon vanilla
1 egg	1 cup sifted self-rising cake flour

Grease 1 (8 x 8 x 2-inch) pan. Blend margarine and sugar. Add egg; beat well. Mix in nuts and vanilla. Fold in sifted self-rising cake flour. Spread in prepared pan. Bake in 350° F. oven 30 to 35 minutes or until golden brown. Cool; cut into squares. (Makes 16 [2-inch] squares.)

HAMENTASHEN
(Fruit-filled pastry)

4 eggs, slightly beaten	Grated rind of 1 orange
¾ cup corn oil	5 cups sifted self-rising cake flour
¾ cup sugar	Apple butter

Combine slightly beaten eggs, corn oil, sugar, and orange rind. Beat until mixture is fluffy and thick. Gently stir in self-rising cake flour. Chill about 1½ hours or until firm. Divide dough into quarters. Roll out each quarter on floured board or cloth to ⅛-inch thickness. Cut into 2½- or 3-inch circles and place on greased cookie sheet. Spoon 1 tablespoon apple butter into center of each. Form tricorns, bringing up edges of dough almost to center and making three seams. (Some filling should show in center.) Pinch seams together tightly. Bake in 350° F. oven 15 to 20 minutes or until golden brown. (Makes about 6 dozen 2½-inch or 4 dozen 3-inch cookies.)

RAISIN NUT SQUARES

¼ cup margarine	1½ cups raisins
1 cup sugar	1 cup coarsely chopped nuts
2 eggs	⅔ cup sifted self-rising cake flour
1 teaspoon vanilla	

Grease 1 (9 x 9 x 2-inch) pan. Blend margarine and sugar; beat in eggs and vanilla. Combine raisins and nuts with self-rising cake flour and stir into egg mixture. Spread batter in prepared pan. Bake in 350° F. oven about 45 minutes or until cake tester inserted in center comes out clean. Cool; cut into squares. (Makes 16 squares.)

238

YELLOW NUT COOKIES

⅓ cup margarine
½ cup sugar
¼ teaspoon almond extract
1 egg yolk

1 cup sifted self-rising cake flour
¼ cup finely chopped blanched
   almonds

Blend margarine, sugar, and almond extract. Add egg yolk; beat well. Blend in flour. Roll into 1-inch balls; then roll balls in chopped almonds. Place on greased cookie sheet. Bake in 350° F. oven 15 to 18 minutes. (Makes about 2 dozen cookies.)

ORANGE NUT SQUARES

2 eggs
1 cup sugar
½ cup corn oil
1¼ cups sifted self-rising cake flour

1 cup chopped nuts
½ teaspoon orange extract
Confectioners' sugar

Grease 1 (9 x 9 x 2-inch) pan. Beat eggs; add sugar and corn oil alternately, beating well after each addition. Sift self-rising cake flour over egg mixture and blend thoroughly. Stir in nuts and orange extract. Spread batter in prepared pan. Bake in 350° F. oven about 35 minutes or until crust is crisp and brown. Cool slightly and sprinkle with confectioners' sugar. Cut into squares. (Makes 16 squares.)

FROSTED FRUIT COOKIES

2¾ cups sifted flour
½ teaspoon soda
1 teaspoon cinnamon
½ teaspoon ground cloves
½ teaspoon nutmeg
½ cup finely chopped, mixed
   candied fruit

½ cup finely chopped nuts
1 egg
1 cup dark corn syrup
¾ cup brown sugar, firmly packed
1 tablespoon lemon juice
1 teaspoon grated lemon rind

Sift flour with soda and spices; mix in candied fruits and nuts. Set aside. Beat egg slightly, stir in syrup, sugar, lemon juice, and rind, then the flour-fruit mixture. Divide dough in half; place each half on a well-greased and floured cookie sheet. Wet palm of hand with cold water and flatten dough to ⅛-inch thickness. Bake in 400° F. oven 12 to 15 minutes or until firm to touch and lightly browned. Immediately brush with Thin Icing. While still warm, cut into bars, squares, or diamonds. Remove from cookie sheet. Cool. Store in tightly covered container to mellow. (Makes about 5 dozen.)

Thin Icing

Mix ½ cup sifted confectioners' sugar with 1 tablespoon water until smooth.

LACE WAFERS

½ cup sifted flour	¼ cup brown sugar, firmly packed
½ cup flaked coconut	¼ cup margarine
¼ cup corn syrup	½ teaspoon vanilla

Mix sifted flour with coconut. Cook and stir syrup, sugar, and margarine in heavy saucepan, over medium heat, until mixture boils. Remove from heat, stir in vanilla, and gradually blend in flour mixture. Drop scant teaspoonfuls about 3 inches apart on ungreased cookie sheet. Bake in 325° F. oven 8 to 10 minutes. Let cookies cool several minutes; remove from cookie sheet. Cool on wire racks covered with paper towels. If cookies cool too much to remove from pan easily, soften a few minutes in oven. (Makes about 2 dozen.)

Rolled Lace Wafers

Bake only 6 wafers at a time. Remove a warm wafer from cookie sheet, roll quickly over handle of wooden spoon. Cool on wire rack.

Chocolate Lace Wafers

Follow recipe for Lace Wafers, using granulated sugar instead of brown sugar. Melt 1 square of unsweetened chocolate with syrup, sugar, and margarine mixture.

PECAN BARS

2 cups sifted flour	⅔ cup brown sugar, firmly packed
1 teaspoon baking powder	½ cup margarine

Sift flour with baking powder. Stir in sugar. Cut in margarine until mixture is well blended. It will look dry and crumbly. Pat evenly into bottom of well-greased baking pan (11 x 7 x 1½ inches or 9 x 9 x 1¾ inches.) Bake in 350° F. oven 15 minutes. Remove from oven. Pour topping mixture evenly over baked mixture. Sprinkle with ¾ cup chopped pecans. Return to oven and bake 40 to 45 minutes more. Cut into squares while warm. (Makes 16 medium bars.)

Topping

Mix ½ cup brown sugar with ⅓ cup flour. Beat 4 eggs; mix in 1½ cups dark corn syrup, 1 teaspoon salt, and 2 teaspoons vanilla, then the flour-sugar mixture.

CARDAMON COOKIES

2 cups sifted flour	1 teaspoon ground cardamon
½ cup sugar	¼ teaspoon ginger
½ teaspoon soda	¼ teaspoon ground cloves
½ cup dark corn syrup	2 teaspoons grated orange rind
½ cup margarine	1 egg

Sift flour with sugar and soda. Stir syrup, margarine, spices, and orange rind in saucepan, over medium heat, until mixture just boils and margarine melts. Remove from heat. Beat egg in large bowl with rotary beater or electric mixer. Slowly stir in syrup mixture. Blend dry ingredients all at once into egg-syrup mixture. Drop by teaspoonfuls onto greased cookie sheet. Bake in 350° F. oven 8 minutes or until lightly browned. (Makes about 4 dozen.)

TWICE-BAKED CREAM COOKIES

Shells

½ cup margarine	1 teaspoon almond extract
½ cup sugar	2 cups sifted flour
2 egg yolks	

Cream margarine and sugar together. Stir in egg yolks, almond extract, and flour, stirring until mixture is smooth and cleans sides of bowl. Pinch off 1-inch balls of dough. Press each evenly in sides and bottom of ungreased (1¾ x 1-inch) muffin cup, forming a shell. (Do not make crust too thick.) Bake in 400° F. oven 8 to 10 minutes or until edges are golden brown. Prepare filling while shells are baking.

Filling

½ cup margarine

⅓ cup dark corn syrup

1 cup sifted confectioners' sugar

1 cup chopped nuts

Bring margarine, syrup, and sugar just to boil, stirring occasionally. Remove from heat. Stir in nuts. Cool slightly. Fill baked shells with mixture. Set oven temperature control to 350° F. and bake cookies 5 minutes. Cool. (Makes 2½ dozen.)

MINCE CHARMING COOKIES

½ cup margarine

½ cup dark corn syrup

½ cup coffee (liquid)

⅓ cup sugar

2 eggs

½ teaspoon anise flavoring

¼ teaspoon anise seed

3¼ cups flour

1½ teaspoons baking soda

½ teaspoon cinnamon

¼ teaspoon salt

¼ teaspoon nutmeg

2 cups ready-to-eat mincemeat

Combine margarine, syrup, coffee, and sugar in saucepan. Bring to boil; then simmer 5 minutes. Cool. Add eggs, anise flavoring, and anise seed. Blend well. Sift flour. baking soda, cinnamon, salt, and nutmeg together. Stir into mixture in saucepan. Stir in mincemeat. Chill at least 4 hours. Drop onto greased cookie sheet by teaspoonfuls. Bake in 350° F. oven 15 to 18 minutes or until lightly browned. If desired, decorate with confectioners' sugar icing. Store in tightly covered container. (Makes 8 dozen.)

PECAN GOODIES

1 cup margarine

1 cup cream-style cottage cheese

2 cups sifted flour

1 cup finely ground pecans

½ cup dark corn syrup

Pecan halves (about 3 dozen)

Dark corn syrup

Blend margarine and cottage cheese. Mix in flour. Shape into ball. Chill 1 hour or overnight. Combine ground pecans and ½ cup syrup. Divide dough into thirds. Roll out each portion on lightly floured board or cloth to 9 x 12 x ⅛-inch rectangle. Cut into 12 (3-inch) squares. Place about 1 teaspoon filling on each square. Fold in corners, overlapping in center. Dip pecan half into syrup and press lightly onto center. Place on ungreased cookie sheet. Bake in 350° F. oven about 25 minutes or until lightly browned. (Makes about 3 dozen.)

X

Pies—The All-American Favorites

Fashions in music and dress may come and go, but young people's well-known fondness for pie stays with us. With these simple, foolproof recipes every "cook-in" is a shoo-in!

CRUSTS AND SHELLS

DOUBLE CRUST PASTRY I

2 cups sifted regular all-purpose
   flour
½ cup corn oil

1 teaspoon salt
3 tablespoons cold water

Combine flour and salt. Blend in corn oil, mixing thoroughly with fork. Sprinkle all water on top; mix well. Press firmly into ball with hands. (If too dry, mix in 1 or 2 tablespoons more oil.) Divide dough almost in half. Flatten larger portion slightly; roll out to 12-inch circle between two pieces of waxed paper. Wipe table with damp cloth to prevent paper from slipping. Peel off top paper; place pastry in pan, paper side up. Peel off paper and fit pastry loosely into pan. Fill as desired; trim if necessary. Roll out remaining pastry for top crust. Peel off paper, cut slits, and place over filling. Trim ½ inch beyond rim of pan; fold edges of both crusts under. Seal and flute edges. Bake as filling recipe directs. (Makes 2 crusts for 9-inch pie pan.)

SINGLE CRUST PASTRY I

1⅓ cups sifted regular all-purpose
   flour
½ teaspoon salt

⅓ cup corn oil
2 tablespoons cold water

Combine as for Double Crust Pastry I. Roll out and place in pie pan as directed above. Trim, fold edge under, and flute. For baked shell, prick thoroughly and bake in 450° F. oven 12 to 15 minutes. Do not prick if crust and filling are to be baked together. Fill and bake as filling recipe directs. (Makes 1 crust for 9-inch pie pan.)

LEMON PASTRY

Follow recipe for Single Crust Pastry I, stirring ½ teaspoon grated lemon rind with flour and salt and substituting lemon juice for water.

CREAM CHEESE PASTRY

Follow recipe for Single Crust Pastry I, cutting 3 ounces cream cheese into flour and salt with pastry blender or 2 knives.

CHOCOLATE PASTRY

Follow recipe for Single Crust Pastry I, sifting ¼ cup cocoa and 1 tablespoon sugar with flour and salt.

DOUBLE CRUST PASTRY II

2 cups sifted regular all-purpose flour
¼ teaspoon salt
⅔ cup margarine
3 tablespoons cold water

Combine flour and salt. Blend in margarine with pastry blender or 2 knives until mixture is very well blended and fine crumbs form. (Do not be afraid to overmix.) Sprinkle water over mixture while tossing to blend well. Press firmly into ball with hands. Divide dough almost in half. Flatten larger portion slightly and roll out to 12-inch circle on lightly floured cloth or board. Fit loosely into pie pan. Fill as desired; trim if necessary. Roll out remaining pastry for top crust. Cut slits and place over filling. Trim ½ inch beyond rim of pan; fold edges of both crusts under. Seal and flute edges. Bake pie according to filling used. (Makes 2 crusts for 9-inch pie pan.)

SINGLE CRUST PASTRY II

1⅓ cups sifted regular all-purpose   ½ cup margarine
    flour   2 tablespoons cold water
⅛ teaspoon salt

Combine as for Double Crust Pastry II. Roll out and place in pie
pan as directed above. Trim, fold edge under, and flute. For baked
shell, prick thoroughly and bake in 450° F. oven 12 to 15 minutes.
Do not prick if crust and filling are to be baked together. Bake as
filling recipe directs. (Makes 1 crust for 9-inch pie pan.)

CHEESE PASTRY

Follow recipe for Single Crust Pastry II, stirring in ¾ cup finely
shredded sharp Cheddar cheese before adding water. Excellent as
a main-dish tart shell.

NUT PASTRY

Follow recipe for Single Crust Pastry II, adding ⅓ cup finely
chopped nuts to flour and salt.

SESAME SEED CRUST

Follow recipe for Single Crust Pastry II, adding ⅓ cup toasted
sesame seeds to flour and salt.

TART SHELLS

Prepare pastry for single crust pie. Place ball of dough on piece
of heavy-duty aluminum foil about 15 inches long. Flatten dough
slightly; cover with waxed paper. Roll dough to 12-inch square.
Remove waxed paper.

Step 1. Mark off 9 (4-inch) squares with edge of knife. (Or make 4-inch circles, 4 x 3-inch rectangles, or triangles 4 inches on each side if you prefer.) Cut through dough and foil with scissors.

Step 2. Turn up sides of dough and foil about 1 inch all around; pinch corners or flute circle to hold dough in place. Prick and place on ungreased cookie sheet. Bake in 450° F. oven about 12 minutes or until golden brown. (Makes 9 tart shells.)

Alternate Method

Roll dough out on a lightly floured board or cloth and cut into 4- to 4½-inch circles. Fit circles into tart pans or over backs of muffin or custard cups, making pleats so pastry will fit closely. Prick. Bake in 450° F. oven about 8 minutes or until lightly browned.

GRAHAM CRACKER CRUST

¼ cup margarine
¼ cup sugar
¼ teaspoon salt
1 cup graham cracker crumbs

Cream margarine; blend in sugar and salt. Thoroughly mix in crumbs. Press evenly on bottom and sides of 9-inch pie pan, making a small rim. Bake in 400° F. oven 8 minutes or until edges are lightly browned.

THE PIES THEMSELVES

APPLE PIE

6 tart apples, pared, cored, and cut in eighths (about 6 cups)
2 tablespoons flour
1 cup sugar
¼ teaspoon salt
1 teaspoon cinnamon
2 tablespoons margarine or butter
1 Double Crust Pastry

Arrange apples in pastry-lined 9-inch pie pan. Combine flour, sugar, salt, and cinnamon. Sprinkle over apples. Dot with margarine. Cover with top crust; seal and flute edges. Cut slits. Bake in 425° F. oven about 50 minutes or until crust is brown and apples tender. Serve à la mode (topped with ice cream) or with a thick square of rich yellow cheese.

CHOCOLATE CREAM PIE

1 envelope unflavored gelatin
¼ cup cold water
1 cup fortified chocolate-flavored
    syrup

1 pint heavy cream
½ teaspoon vanilla
1 baked 9-inch pastry shell or
    Graham Cracker Crust

Soften gelatin in water. Bring chocolate syrup to full boil in medium saucepan. Remove from heat. Add softened gelatin; stir until gelatin is completely dissolved. Chill, stirring occasionally, until mixture is thick and syrupy. (Do not let mixture become too stiff.) Whip cream; gently fold into chilled chocolate mixture. Fold in flavoring. Pile into baked pastry shell. Chill until firm. (May also be used in baked tart shells.)

CHERRY PIE

3 tablespoons cornstarch
⅔ cup sugar
½ teaspoon salt
1 cup juice, drained from cherries
2 tablespoons margarine

1 (1-pound) can pitted, sour red
    cherries, drained
1 teaspoon lemon juice
1 Double Crust Pastry

Combine cornstarch, sugar, salt, and cherry juice in a saucepan. Cook and stir over medium heat until mixture thickens and boils. Add margarine, cherries, and lemon juice. Pour into pastry-lined 9-inch pie pan. Cover with top crust; seal and flute edges. Cut slits. Bake in 400° F. oven 15 minutes; reduce heat to 350° F. and bake 30 minutes longer or until crust is browned.

LEMON OR LIME CHIFFON PIE

1 envelope unflavored gelatin
½ cup cold water
½ cup sugar
½ cup lemon or lime juice
2 drops yellow or green food
   coloring
½ teaspoon grated lemon or lime
   rind

3 egg whites
¼ teaspoon salt
½ cup light corn syrup
1 baked 9-inch Graham Cracker
   Crust

Soften gelatin in water. Add sugar and stir over hot water until gelatin and sugar are completely dissolved. Remove from heat; stir in juice, rind, and food coloring. Chill to unbeaten-egg-white consistency. (*Caution:* If gelatin mixture becomes too stiff, texture of filling is less smooth and creamy.) Add salt to egg whites and beat until stiff but not dry. Slowly add syrup, beating until smooth and glossy. Fold chilled gelatin mixture into beaten whites; chill until thick enough to pile up (about ½ hour). Stir mixture occasionally while chilling for a smoother filling. Pile lightly into crust and chill until ready to serve. (May be used in baked tart shells.)

CRANBERRY CHIFFON PIE

Follow recipe for Lemon or Lime Chiffon Pie, replacing water and lemon juice with one cup cranberry juice. Use ½ cup of the juice for dissolving gelatin. Omit food color. Reduce sugar to ¼ cup.

GRAPE CHIFFON PIE

Follow recipe for Lemon or Lime Chiffon Pie, replacing water and lemon juice with one cup grape juice. Reduce sugar to ¼ cup.

ORANGE CHIFFON PIE

Follow recipe for Lemon or Lime Chiffon Pie, replacing water and lemon juice with one cup orange juice. Reduce sugar to ¼ cup.

PUMPKIN PIE

½ cup sugar
2 teaspoons cornstarch
½ teaspoon salt
½ teaspoon cinnamon
¼ teaspoon ginger

2 eggs, slightly beaten
1 cup canned pumpkin
1 cup milk
1 unbaked 9-inch pastry shell

Combine sugar, cornstarch, salt, cinnamon, ginger, and eggs. Add pumpkin and milk; blend well. Pour into pastry shell. Bake in 300° F. oven 15 minutes; reduce heat to 350° F., and bake 30 minutes longer or until a knife inserted in filling 2 inches from edge comes out clean. Center of pie will be soft.

PECAN PIE

3 eggs, slightly beaten
1 cup dark corn syrup
1 cup sugar
2 tablespoons margarine, melted

1 teaspoon vanilla
⅛ teaspoon salt
1 cup pecans
1 unbaked 9-inch pastry shell

Combine ingredients, adding nuts last. Pour into pastry shell. Bake in 400° F. oven 15 minutes, reduce heat to 350° F., and continue to bake 30 to 35 minutes longer. (Filling should be slightly less set in the center than around edges.)

DATE NUT PIE

Follow recipe for Pecan Pie, substituting 1 cup finely chopped dates and ½ cup walnut halves for pecans.

FUDGE NUT PIE

Follow recipe for Pecan Pie, melting 2 ounces unsweetened chocolate with margarine and reducing eggs to 2.

PECAN TARTS

Pour Pecan Pie into tart shells and bake in 400° F. oven 20 to 25 minutes.

LEMON MERINGUE PIE

1 cup sugar	⅓ cup lemon juice
4 tablespoons cornstarch	1½ teaspoons grated lemon rind
¼ teaspoon salt	3 egg whites
1½ cups water	6 tablespoons sugar
3 egg yolks	1 baked 9-inch pastry shell
2 tablespoons margarine	

Combine ½ cup sugar, cornstarch, and salt in double boiler top. Gradually blend in water. Cook over boiling water, stirring constantly until thickened. Cover; cook 10 minutes longer, stirring occasionally. Meanwhile, beat together egg yolks and ½ cup sugar. Blend a little hot mixture into egg yolks, then stir into remaining hot mixture. Stirring, cook over boiling water 2 minutes. Remove from boiling water. Add margarine, lemon juice, and lemon rind. Cool. Pour into baked shell. To prepare meringue, beat egg whites until foamy. Add sugar, one tablespoon at a time, beating well after each addition. Continue beating until stiff peaks form when beater is raised. Spread meringue around edge of filling first, to touch crust; then fill in center. Bake in 350° F. oven 15 to 20 minutes or until meringue is lightly browned; or about 5 minutes in 425° F. oven. Cool at room temperature away from drafts.

Note: For firmer filling, use 5 tablespoons cornstarch.

CURRANT LEMON TARTS

2 teaspoons cornstarch
½ cup sugar
¼ teaspoon salt
1 egg, well beaten
½ cup light corn syrup

2 teaspoons grated lemon rind
⅓ cup melted margarine
1 tablespoon lemon juice
⅔ cup currants or raisins
8 unbaked 3-inch pastry tart shells

Combine cornstarch, sugar, and salt. Blend in egg. Mix in remaining ingredients. Chill. Pour into tart shells. Bake in 400° F. oven 15 minutes. Reduce heat to 350° F.; bake 10 minutes longer. Cool in pans.

ENGLISH RAISIN APPLE TART

2 medium tart cooking apples,
    pared, cored, and sliced
    (about ½-inch thick)
½ cup light corn syrup
2 tablespoons flour
½ cup raisins

3 eggs
⅓ cup sugar
¼ teaspoon vanilla
¾ cup sifted flour
1 unbaked 9-inch pastry shell

Combine syrup with 2 tablespoons flour. Toss with apples and raisins to mix well. Spread evenly in pastry shell. Beat eggs and sugar until thick and fluffy. Stir in vanilla. Fold in ¾ cup flour, sifting a little at a time over top. Pour over apple mixture to cover completely. Bake in 400° F. oven 10 minutes. Reduce heat to 350° F. and bake 40 minutes longer, or until apples are tender and topping is brown and firm.

SHOOFLY PIE

1½ cups sifted flour
¾ cup granulated or brown sugar
½ teaspoon salt
⅓ cup margarine
½ teaspoon soda

⅓ cup hot water
⅓ cup dark corn syrup
Cinnamon
1 unbaked 9-inch pastry shell

Sift flour with sugar and salt. Cut in margarine until mixture is crumbly. Spread one cup of crumb mixture over bottom of pastry shell. Stir soda into hot water; mix in syrup. Spoon this liquid mixture over the crumbs. (*Do not pour all in one spot.*) Spread remaining crumb mixture evenly over top. Sprinkle with cinnamon. Bake in 400° F. oven 15 minutes, reduce heat to 350° F., and continue baking 30 minutes longer. Serve warm.

Note: For a pie that is more moist, pour all of liquid mixture into pastry shell; then top with all of crumb mixture, spreading evenly.

HARVEST TABLE APPLE PIE

6 to 8 medium apples	3 tablespoons sugar
1 tablespoon cornstarch	3 tablespoons melted margarine
1 teaspoon cinnamon	⅓ cup dark corn syrup
¼ teaspoon salt	1 Double Crust Pastry

Prepare pastry and roll out half for bottom crust. Fit into 9-inch pie pan. Peel, core, and slice apples. Arrange in crust. Combine cornstarch, cinnamon, salt, sugar, margarine, and syrup. Pour over apples. Roll out pastry for top crust; cut slits. Place over apples, fold edges under, seal, and flute. Bake in 425° F. oven 45 minutes or until crust is browned and apples tender. Remove from oven. Spread topping over top of pie; return to oven for 10 minutes or until topping is bubbly. (Place large pan under pie to catch any topping that may run off.)

Topping

Mix ¼ cup brown sugar, 2 tablespoons flour, 3 tablespoons dark corn syrup, 2 tablespoons softened margarine, and ¼ cup chopped nuts.

DATE NUT PIE

1 (8-ounce) package dates, finely
    chopped
¾ cup water
½ cup dark corn syrup
2 tablespoons margarine
1 teaspoon vanilla
¼ cup chopped walnuts

1 (8-ounce) package cream cheese,
    softened
½ cup light corn syrup
1 egg, beaten
1 teaspoon vanilla
Whipped cream
1 unbaked 9-inch pastry shell

Combine dates, water, and ½ cup dark corn syrup in saucepan.
Cook over medium heat 8 to 10 minutes or until thickened.
Remove from heat. Stir in margarine, 1 teaspoon vanilla, and
walnuts. Cool. Blend cream cheese, ½ cup light corn syrup, egg,
and remaining 1 teaspoon vanilla. Pour into unbaked pastry shell.
Gently spread date mixture on top. Bake in 375° F. oven 35 to
40 minutes or until edge of filling is set and crust lightly browned.
Cool. Serve garnished with whipped cream.

GRAHAM NUT APPLE PIE

1 (1-pound, 9½-ounce) can apple
    pie filling
1 egg yolk
1 tablespoon cold water
1 (3-ounce) package cream cheese,
    softened
⅓ cup graham cracker crumbs
2 tablespoons sugar

¼ teaspoon baking powder
½ teaspoon vanilla
1 egg white
¼ cup dark corn syrup
¼ cup chopped nuts
1 unbaked 9-inch pastry shell witl
    high, fluted edge

Empty pie filling into pastry shell. Beat egg yolk and water until
foamy. Blend in cream cheese. Combine graham cracker crumbs,
sugar, and baking powder. Stir into cream cheese mixture. Add
vanilla. Beat egg white until soft peaks form when beater is
raised. Gradually add syrup, beating until stiff peaks form when
beater is raised. Fold crumb mixture and nuts into egg white.
Lightly spread over apple filling, covering it completely and seal-

ing to the edge. Bake in 375° F. oven about 50 minutes or until knife inserted in center of pie comes out clean.

SOUR CREAM RAISIN PIE

1 cup raisins
3 egg yolks, slightly beaten
1 cup dark corn syrup
½ cup dairy sour cream
1½ tablespoons cornstarch
1 teaspoon vinegar

½ teaspoon cinnamon
½ teaspoon grated lemon rind
¼ teaspoon nutmeg
¼ teaspoon ground cloves
1 baked 9-inch pastry shell

Simmer raisins in water to cover 5 minutes; drain well. Combine egg yolks, syrup, sour cream, cornstarch, vinegar, cinnamon, lemon rind, nutmeg, and cloves in saucepan. Cook over medium heat, stirring constantly, about 5 minutes or just until mixture comes to a boil. Stir in raisins. Pour into pastry shell.

Meringue

3 egg whites
6 tablespoons sugar

Beat egg whites until foamy. Add sugar, 1 tablespoon at a time, beating well after each addition. Beat constantly until stiff peaks form when beater is raised. Spread some meringue around edge of filling first, to touch crust all around; then fill in center. Bake in 350° F. oven 15 to 20 minutes or until meringue is lightly browned, or in 425° F. oven about 5 minutes. Cool at room temperature away from drafts.

APPLE PIE WITH CUSTARD TOPPING

1 (1-pound, 6-ounce) can apple
   pie filling
¼ cup sugar
¼ cup margarine, softened
⅓ cup dark corn syrup

3 eggs, beaten
1 teaspoon vanilla
Nutmeg
1 unbaked 9-inch pastry shell

Spoon apple filling into pastry shell. Bake in 450° F. oven 10 minutes. Meanwhile, blend margarine and sugar; mix in syrup, eggs, and vanilla, blending well. Pour over hot apple filling. Sprinkle with nutmeg. Reduce oven temperature control to 350° F. Continue baking about 40 to 45 minutes or until topping is well browned and set.

FROZEN DESSERT PIE

¾ cup corn syrup
1 (8-ounce) package cream cheese, softened
¼ cup margarine

⅓ cup brown sugar, firmly packed
¾ cup milk
½ cup chopped pecans
1 baked 9-inch pastry shell

Blend syrup into cream cheese a little at a time. Heat margarine and brown sugar in small saucepan, over medium heat, stirring constantly, just to melt margarine and sugar. Gradually stir into syrup mixture. Stir in milk and pecans. Pour into baked pastry shell. Freeze until firm, 4 to 6 hours. Serve without thawing.

MAPLE NUT PIZZA

½ cup margarine
1 cup sugar
2 eggs
2 cups chopped walnuts

1 teaspoon vanilla
½ cup pancake and waffle syrup
1 Double Crust Pastry

Line 1 (14-inch-diameter) pizza pan with pastry. Place dough carefully to avoid breaks in bottom. (It is not necessary to flute.) Blend margarine, sugar, and eggs. Mix in walnuts and vanilla. Turn into pastry shell. Drizzle syrup evenly on top. Bake in 375° F. oven 35 to 40 minutes or until top is golden brown and set. Cool. Cut into wedges to serve. (Makes 12 servings.)

XI

Dessert Treats

No matter how sophisticated, today's young crowd is not so far removed from childhood and the special magic of "sweets" that such traditional delights as ice cream and candy have lost their appeal. The following favorites are fun to make as well as to eat.

259

ICE CREAM DELIGHTS

HOMEMADE VANILLA ICE CREAM I (REFRIGERATOR METHOD)

2 eggs	1 cup heavy cream
⅓ cup sugar	1½ cups milk
⅔ cup light corn syrup	1½ teaspoons vanilla

Beat eggs in large bowl until foamy. Gradually add sugar, then syrup, beating until mixture is thick. Stir in cream, milk, and vanilla. Turn into freezing tray or trays. Freeze about 1 hour or until almost firm. Turn into a chilled bowl; cut apart and beat until smooth. Return to tray or trays and freeze until firm. (Makes 1 quart ice cream.)

CHOCOLATE ICE CREAM

Follow recipe for Homemade Vanilla Ice Cream I, reducing vanilla to one teaspoon. Combine in saucepan ⅓ cup cocoa, syrup, and ½ cup of the milk. Bring to boil over medium heat, stirring constantly. Cool slightly; add to egg-sugar mixture.

LEMON ICE CREAM

Follow recipe for Homemade Vanilla Ice Cream I, increasing sugar to ½ cup, and substituting ½ cup lemon juice for ½ cup of the milk, and 1 teaspoon grated lemon peel for vanilla.

MAPLE ICE CREAM

Follow recipe for Homemade Vanilla Ice Cream I, reducing vanilla to one teaspoon and milk to one cup, and substituting light brown sugar for granulated and mapley waffle syrup for light corn syrup.

BUTTER PECAN ICE CREAM

Follow recipe for Homemade Vanilla Ice Cream I, reducing vanilla to one teaspoon and milk to one cup. Substitute ⅓ cup light brown sugar for granulated. Combine ½ cup chopped pecans, 2 tablespoons butter, ⅛ teaspoon salt. Toast in 350° F. oven about 10 minutes, stirring once or twice. Fold in just before freezing.

HOMEMADE VANILLA ICE CREAM II (ELECTRIC OR CRANK FREEZER)

⅓ cup light corn syrup	3 cups milk
2 tablespoons cornstarch	2 eggs, beaten slightly
¾ cup sugar	2 teaspoons vanilla
½ teaspoon salt	1 cup light cream

Combine syrup, cornstarch, sugar, salt, and milk in top of double boiler. Mix in eggs. Cook over boiling water, stirring constantly, about 5 minutes or until mixture is slightly thickened. Chill. Add vanilla and light cream. With electric freezer, follow manufacturer's directions. With crank freezer, pour chilled custard mixture into can, filling can no more than ⅔ full. Pack tub with alternate layers crushed ice and rock salt, using 8 parts ice to 1 part salt. Turn crank slowly, increasing speed and turning until crank no longer turns easily. Remove dasher. Pack ice cream; cover. Repack tub with ice and salt, using 4 parts ice to 1 part salt. Let stand 2 hours. (Makes about 2 quarts ice cream.)

CHOCOLATE ICE CREAM

Follow recipe for Homemade Vanilla Ice Cream II, adding 4 ounces unsweetened chocolate to egg-milk mixture before cooking. When mixture thickens, remove from heat, beat until smooth. Add vanilla.

BANANA ICE CREAM

Follow recipe for Homemade Vanilla Ice Cream II; but mix together 1½ cups mashed bananas and 1 tablespoon lemon juice, and add to chilled custard mixture just before freezing.

†SUNDAE SUGGESTIONS

VANILLA ICE CREAM

SERVE WITH:
  honey
  hot maple syrup
  butterscotch sauce
  caramel sauce
  hot or cold chocolate sauce
  chocolate mints melted in a little cream or milk
  shredded coconut toasted in the oven
  crushed peanut brittle
  crushed peanut brittle melted in a little water
  crumbled macaroons
  chopped nuts
  raspberry sauce garnished with chopped nuts
  strawberry sauce
  crushed pineapple with chopped pecans or minced fresh mint
  sweetened fresh peaches
  minced maraschino cherries
  butterscotch sauce with thin slices of banana
SERVE ON:
  brandied peach halves with strawberry sauce
  finely diced and chilled honey dew melon sweetened and
    flavored to taste with lime juice and topped with mashed,
    sweetened strawberries
  chocolate waffles and topped with hot maple syrup and
    chopped nuts

sliced sweetened peaches and topped with crushed raspberries or strawberries or slightly melted currant jelly

chocolate pudding

apple or other fruit pies

SERVE IN:

cantaloupe halves

scooped out pineapple halves from which the green leaves have not been removed

CHOCOLATE ICE CREAM

SERVE WITH:

shredded coconut toasted in oven

chopped nuts

marshmallow sauce

honey

hot maple syrup

butterscotch sauce

crushed peanut brittle

crushed peanut brittle melted in a little water

SERVE ON:

sliced bananas topped with butterscotch sauce

angel food cake and topped with marshmallow sauce

peppermint flavored waffles and topped with marshmallow sauce

puddings

apple pie

COFFEE ICE CREAM

SERVE WITH:

sweetened fresh peaches flavored with a little almond extract

cold or hot chocolate sauce

crumbled macaroons

sweetened crushed pineapple

sweetened apricot purée and whipped cream

shredded coconut toasted in the oven
chopped nuts

SERVE ON:

coffee-flavored waffles and topped with chocolate or marshmallow sauce
peach pie
coffee-flavored pudding
vanilla butterscotch sauce and chopped nuts
butter cake or angel food cake topped with vanilla butterscotch
sauce and chopped nuts

SERVE IN:

cream puffs and topped with butterscotch sauce sprinkled with
chopped almonds

SWEET CREATIONS

† WALDORF ICE CREAM

1 quart strawberry ice cream
1 pint vanilla ice cream

Line refrigerator tray with waxed paper. Put ¾ of the strawberry
ice cream in tray; using a spoon, pack the ice cream so it lines the
bottom and sides of tray. Fill the center with vanilla ice cream;
cover with remaining strawberry ice cream. Cover with waxed
paper. Place in refrigerator freezing compartment with the dial
set at coldest temperature. Chill 3 to 4 hours. Place on chilled
serving dish; peel off waxed paper. Slice into individual servings
at the table. Serve on chilled plates. (Makes 6 to 8 servings.)

† ICE CREAM PIE

1½ quarts strawberry ice cream
1 pint coffee ice cream

Carefully line 9-inch pie plate with waxed paper; put in refrigerator freezing compartment to chill. Mix coffee ice cream with spoon until pliable but not melted. Put into chilled pie plate. Using a spoon, press the ice cream so that it lines the bottom and sides of the pie plate. Fill the center with strawberry ice cream. Cover with waxed paper. Put into refrigerator freezing compartment with dial set at coldest temperature. Chill 3 to 4 hours. Place on chilled serving dish; peel off waxed paper. Top with whipped cream that has been sweetened and flavored with instant coffee to taste. Cut into individual servings at the table. Serve on chilled dessert plates. (Makes 8 to 10 servings.)

† ICE CREAM TART

4 egg whites	½ teaspoon peppermint extract
½ teaspoon cream of tartar	1½ quarts chocolate ice cream
1 cup fine granulated sugar	

Beat egg whites until foamy; add cream of tartar and beat until stiff but not dry. Gradually add ⅔ cup sugar while continuing to beat. Add peppermint extract. Fold in remaining sugar. Cover cookie sheet with thick brown paper. Fill pastry tube with mixture and make solid bottom about 8 inches in diameter. Make two rings with outside diameter 8 inches, inside diameter 6 inches. Bake in a 235° F. to 250° F. oven about 1 hour or until dry. Cool; remove from paper. Put bottom on serving plate; fasten the rings to the bottom by moistening edges with water. Fill center with large spoonfuls of chocolate ice cream. Decorate with sprigs of mint. Serve with chocolate sauce. (Makes 8 to 10 servings.)

LEMON SHERBET

2 eggs	2 cups buttermilk
½ cup sugar	½ cup lemon juice
¾ cup light corn syrup	1 tablespoon grated lemon peel

266

Beat eggs in large bowl until foamy. Gradually beat in sugar, then syrup, beating until mixture is thick. Stir in buttermilk, lemon juice, and grated lemon peel. Turn into freezing tray. Freeze about 1 hour until almost firm. Turn into a chilled bowl; cut apart and beat until smooth. Return to tray and freeze about 3 hours or until firm. (Makes about 1 quart.)

FRUIT ICE

1 (1-pound, 14-ounce) can apricots, plums, peaches, or pears in syrup	¾ cup light corn syrup
	⅔ cup sugar
	⅓ cup lemon juice
½ cup water	2 egg whites

Empty fruit and syrup into strainer placed over a bowl; make a purée by pressing fruit through strainer; reserve. Combine water, syrup, and sugar in a saucepan. Bring to boil over medium heat, stirring until sugar dissolves. Boil 5 minutes. Cool. Add lemon juice and reserved fruit purée. Turn into freezing tray or trays. Freeze about 1 hour or until mixture is almost firm. While mixture is in freezer, beat egg whites until stiff but not dry. Turn almost-frozen mixture into a chilled bowl. Cut apart and beat until smooth. Fold in beaten egg whites. Return to tray or trays and continue freezing 2 to 3 hours or until firm. (Makes about 1 quart.)

Note: 2 (12-ounce) cans (3 cups) nectar may be substituted for the puréed canned fruit.

EYE-FULL TOWER PEACH DESSERT

¼ cup orange juice	1 teaspoon rum extract
¼ cup dark corn syrup	6 canned peach halves, drained
¼ cup light corn syrup	Vanilla ice cream

Combine syrup and orange juice in small saucepan. Bring to boil, stirring constantly, and boil one minute. Remove from heat. Stir in rum extract. Keep warm. Broil peach halves about 3 to 4 minutes or until completely heated. Spoon ice cream into individual dishes. Top each serving with broiled peach half. Pour warm syrup over all. Serve immediately. (Makes ¾ cup sauce, enough for about 6 servings.)

MOCK CREME DE MENTHE PARFAIT

1 (8½-ounce) can crushed pineapple
½ cup light corn syrup
½ cup sugar
½ cup water

Dash salt
¼ teaspoon peppermint flavoring
2 drops green food coloring
Vanilla ice cream

Combine pineapple, syrup, sugar, water, and salt in saucepan. Bring to boil, stirring constantly. Boil 10 minutes. Remove from heat. Stir in peppermint flavoring and food coloring. Chill. Arrange alternate layers of ice cream and sauce in parfait glasses. (Makes about 2 cups sauce.)

CHOCO-CUPS DESSERT

¼ cup sugar
¼ teaspoon salt
½ cup light corn syrup

1 (6-ounce) package semi-sweet chocolate pieces
3 cups crisp rice cereal
Ice cream or sherbet

Combine syrup, sugar, and salt in large skillet. Bring to boil, stirring constantly. Remove from heat. Add chocolate pieces; stir until melted. Add cereal; stir until well coated. Cool slightly. Shape by hand into 8 (3-inch-diameter) cups, or press onto sides and bottoms of 8 (5-ounce) custard cups. Allow to set at room temperature until firm enough to hold shape. Serve filled with ice cream or sherbet. (Makes 8 servings.)

Choco-Bar Desserts

Spread Choco-Cups mixture in lightly greased 9-inch-square baking pan. Cool at room temperature until firm enough to cut into bars.

TOASTED ALMOND PARFAIT

¾ cup light corn syrup
¼ cup sugar
3 egg whites
1 cup heavy cream, whipped

½ teaspoon vanilla
½ cup blanched, finely chopped
    almonds, toasted

Heat and stir syrup and sugar in saucepan over medium heat until sugar dissolves and mixture boils. Boil 1 minute. Beat egg whites to soft peaks; beat in syrup mixture a little at a time, beating to soft peaks. Cool to room temperature (about 10 minutes). Fold in whipped cream, vanilla, and nuts. Freeze in refrigerator freezing tray with cold control set for fast freezing, about 3 hours or until firm. Set control midway between fast freezing and normal for storage. (Makes 1 quart.)

Note: Do not use warm bowl and beaters to whip cream. Chill if used for syrup-egg white mixtures.

PEPPERMINT PARFAIT

Follow recipe for Toasted Almond Parfait, omitting sugar and almonds, and folding ¼ cup coarsely crushed peppermint candy into mixture after whipped cream.

CINNAMON PARFAIT

Follow recipe for Toasted Almond Parfait, omitting sugar, and heating 2 tablespoons cinnamon candies with syrup until melted.

BAKED ALASKA PIE

4 eggs
¼ cup sugar
1 cup light corn syrup
1 teaspoon vanilla

1 cup heavy cream, whipped
1 baked 9-inch pastry shell, chilled
3 egg whites
¼ teaspoon cream of tartar

Beat eggs until foamy. Gradually add sugar, then ½ cup syrup; beat until thick. Stir in vanilla. Fold in whipped cream. Turn into freezing tray. Freeze until almost firm. Turn into chilled bowl; beat until smooth. Turn into pastry shell and freeze until firm. Just before serving, beat egg whites until frothy; add cream of tartar, beat until stiff peaks form. Gradually beat in remaining ½ cup syrup; beat until very stiff. Cover pie with meringue; seal edges. Place on several thicknesses of wrapping paper on a wet board. Bake in a 500° F. oven about 5 minutes. Serve immediately.

STRAWBERRY MOUSSE

2 (10-ounce) packages frozen
    strawberries
⅔ cup light corn syrup
⅓ cup sugar
⅓ cup water

3 egg whites
1½ teaspoons vanilla
3 egg yolks
2 cups heavy cream, whipped

Thaw strawberries and drain all juice or syrup. Combine syrup, sugar, and water in a saucepan. Bring to a boil, and boil 2 minutes. Beat egg whites until stiff but not dry. Gradually beat in hot syrup, continuing until mixture is thick and creamy. Add vanilla. Beat egg yolks until thick; fold into egg whites. Fold in cream and strawberries. Pour into freezing trays lined with aluminum foil or into a 2-quart mold. Freeze without stirring. Turn out of trays; remove foil and cut into blocks. Or, to remove mousse from mold, cover outside of mold for a few seconds with a cloth wrung out of hot water. (Makes about 2 quarts.)

FINNISH FRUIT DESSERT

1 package (11-ounce) mixed dried fruits
2 cups water
1 cup corn syrup

¼ cup quick-cooking tapioca
¼ teaspoon cinnamon
¼ teaspoon nutmeg
⅛ teaspoon salt

Simmer (do not boil) fruit with water for ½ hour. Drain. Set fruit aside. Add water to liquid to make 1½ cups total. Add syrup. Mix tapioca, spices, and salt, and stir into liquid mixture in saucepan. Let stand 5 minutes. Bring to boil over medium heat, stirring occasionally. Remove from heat; let stand until slightly thickened. Arrange fruit pieces in 8 dessert dishes; pour sauce over fruit. Cool. Decorate with whipped cream. (Makes 8 servings.)

FRESH FRUIT COMPOTE

Wash, peel, core, and cut up, if needed, any desired combination of fruits: oranges, bananas, pineapple, apple, grapefruit, grapes, berries, etc. If no citrus fruits are included, add a little lemon juice to prevent discoloring of apples, bananas. Add light corn syrup or sugar to give desired sweetness; toss to mix well. Do *not* prepare cut-up fruits too far in advance, or vitamins are lost. Refrigerate until served.

PINEAPPLE IN GINGERED SOUR CREAM

1 (1-pound, 13-ounce) can pineapple chunks, drained, or 1 fresh pineapple, cut into chunks
½ pint dairy sour cream

¼ cup corn syrup
1 tablespoon chopped crystallized ginger
Mint sprigs (optional)

Chill pineapple chunks. Combine sour cream, syrup, and ginger. Pour over pineapple in serving dishes. If desired, garnish with mint sprigs. (Makes 6 servings.)

RAISIN AND NUT BAKED APPLES

6 baking apples
⅓ cup chopped walnuts
⅓ cup raisins

⅓ cup dark corn syrup
⅓ cup light cream

Core apples, making well at least 1 inch in diameter; place in shallow baking dish. Combine walnuts, raisins, syrup, and cream. Fill centers of apples with mixture. Add any leftover mixture to apples while baking. Bake in 350° F. oven about 30 minutes or until apples are tender. Serve with Sauce. (Makes 6 servings.)

Sauce

1 cup light cream
⅓ cup dark corn syrup
3 tablespoons margarine

1 teaspoon vanilla
½ teaspoon cinnamon

Combine all ingredients in saucepan. Cook over low heat, stirring frequently, about 30 minutes or until thickened. Serve warm over apples. (Makes about 1½ cups sauce.)

CHILLED CHOCOLATE DESSERT

3 tablespoons flour
3 tablespoons cocoa
2 tablespoons sugar
⅛ teaspoon salt
1¼ cups water
½ cup light corn syrup
1 tablespoon margarine

1 teaspoon vanilla
12 graham crackers
1 cup heavy cream, whipped, *or* (2-ounce) package whipped topping mix, prepared according to package directions

Combine flour, cocoa, sugar, and salt in saucepan. Gradually stir in water and syrup. Stirring constantly, bring to boil and boil 2 minutes. Remove from heat. Stir in margarine and vanilla. Cool. Spread thin layer of pudding in serving dish. Top with layer of graham crackers, then whipped cream. Repeat until all ingredients are used, ending with layer of whipped cream. Chill at least 2 hours. (Freeze, if desired.) (Makes 4 to 6 servings.)

APPLE TAPIOCA

3 cups pared, cut-up cooking apples
(3 or 4 medium apples)
¾ cup light corn syrup
1 teaspoon grated lemon rind
1 tablespoon lemon juice

½ teaspoon salt
½ teaspoon cinnamon
¼ teaspoon nutmeg
⅓ cup quick-cooking tapioca
2½ cups water

Combine apple, syrup, lemon rind, lemon juice, salt, cinnamon, and nutmeg in saucepan. Cover. Cook gently, stirring occasionally, about 20 minutes or until apple is tender. Pour into serving dish. Pour tapioca into water in saucepan. Let stand 5 minutes. Bring to boil over medium heat, stirring frequently. Stir hot tapioca into apple mixture, just enough to blend. Let stand 20 minutes. Stir gently. If desired, serve with hard sauce. (Makes 6 to 8 servings.)

PECAN CUSTARD

1 cup light corn syrup
3 tablespoons sugar
⅛ teaspoon salt
1 tablespoon margarine
1 cup evaporated milk or light
cream

⅓ cup raisins
3 eggs
1 cup chopped pecans
1 teaspoon vanilla

Combine syrup, sugar, salt, and margarine in saucepan. Stirring constantly, bring to boil and boil 1 minute. Remove from heat. Stir in evaporated milk or cream. Cool. Set 8 (5-ounce) custard cups into baking pan. Divide plumped raisins evenly among custard cups. Beat eggs. Gradually stir cooled syrup-milk mixture into eggs, blending well. Stir in pecans and vanilla. Pour into custard cups. Pour hot water into baking pan to depth of ½ inch. Bake in 375° F. oven 25 to 30 minutes or until nut topping is golden brown and custard is set. Nuts will form crusted top. (Makes 8 servings.)

FRUIT BARS ALASKA

1⅓ cups sifted flour	½ cup raisins
1 teaspoon baking powder	3 eggs
¼ teaspoon salt	1 cup light corn syrup
1¾ cups chopped pitted dates	1 teaspoon vanilla
1 cup chopped nuts	Confectioners' sugar

Sift flour, baking powder, and salt together into mixing bowl. Stir in dates, nuts, and raisins. Beat eggs well. Add syrup and vanilla. Stir into flour mixture. Spread evenly in greased (13 x 9½ x 2-inch) baking pan. Bake in 350° F. oven about 45 minutes or until lightly browned and springy to the touch. Cut into 3 x 1-inch bars. If desired, roll in confectioners' sugar. Store in tightly covered container. (Makes about 3 dozen.)

ORANGE DIVINITY FROZEN DESSERT

1 cup light corn syrup	1 cup well-chilled undiluted
2 eggs, separated	evaporated milk [1]
1 (6-ounce) can frozen orange juice concentrate, partially thawed	1 cup ginger snap crumbs

Bring syrup to a boil. Meanwhile, beat egg whites until soft peaks form when beater is raised. Beating constantly, pour continuous fine stream of hot syrup over beaten egg whites. Continue beating until mixture holds stiff peaks. Beat egg yolks well; fold into egg white mixture. Fold in orange juice concentrate. Whip chilled evaporated milk until thick and fluffy. Lightly fold into egg mixture.

Sprinkle 9-inch-square pan with ½ cup crumbs. Pour in orange

---

[1] Pour evaporated milk into freezing tray. Chill in freezing unit until ice crystals begin to form around edges.

274

mixture. Sprinkle with remaining crumbs. Freeze until firm.
(Makes 8 to 10 servings.)

BLANC MANGE

½ cup sugar
6 tablespoons cornstarch
¼ teaspoon salt

4 cups milk
1 teaspoon vanilla

Mix sugar with cornstarch and salt in double boiler top. Slowly
stir in 4 cups milk. Stir over boiling water until mixture thickens.
Cover, cook 10 minutes; stir once. Remove from heat. Gently
stir in vanilla. Pour into serving dish or mold or individual dishes.
Cool; chill about 2 hours for small dishes, 4 hours for large. Unmold; serve with garnish or sauce if desired. (Makes 6 to 8
servings.)

Custard Blanc Mange

Follow above recipe. Stir a little of the cooked hot Blanc Mange
mixture into 2 well beaten egg yolks; then stir this back into
remaining hot mixture. Cook 2 more minutes. Cool to lukewarm.
Beat 2 egg whites to stiff peaks and fold gently into pudding.
Pour into molds, cool, and chill until set.

VANILLA SOUFFLE

2 tablespoons cornstarch
3 tablespoons margarine
1 cup milk
4 egg yolks

3 tablespoons sugar
4 egg whites
1 teaspoon vanilla
Sugar

Blend cornstarch with margarine in a saucepan over low heat.
Remove from heat; slowly stir in milk. Cook and stir over medium
heat until sauce thickens. Beat egg yolks light and thick with
sugar. Stir into sauce. Beat egg whites to stiff peaks; fold in sauce

mixture with vanilla. Sprinkle an oiled 2-quart heatproof casserole or soufflé dish with sugar to coat inside. Pour in soufflé mixture. Set in pan of hot water. Bake in 350° F. oven about 1 hour or until soufflé is puffed and golden brown. (Makes 4 to 6 servings.)

To Re-Puff Soufflé

Set casserole in pan hot water, and place in 350° F. oven about ½ hour or until soufflé re-puffs.

CHOCOLATE SOUFFLE

Follow recipe for Vanilla Soufflé, but reduce cornstarch to 1 tablespoon, and stir 1½ squares of melted unsweetened chocolate into sauce mixture before adding egg yolks.

SAUCES

The first seven sauces are delicious served on fritters, waffles, pancakes, plain cake, French toast, ice cream, or pudding.

HASTY CHOCOLATE SAUCE

> 1 (6-ounce) package semi-sweet chocolate pieces
> 2 cups light corn syrup

Put chocolate pieces into small mixing bowl. If cold, let come to room temperature. Bring syrup to boil in saucepan. Stir gradually into chocolate pieces. Stir until chocolate is melted and sauce is smooth. Use hot or cold. When cooled, sauce thickens. To thin, add small amount warm water or cream, or thin over hot water. (Makes 2⅔ cups.)

276

SPEEDY FRUIT SAUCE I

Blend ½ cup light corn syrup with 1 cup fruit preserves or jam (any flavor you like). For thinner sauce, use ¾ cup syrup. (Makes 1 to 1¼ cups.)

SPEEDY FRUIT SAUCE II

Stir ½ to ⅔ cup light corn syrup with 1½ cups fresh, crushed fruit such as strawberries, raspberries, peaches, or sweet cherries. Chill. (Makes 1½ to 2 cups.)

SPEEDY PEANUT BUTTER SAUCE

Mix ⅓ cup creamy or chunk-style peanut butter with ⅔ cup pancake syrup. (Makes about 1 cup.)

SPEEDY HOT BUTTERY SAUCE

Stir 1 cup corn syrup with ¼ cup margarine in a saucepan and bring to boil. Serve hot. (Makes about 1 cup.)

SPEEDY FLUFF SAUCE

Cream ½ cup margarine until light and fluffy. Beat in 1 cup corn syrup, 2 tablespoons at a time. For flavor variety fold in: chopped nuts, grated orange rind, grated chocolate, or a dash of nutmeg or cinnamon. (Makes 2 cups.)

SPEEDY HOT SPICY APPLE SAUCE

Bring to a boil in saucepan and boil 5 minutes: 2 cups canned apple sauce, 1 cup pancake syrup, ¼ teaspoon nutmeg, ½ teaspoon cinnamon, and 2 tablespoons margarine. Serve hot. (Makes about 2½ cups.)

DELUXE BUTTERSCOTCH SAUCE

1 cup firmly packed light brown sugar	2 tablespoons margarine
1 cup light cream	Dash salt
½ cup light corn syrup	½ teaspoon vanilla

Combine sugar, ½ cup light cream, syrup, margarine, and salt in saucepan. Bring to boil over medium heat, stirring constantly. Cook, stirring occasionally, until temperature reaches 246° F. or until a small amount of mixture dropped into very cold water forms a firm ball which does not flatten on removal from water. Remove from heat. Stir in remaining ½ cup light cream. Cook over medium heat about 1 minute. Mix in vanilla. Serve warm. Store in covered jar in refrigerator. (Makes about 1¾ cups.)

To reheat: place jar of sauce in hot water.

HOT FUDGE SAUCE

½ cup cocoa	¼ teaspoon salt
1 cup sugar	3 tablespoons margarine
1 cup light or dark corn syrup	1 teaspoon vanilla
½ cup light cream, or undiluted evaporated milk	

Combine all ingredients except vanilla in saucepan. Cook over medium heat, stirring constantly, until mixture comes to a full rolling boil. Boil briskly 3 minutes, stirring occasionally. Remove from heat. Add vanilla. Serve hot. (Makes about 2½ cups.)

LEMON DESSERT TOPPING

1 cup milk	⅔ cup chopped walnuts (optional)
1 cup light corn syrup	
1 (3-ounce) package instant lemon pudding mix	

Stir milk and syrup into pudding mix. Beat until well blended. Stir in nuts. Serve on ice cream, pudding or cake. (Makes 2 cups.)

278

CREAMY RICH DESSERT SAUCE

1 cup sugar
1 cup dark corn syrup
1 cup heavy cream

⅛ teaspoon salt
½ teaspoon vanilla

Combine syrup, sugar, cream, and salt in saucepan. Stirring constantly, bring to boil over medium heat and boil 10 minutes. Remove from heat. Add vanilla. Serve hot or cold on ice cream, sponge cake, waffles, etc. (Makes about 2½ cups.)

CANDIES

10-MINUTE FUDGE

4 tablespoons margarine
3 ounces unsweetened chocolate
4½ cups sifted confectioners' sugar
⅓ cup instant non-fat dry milk
½ cup light or dark corn syrup

1 tablespoon water
1 teaspoon vanilla
½ cup chopped nuts *or* 1 cup
  miniature or cut-up
  marshmallows (optional)

Melt margarine and chocolate in top of 2-quart double boiler or saucepan over boiling water. Meanwhile, sift confectioners' sugar and non-fat dry milk together; set aside. Stir syrup, water, and vanilla into chocolate mixture over boiling water. Blend in sifted dry ingredients in 2 additions, stirring until mixture is well blended and smooth. Remove from boiling water. Mix in nuts or marshmallows. Turn into greased 8-inch-square pan. Cool. Cut into squares. (Makes 1¾ pounds.)

BROWN SUGAR FUDGE

Follow recipe for Ten-Minute Fudge, omitting chocolate and water. Melt ½ cup brown sugar with margarine. Use dark corn syrup.

OLD-FASHIONED CHOCOLATE FUDGE

3 tablespoons margarine
3 cups sugar
2 tablespoons light or dark corn syrup
2 squares unsweetened chocolate

¾ cup milk
1 teaspoon vanilla
1 cup walnuts, coarsely chopped (optional)

Place margarine, sugar, corn syrup, chocolate, and milk in a heavy 3-quart saucepan. Cook over medium heat, stirring constantly, until mixture boils. Continue cooking, stirring occasionally, to 238° F. or until a small amount of mixture forms a soft ball when tested in cold water. Remove from heat. Add vanilla. Cool to lukewarm (110° F.) Beat until fudge begins to thicken and loses its gloss. Fold in nuts. Quickly pour into greased (8 x 8 x 2-inch) pan. For best results do not spread fudge or scrape out of pan. When cold, cut in squares. (Makes 2 pounds.)

NO-COOK FONDANT

⅓ cup margarine
⅓ cup light corn syrup
1 teaspoon vanilla

½ teaspoon salt
1 pound confectioners' sugar, sifted

Cream margarine slightly in large mixing bowl; blend in syrup, vanilla, and salt. Add confectioners' sugar all at once and mix in, first with spoon, then kneading with hands. Turn out onto board and continue kneading until mixture is well blended and smooth. Store in cool place. Shape as desired. (Makes 1⅓ pounds.)

MINT PATTIES

Follow recipe for No-Cook Fondant, substituting 1 teaspoon peppermint or wintergreen flavoring for vanilla. Tint to desired color, using red or green food coloring. Shape into balls or roll thin and cut into desired shapes.

CANDIED FRUIT SHAPES

Follow recipe for No-Cook Fondant, substituting rum or rum extract for vanilla, if desired. Mix in ½ cup finely chopped mixed candied fruit. Roll out to ½-inch thickness. Cut squares.

ORANGE OR LEMON CREAMS

Follow recipe for No-Cook Fondant, substituting 2 teaspoons orange extract or 1 teaspoon lemon extract for vanilla. Tint to a delicious orange or yellow using vegetable coloring. Shape as desired.

ALMOND DIAMONDS

Follow recipe for No-Cook Fondant, substituting 1 teaspoon almond extract for vanilla. Add ½ cup coarsely chopped blanched and toasted almonds. Roll out or pat to ½-inch thickness. Cut into diamonds.

MOCHA LOGS

Follow recipe for No-Cook Fondant, adding 2 teaspoons powdered instant coffee. Shape into small rolls about ½ inch in diameter and 2 inches long. Roll in chocolate candy cake decorations.

CHRISTMAS BALLS

Shape No-Cook Fondant into ½-inch balls. Roll in multicolored decorations.

NUT CREAMS

Shape No-Cook Fondant into ½-inch balls. Press between 2 walnut or pecan halves.

STUFFED DATES

Shape No-Cook Fondant into very small finger-shaped rolls and stuff into pitted dates. Roll in granulated sugar. (Recipe makes enough fondant to stuff about 1¾ pounds dates.)

QUICK-COOK FONDANT

⅓ cup margarine
½ cup light corn syrup

1 pound sifted confectioners' sugar
1 teaspoon vanilla

Stir margarine, syrup, and ½ of sugar in 3-quart saucepan over low heat until mixture bubbles throughout. Quickly stir in remaining sugar and vanilla. Remove at once from heat; stir until mixture just holds shape. Pour into greased pan; let cool just enough to handle; knead well. If candy seems to harden too much before cooling, work with spoon, then knead. Flavor and color; then shape with lightly greased hands as desired or in any of the following ways. (Makes 1⅓ pounds.)

Bon-Bons

Form into small balls with nut piece in center. Roll balls in colored or white sugar or in candy cake decorations.

Filled Fruits or Nuts

Place small piece of candy in center of pitted prunes, dates, or apricots. Roll fruit in granulated sugar.

Peppermint Popcorn Tree

Prepare 14 cups popped corn. Line 13 x 9 x 2-inch pan with aluminum foil; let ends extend beyond pan sides. Prepare candy mixture, replacing margarine with 2 tablespoons water, increasing syrup to 1 cup. After all of sugar is added, remove from heat. Stir in 32 marshmallows (not miniature) and 1 teaspoon peppermint flavoring. Pour over popped corn in large bowl; toss to coat well. Press into pan; cool about 15 minutes or until set. Remove from pan and foil. Cut into pieces: two each about 5 x 5 inches, 4 x 4 inches, 2 x 2 inches, and three about 3 x 3 inches. Stack pieces, largest on bottom, smallest on top, alternating square corners over straight sides. Support with dowel stick through center if needed. Decorate with green sugar, small candies, and birthday cake candles.

Easter Eggs

Tint candy mixture pink, green, or yellow with food color. Flavor as desired. Form into egg shapes. Decorate with frosting. (Stir about 1 tablespoon water into 1 cup confectioners' sugar to give good consistency. Color if desired.) Nest eggs in colored coconut. (Toss coconut with few drops food coloring.)

DIVINITY

2½ cups sugar
½ cup light corn syrup
½ cup water
¼ teaspoon salt

2 egg whites
1 teaspoon vanilla
1 cup coarsely chopped walnuts or
    pecans (optional)

Combine sugar, syrup, water, and salt in 2-quart saucepan. Cook over medium heat, stirring constantly, until mixture comes to a boil. Reduce heat; cook without stirring until temperature reaches 248° F. or until a small amount of mixture dropped into very cold water forms a firm ball which does not flatten on removal from water. Just before temperature reaches 248° F., beat egg whites until stiff but not dry. Beating constantly, slowly pour about ½ the hot syrup over egg whites. Meanwhile, cook remaining syrup to 272° F. or until a small amount separates into threads which are hard but not brittle when dropped into very cold water. Beating constantly, pour hot syrup over first mixture about 1 tablespoon at a time, beating well after each addition.

Continue beating until mixture begins to lose its gloss and a
small amount of mixture holds soft peak when dropped from
spoon. (If mixture becomes too stiff for mixer, beat with wooden
spoon.) Mix in vanilla and nuts. Drop by teaspoonfuls onto waxed
paper. (Makes about 1¼ pounds.)

APPLE-ON-A-STICK

8 medium-sized apples	½ cup water
8 wooden skewers or spoons	1 drop oil of cinnamon
3 cups sugar	1 teaspoonful red food coloring
½ cup light corn syrup	

Wash and dry apples; remove stems and insert skewers into stem
ends. Combine sugar, syrup, and water in deep, heavy saucepan.
Cook over medium heat, stirring constantly, until mixture boils.
Then cook without stirring until temperature reaches 285° F.
(soft-crack stage) or until a small amount of syrup dropped into
very cold water separates into threads which are hard but not
brittle. Remove from heat. Add flavoring and coloring; stir only
enough to mix. Hold each apple by skewer and quickly twirl in
syrup, tilting pan to cover apple with syrup. Remove from syrup,
allow excess to drip off, and then twirl to spread syrup smoothly
over apple. Place on lightly buttered baking sheet to cool. Store
in cool place. (Makes 8.)

CRUNCHY APPLE-ON-A-STICK

Follow recipe for Apple-on-a-Stick, rolling bottom quarter of apples in slightly crushed corn flakes before placing on buttered
baking sheet to cool.

CRAZY CRUNCH

⅔ cup sugar	4 cups popcorn
½ cup margarine	⅔ cup toasted pecans
¼ cup light or dark corn syrup	⅓ cup toasted almonds
½ teaspoon vanilla	

Combine sugar, margarine, and syrup in small saucepan. Bring to boil over medium heat, stirring constantly. Continue boiling, stirring occasionally, 10 to 15 minutes or until mixture turns light caramel color (290° F.). Remove from heat. Stir in vanilla. Pour syrup over popcorn and nuts on baking sheet. Toss with two large spoons until popcorn and nuts are coated. Spread out to dry. Break apart and store in tightly covered container. (Makes about 1 pound.)

SPICY CEREAL CRUNCH

½ cup margarine
1⅓ cups firmly packed brown sugar
¼ cup light corn syrup
2 teaspoons cinnamon
½ teaspoon salt
3 cups toasted round oat cereal

2 cups bite-size shredded wheat cereal
2 cups bite-size toasted corn cereal
1 cup raisins
1 cup pecan halves or walnut pieces

Combine margarine, brown sugar, syrup, cinnamon, and salt in heavy 1-quart saucepan. Stirring constantly, bring to boil over medium heat and boil 2 minutes. Toss cereals, raisins, and nuts together in large greased bowl. Pour hot syrup over mixture. Stir well to coat completely. Spread on 2 greased cookie sheets. When cool and firm, break into pieces. (Makes about 2½ quarts.)

CHOCOLATE CARAMEL ROLL

1 cup unsalted nuts, very finely chopped
1 cup sugar
1 cup dark corn syrup
3 tablespoons cocoa

¼ teaspoon salt
1 cup evaporated milk
¼ cup margarine
1 teaspoon vanilla

Spread nuts on lightly greased (12 x 15-inch) cookie sheet, leaving 2-inch margin all around. Combine syrup, sugar, cocoa, and salt in heavy 2-quart saucepan. Cook over medium heat, stirring constantly, until mixture comes to a boil and sugar is completely

dissolved. Boil, stirring frequently, until temperature reaches 244°
F. or until small amount of mixture dropped into very cold water
forms a firm ball which does not flatten on removal from water.
Meanwhile, heat evaporated milk and margarine until margarine
melts. Slowly stir into sugar mixture so it does not stop boiling.
Cook until temperature again reaches 244° F. Remove from heat.
Stir in vanilla. (If mixture appears curdled, stir just until smooth
and blended.) Pour over nuts. Let stand 15 minutes. Roll up
jelly-roll fashion, starting at one long side. Wrap in waxed paper.
Store at room temperature. Cut into ¼-inch slices when firm.
(Makes about 4½ dozen.)

VANILLA TAFFY

1 cup sugar	¼ teaspoon cream of tartar
¾ cup light corn syrup	1 teaspoon vanilla
½ cup water	1 tablespoon margarine

Combine sugar, corn syrup, water, and cream of tartar in saucepan. Bring to a boil over medium heat, stirring constantly until
sugar dissolves. Continue cooking without stirring, to 266° F. or
until a small amount of mixture forms a hard ball when tested
in very cold water. Remove from heat; stir in vanilla and margarine. Pour into a greased 8 x 8 x 2-inch-square pan; let stand until
cool enough to handle. Pull candy with fingers until it has a
satinlike finish and milky-white color. Pull into long strips ¾
inch in diameter. Cut into 1-inch pieces with scissors. Wrap in
waxed paper. (Makes about ½ pound.) Recipe may be doubled.

CANDIED ORANGE PEEL

2 medium oranges	1 cup sugar
1 teaspoon salt	1 cup water
½ cup light corn syrup	

Select thick-skinned oranges of a good color and free from blem-
ishes. Wash oranges, and remove peel in 4 to 6 sections. Cover

peel with cold water; add salt. Bring to a boil; boil 10 minutes. Drain. Repeat operation 3 times, omitting salt. After each cooking period, gently scrape off moist, white membrane with the bowl of a spoon. Peel should be about ¼ inch thick. Cut peel into strips. Combine corn syrup, sugar, and water in 3-quart saucepan. Cook over medium heat, stirring constantly, until sugar is dissolved. Add orange peel; bring to a boil. Reduce heat and boil gently 45 minutes. Drain in coarse strainer or colander, reserving syrup. Bring syrup to a full, rolling boil. Cool; store covered in refrigerator. Roll peel, a few pieces at a time, in granulated sugar. Arrange in a single layer on trays; let dry about 24 hours. Store covered. (Makes about 1 pound.)

Note: Use syrup as a dessert sauce or for pancakes.

Chocolate Tipped Orange Peel

Melt ½ cup chocolate semi-sweet bits in top of double boiler over hot water. Dip ends of peel. Put on waxed paper until chocolate is hardened.

SPICED GLACE NUTS

1½ cups sugar	½ cup light or dark corn syrup
1 teaspoon cinnamon	½ cup water
¼ teaspoon cloves	½ teaspoon salt
⅛ teaspoon ginger	3 cups nuts
⅛ teaspoon nutmeg	2 tablespoons margarine

Combine sugar, spices, corn syrup, water, and salt in a heavy saucepan. Stir over low heat until sugar is dissolved; then cook over medium heat, without stirring, to hard-crack stage (300° F. or until a small amount of syrup separates into threads which are hard and brittle when dropped into very cold water). Meanwhile, spread nuts in a shallow pan and heat in a 350° F. oven for 10 minutes. Reduce heat under candy mixture to very low. Add heated nuts and margarine. Stir just until nuts are coated and margarine is melted. Remove from heat. Turn out into a large, coarse sieve, and set over a pan for 1 minute to drain off excess syrup. Then spread nuts on a greased pan and separate with forks. If desired, saucepan can be placed over boiling water to keep warm and nuts removed separately with forks onto a greased pan.

PEANUT BRITTLE

1 cup light or dark corn syrup	2 tablespoons margarine
⅛ teaspoon salt	1½ cups shelled peanuts
1 cup sugar	2 teaspoons hot water
¼ cup water	1 teaspoon baking soda

Stir together corn syrup, salt, sugar, water, and margarine; then cook to soft-crack stage (280° F. or until a small amount separates into threads which are hard but not brittle when tested in very cold water). Stir in peanuts gradually so that mixture will continue to boil. Cook, stirring frequently, to hard-crack stage (300° F. or until a small amount separates into threads which are hard and brittle when tested in very cold water). Color of mixture will darken slightly. Remove from heat. Stir hot water into baking soda and beat thoroughly into brittle. Turn out onto heavily greased baking sheet and with spatula spread out as thin as possible. Let cool slightly, about 5 minutes; then turn warm brittle upside-down. Sheet of brittle may be cut into strips to make it easier to turn. Stretch brittle to desired thickness. With this method the nuts are covered more evenly with brittle mixture. Let cool, and break into irregular shaped pieces. (Makes about 1¼ pounds.)

Note: One 7¼-ounce can salted peanuts may be used. Omit salt in recipe.

QUICK POPCORN BALLS

¼ cup corn oil	½ cup sugar
½ cup popcorn	½ teaspoon salt
½ cup dark corn syrup	

Heat corn oil in a 4-quart kettle over medium heat for 3 minutes. Add popcorn. Cover, leaving small air space at edge of cover. Shake frequently over medium heat until popping stops. Meanwhile mix together dark corn syrup, sugar, and salt. Add to popped corn in kettle and stir constantly over medium heat 3 to 5 minutes or until corn is evenly and completely coated with mixture. Remove from heat. Form into balls, using as little pressure as possible. Use margarine on hands, if desired. (Makes 6 popcorn balls about 2½ inches in diameter.)

Note: Do *not* double recipe.

Caramel Corn

Follow recipe for Quick Popcorn Balls. After removing from heat, spread on waxed paper and separate the pieces of popped corn. (Makes about 2 quarts.)

Pastel Popcorn Balls

Follow recipe for Quick Popcorn Balls, using light corn syrup for dark corn syrup, and tint corn syrup mixture with pink or green vegetable coloring before adding popped corn. Flavor green syrup with wintergreen, and pink syrup with peppermint.

XII

Traditional Christmas Favorites for the Now Generation

HOLLYBERRY DIP

1 (8-ounce) package cream cheese
½ cup light corn syrup
½ cup dairy sour cream

1 cup chopped fresh cranberries
3 tablespoons grated orange rind

Place cream cheese in small mixing bowl. Add syrup; beat until fluffy. Fold in remaining ingredients in order listed. Serve with crackers. (Makes about 2 cups.)

FRUIT CAKE

2¼ cups sifted flour
1 teaspoon cinnamon
½ teaspoon baking soda
½ teaspoon nutmeg
½ teaspoon clove
¼ teaspoon salt
6 cups fruit—chopped candied figs
    dates, raisins, currants
½ cup chopped nuts

½ cup margarine
1 cup firmly packed brown sugar
2 egg yolks
½ cup dark corn syrup
1 cup grape juice
½ cup buttermilk
2 egg whites
Brandy or rum

Sift flour, cinnamon, baking soda, nutmeg, clove, and salt together. Combine fruit and nuts in large bowl; dredge with ¼ cup flour mixture. Blend margarine and brown sugar in mixing bowl. Add egg yolks, one at a time, beating after each addition. Stir in syrup, then fruit mixture, then grape juice. Add flour mixture alternately with buttermilk. Beat egg whites until soft peaks form when beater is raised. Fold into batter. Turn into prepared pan(s). Bake in 300° F. oven until cake(s) tests done. Cool thoroughly. Wrap in brandy or rum-soaked cheesecloth or sprinkle tops of cupcakes with liquor if paper cups are not removed. Store in tightly covered container, moistening cheesecloth with brandy or rum as it dries.

Pan Sizes: 2 (8½ x 4½ x 2½-inch) loaf pans
Preparation: Grease, line bottom with waxed paper and grease again.
Baking Time: 2½ hours

Pan Sizes: 32 (2½ x 1¼-inch) cupcake cups
Preparation: Line with paper baking cups.
Baking Time: 1¼ hours

Pan Sizes: 64 (1¾ x 1-inch) cupcake cups
Preparation: Grease well or line with paper baking cups.
Baking Time: 1 hour

Note: Batter may be refrigerated several days before baking. Store in tightly covered bowl; turn cold batter into prepared pan(s) and increase baking time by 15 minutes for all pan sizes.

HOLIDAY RUM BALLS

5 cups finely crushed vanilla cookies	½ cup (4 ounces) rum
	¼ cup light corn syrup
1 cup chopped pecans	2 tablespoons cocoa
1 cup confectioners' sugar	Confectioners' sugar

Combine crumbs, pecans, one cup confectioners' sugar, rum, syrup, and cocoa. Shape into 1-inch balls with hands dusted with confectioners' sugar. Roll balls in confectioners' sugar. Store in tightly covered container several days to mellow. (Makes about 4 dozen.)

PFEFFERNUESSE
(Very hard, spicy Christmas cookie)

2¼ cups sifted flour	¼ teaspoon freshly ground pepper
1½ teaspoons baking powder	1 egg, slightly beaten
¾ cup sugar	¼ cup dark corn syrup
1½ teaspoons cinnamon	2 tablespoons corn oil
¼ teaspoon ginger	⅓ cup finely cut citron
¼ teaspoon cardamon	1 tablespoon flour
¼ teaspoon clove	Confectioners' sugar

Sift 2¼ cups flour, baking powder, sugar, and spices together into mixing bowl. Make well in center, and add beaten egg, syrup, and corn oil. Stir with spoon, beginning at center and working out to edge; then blend with hands to completely mix in flour. Coat citron with one tablespoon flour; mix into dough. Shape into 1-inch balls. Place on greased cookie sheet. Bake in 350° F. oven 20 minutes. Roll in confectioners' sugar while still warm. Store in tightly covered container. (Makes about 2 dozen.)

MINTED WALNUTS

1 cup sugar	10 regular marshmallows
½ cup water	1 teaspoon essence of peppermint
¼ cup light corn syrup	3 cups walnut halves

Combine sugar, water, and syrup in heavy saucepan. Cook over medium heat, stirring constantly, until mixture boils. Continue cooking to 238° F. or until a small amount of mixture dropped into very cold water forms a soft ball which flattens on removal from water. Remove from heat. Quickly add marshmallows and essence of peppermint. Stir until marshmallows are completely dissolved. Add walnut halves. Stir until well-coated. Pour onto waxed paper. Separate halves while still warm. (Makes 1¼ pounds.)

CANDIED CHRISTMAS POPCORN

¼ cup corn oil	⅔ cup sugar
½ cup popcorn	½ teaspoon salt
⅔ cup light or dark corn syrup	

Heat corn oil in 4-quart kettle over medium heat 3 minutes. Add popcorn. Cover, leaving small air space at edge. Shake frequently over medium heat until popping stops. Mix syrup, sugar, and salt in heavy saucepan. Cook over medium heat about 2 minutes, stirring constantly, until sugar and salt are dissolved. If desired, flavor with essence of peppermint or wintergreen. Add popped corn and stir over medium heat 3 to 5 minutes or until corn is evenly and completely coated with syrup mixture. Remove from heat. Use in one or more of the following ways:

Popcorn Balls

Form popcorn into balls, using as little pressure as possible. Insert wooden stick into balls, if desired. (Makes 6 [2½-inch] balls.)

Popcorn Wreaths

Shape popcorn on waxed paper, making wreaths 5 to 6 inches in diameter for hanging and about 9 inches in diameter for centerpiece. Decorate with holly leaves cut from angelica, small red cinnamon candies, and silver dragees. (Makes 2 small wreaths or 1 large one.)

Popcorn Candle

Cut top off ½-pint cream carton. Wash and dry carton. Pack with popcorn. Insert small candy cane into top for wick. Remove carton when popcorn is cool and set.

Note: Do *not* double popcorn recipe. Use margarine on hands in forming balls, etc.

If popcorn mixture cools during shaping and does not stick together, place over low heat a few minutes. When using light corn syrup, mixture may be tinted with food coloring before adding the popped corn.

HOT YULE PUNCH

2 quarts cider
2 cinnamon sticks
1 (12-ounce) can pineapple juice
1 cup light corn syrup
½ cup lemon juice
½ teaspoon nutmeg
Baked oranges

Combine cider and cinnamon in large saucepan. Cover. Bring to boil; then simmer 5 minutes. Add pineapple juice, syrup, lemon juice, and nutmeg. Heat well. Remove cinnamon sticks. Pour over Baked Oranges in punch bowl. Serve hot. (Makes about 2 to 3 quarts.)

Baked Oranges

> 3 small perfect oranges (preferably navel)
> Whole cloves

Stud oranges with cloves about ½ inch apart. Place in baking pan with water covering bottom. Bake in 300°F. oven about 30 minutes.

XIII

Gourmet Cooking for the Budding Palate— A Guide for Mothers

An Introduction to Gourmet Foods

"Ugh!" "What's *that?*" "Can't I just have a hamburger?"

If comments like these are all too familiar, if you ever have second thoughts about serving yourself and your husband the bland, nourishing but generally unexciting meals that too easily become the habit when your children join you at the dinner table, some palate-educating is surely in order.

The recipes and menus for one week of dinners that follow are designed to tempt the young palate gradually into more adventurous paths. All recipes are simple and relatively inexpensive to prepare. They lean on flavors most likely to appeal to the budding gourmet, and include a discreet use of herbs interesting enough to provide a new taste experience without being so strong as to discourage further adventurousness.

Since this first week's menus are based on a theory of gradual progression, the Monday menu features a solid and familiar main dish with new taste experiences provided in the appetizer, salad, and dessert.

The table wines suggested with each menu are all American wines, economically priced and of good quality and flavor.

All recipes in this chapter serve 6.

One Week of Dinner Menus and Recipes

MONDAY

BOUILLON-ON-THE-ROCKS SERVED WITH

CELERY STUFFED WITH ROQUEFORT CHEESE

OPEN-FACE STEAK SANDWICH WITH GARLIC BUTTER

WATERMELON-RIND PRESERVE GARNISH

SHOESTRING POTATOES

LETTUCE, TOMATO, AND

HEART OF PALM SALAD WITH
VINAIGRETTE SAUCE

PINOT NOIR—A FULL-BODIED RED WINE
MADE FROM THE GRAPES USED IN THE WORLD'S
GREAT RED BURGUNDIES

CHERRIES JUBILEE IN-A-HURRY

Bouillon-on-the-Rocks is a sure success for several reasons—not the least of these being its surprise value. It sounds sophisticated and looks unusual served in a chilled glass over ice, yet it has a faintly familiar flavor despite the change in its temperature. I find it most satisfactory to serve it filled to the brim in old fashioned glasses—not only for eye appeal but because seconds will be called for. Steak seems to be irresistible to young and old alike, especially when topped with a sizzling hot melted garlic butter sauce—a new and distinctive combination of tastes for the younger set. There is nothing to be said about the salad— it is a "hazard of new fortunes." But the dessert can't miss. The fun and dramatic possibilities of serving Cherries Jubilee are incalculable. The basic luscious flavor of ice cream and fruit can be relied on to delight everyone, while the awe-struck countenances of the young as you set this flaming wonder before them will be reward enough. Dad will appreciate the gently identifiable flavor of brandy, too.

BOUILLON-ON-THE-ROCKS

2 cans undiluted Beef Bouillon poured over ice cubes. (Packages of powdered bouillon or cubes need to be dissolved in *boiling* water first.)

OPEN-FACE STEAK SANDWICH WITH GARLIC BUTTER

Sear and pan-broil a boneless sirloin steak quickly over medium-to-high heat. Dot generously with Garlic Butter and season with salt and pepper as it browns. Carve thin slices and serve on toast, spooning juice and butter over all.

Quick Garlic Butter

Can be made by thoroughly mixing garlic powder with creamed butter to taste.

SHOESTRING POTATOES

Peel and slice 2 pounds potatoes into thin, matchlike pieces. Fry in hot, deep fat (375° F.) until they are crisp, crunchy, and golden-brown. (Can also be bought oven-ready in frozen packages.)

TOMATO AND HEART OF PALM SALAD

Decorate very crisp Bibb lettuce with tomato wedges and 1-inch pieces of heart of palm and serve icy cold with Vinaigrette Sauce.

Easy Vinaigrette Sauce

Combine 4 tablespoons olive oil with one tablespoon vinegar and add ¼ teaspoon prepared mustard, 1 teaspoon salt, and 1 teaspoon mixed chopped parsley, tarragon, chives, chervil. Sprinkle with ½ chopped hard-cooked egg.

CHERRIES JUBILEE IN-A-HURRY

½ cup sugar
Dash salt
1 tablespoon cornstarch
½ cup water

1 pound cherries
1 pint vanilla ice cream
4 tablespoons brandy

Combine sugar, salt, and cornstarch in saucepan; add water and pitted cherries (frozen or canned). Cook until thickened, stirring constantly. When cherries are cool, spoon over ice cream in individual dishes. Pour one tablespoon brandy over each serving, ignite with match, serve flaming with characteristic blue flame.

Note: Warm brandy gently in saucepan over low flame before spooning over cherries.

TUESDAY

BAKED STUFFED CLAMS

VEAL AND PEPPERS ITALIANO

SPAGHETTI WITH PARSLEY BUTTER SAUCE

HEARTS OF ROMAINE SALAD WITH

GORGONZOLA CHEESE DRESSING

ITALIAN BREAD LOAF

GAMAY ROSE (CHILLED)—A SPRIGHTLY PINK WINE
MADE FROM THE SAME GRAPES AS BEAUJOLAIS

BEL PAESE CHEESE, CRACKERS, AND FRESH PEARS

Baked Stuffed Clams, bubbling hot and tasty from the oven—
they can be bought all prepared, stored in your freezing compartment and require only heating time in your oven. They are to be
found packaged at the fish and seafood counter of most super-
markets as well as at your favorite fish stores and are quite reason-
ably priced. Veal and Peppers Italiano may be served over buttered spaghetti *al dente* or stand alone as the entrée with Spaghetti
with Parsley Butter Sauce as a side dish. Either way it is a hearty,
filling, and most desirable dish, especially in cold weather. The
secret here is to charm your butcher into giving you a good quality and cut of veal, a grade better than ordinary stewing veal
to cut down on cooking time and insure tender and non-chewy
meat. This savory dish is sure-fire and will probably incite the
most finicky eater in your family to inquire when dinner will be
ready as its fragrant cooking odors escape the sanctum sanctorum
of your kitchen. A crusty Italian Bread Loaf, oven-warmed, and
a tangy Hearts of Romaine Salad with Gorgonzola Cheese Dressing are its perfect foils. By the time the continental dessert is
served, your children should be in a delightfully dazed condition
and your husband radiating a rosy glow reminiscent of an earlier
period of wedded bliss. *Ciao!*

BAKED STUFFED CLAMS

Buy already prepared. Heat in moderately high oven until lightly browned on top and bubbling hot.

VEAL AND PEPPERS ITALIANO

1½ pounds veal, boneless, cut into 2-inch pieces
3 tablespoons corn oil
2 green peppers
1 (3-ounce) can mushrooms, sliced
1 (16-ounce) can tomatoes
1 teaspoon basil
1 teaspoon salt
⅛ teaspoon pepper

Brown veal in hot oil over low heat. Chop peppers, add them to veal, and cook, stirring, until soft. Add mushrooms, tomatoes, and seasonings; cover and simmer 30 minutes or until meat is tender.

SPAGHETTI WITH PARSLEY BUTTER SAUCE

Mince a handful of parsley stripped from the stems. Add parsley and ¼ pound butter to one pound steaming hot spaghetti (see p. 164). Mix well until butter is completely melted.

HEARTS OF ROMAINE SALAD

Sprinkle liberally with freshly ground pepper before adding bottled Gorgonzola Cheese Dressing.

ITALIAN BREAD LOAF

Warm in moderate oven for about 10 minutes.

BEL PAESE CHEESE

Serve at room temperature in wedges on crackers with fresh pears that have been chilled in the refrigerator.

WEDNESDAY

VICHYSOISSE

QUICK SHRIMP JAMBALAYA

HOT BUTTERED CROISSANTS

AVOCADO SALAD WITH FRENCH DRESSING

JOHANNESBERG RIESLING—A WHITE WINE
PRESSED FROM THE SAME GRAPES USED IN
MAKING THE FINEST RHINE WINES

HAITIAN PINEAPPLE WITH CINNAMON COOKIES

ICED TEA

This next no-nonsense menu requires so little time to prepare and provides such glorious results as to be truly incredible. A good brand of canned Vichyssoise, chilled, requires only the addition of heavy sweet cream to taste and a sprinkling of chives, fresh or frozen. The main dish requires precisely 35 minutes to make and it is both delectable and substantial. Frozen packaged croissants, now available at any supermarket, are delicious and need only to be warmed in the oven for 15 minutes. The avocado salad is the only real taste challenge in this meal. However, the delicate coloring of a freshly ripe, peeled avocado on a bed of iceberg lettuce vies with a Dufy painting to some gourmet minds and will do much to captivate the subject who is about to acquire a taste for this delicious food. Haitian Pineapple is a cool, refreshing dessert with a sparkling flavor that is pleasing to the palate after the predominantly ham and seafood taste of the entrée.

VICHYSOISSE

Use canned soup. Add heavy sweet cream to taste, mix, chill, and sprinkle with chives (fresh or frozen).

QUICK SHRIMP JAMBALAYA

1 large green pepper, sliced
1 clove garlic, minced
2 medium onions, sliced
1 (16-ounce) can tomatoes, peeled
1 pound fresh, cooked or 1
   (12-ounce) can chopped ham
¼ teaspoon thyme

½ teaspoon basil
½ teaspoon paprika
1 teaspoon salt
½ cup dry white wine
1 cup raw rice
1 pound shrimp, cooked and
   cleaned or 2 (7-ounce) cans

Sauté green pepper, garlic, and onion in butter until soft. Add tomatoes, ham, seasonings, and wine. Bring mixture to a boil, add rice slowly, stirring constantly. Cover, simmer over low heat for 25 minutes or until rice is tender, adding water if necessary. Add shrimp, heat thoroughly, and serve immediately.

AVOCADO SALAD

Peel and cut into medium-sized slices a newly ripe avocado. (If pit rattles loosely within avocado when it is shaken, it is ripe enough to be marvelously edible.) Arrange these slices on a bed of iceberg lettuce, squeeze over them a small amount of lemon juice, add freshly ground pepper, and serve with bottled French dressing. (Lemon juice will also prevent avocado from darkening.)

HOT BUTTERED CROISSANTS

Heat frozen croissants for 15 minutes and serve.

HAITIAN PINEAPPLE WITH CINNAMON COOKIES

1 can pineapple cubes   Crème de menthe
Grated coconut   Packaged cinnamon cookies

Drain pineapple, chill, and serve piled in individual sherbet dishes. Sprinkle liberally with grated coconut and top with a couple of generous tablespoons of crème de menthe. Two or three cinnamon cookies on each serving plate and a large frosty pitcher of iced tea will successfully complete Phase III of your campaign.

THURSDAY

TOMATO MADRILENE A LA RUSSE

SIMPLIFIED BEEF STROGANOFF ON WILD RICE

BUTTER GEM ROLLS

ENDIVE AND WATERCRESS SALAD WITH RUSSIAN DRESSING

CABERNET SAUVIGNON—MADE FROM GRAPES USED
IN THE FINEST CLARETS (RED BORDEAUX)

STRAWBERRIES ROMANOFF

Bring on the balalaikas and sour cream! You may not remind your husband of a lady spy, but this dinner should elicit kudos from your family if the past three have been even mildly successful.

TOMATO MADRILENE A LA RUSSE

Canned tomato madrilene

Keep in the refrigerator until ready to serve to maintain jellied consistency. Garnish with a generous dollop of sour cream which is topped by a spoonful of red caviar.

SIMPLIFIED BEEF STROGANOFF

1½ pounds fillet of beef, cut into
    2-inch strips, ¼ inch wide
3 medium-sized onions, sliced
1 (8-ounce) can button
    mushrooms

3 tablespoons butter
¼ pint sour cream
1½ teaspoons salt
⅛ teaspoon ground pepper

Sauté onions slowly in about half the butter. Add the mushrooms and fry for a few minutes. Remove mushrooms and onions. Add remaining butter, allowing it to get thoroughly hot; put in beef, and fry quickly 3 or 4 minutes, allowing beef to brown but not frizzle. Put back onions and mushrooms, add seasonings, and stir all together over the fire for a minute. Remove from heat, add sour cream, and return to heat for another minute, stirring in cream well. Serve at once on a bed of wild rice.

Wild Rice

May now be purchased packaged with clear directions on the box to follow for quick and simple final cooking.

BUTTER GEM ROLLS

May be bought packaged and partly baked. To finish the baking process requires only 20 minutes in the oven.

ENDIVE AND WATERCRESS SALAD WITH RUSSIAN DRESSING

Break up a chilled head of Simpson lettuce; add endive and young watercress. Sprinkle with freshly ground pepper and a squeeze of lemon. Top with several liberal spoonfuls of Russian Dressing.

Russian Dressing

Add 3 tablespoons of chili sauce to one cup of mayonnaise. (Be sure to cream the mayonnaise first to eliminate little lumps when it is mixed with the chili sauce.) Stir in one tablespoon of chopped pimiento and mix thoroughly.

STRAWBERRIES ROMANOFF

1 pint vanilla ice cream	6 tablespoons Cointreau
1 cup heavy sweet cream	2 quarts strawberries
1 lemon	2 tablespoons sugar

Whip the vanilla ice cream slightly and fold in the cream beaten stiff. Add the juice of the lemon and the prescribed quantity of Cointreau, and pour over well-chilled strawberries which have already been slightly sweetened with a little sugar. Mix thoroughly and quickly.

FRIDAY

CLAMATO COCKTAIL

JIFFY SOLE BERCY

RISSOLE POTATOES

GREEN BEANS AMANDINE

ARTICHOKE HEART SALAD WITH FRENCH DRESSING

PINOT CHARDONAY—AMERICAN COUSIN OF THE
FRENCH CHABLIS

MERINGUES GLACEES CHANTILLY AU CHOCOLAT

T.G.I.F. The great thing about tonight's menu is that it is elegant and sophisticated, offering several new taste experiences, yet is uncommonly easy to prepare quickly.

The delicious appetizer may be bought canned, requiring only garnishes to taste, or it may be quickly prepared. Jiffy Sole Bercy is a breeze to fix and a delight to eat even for that very special genus that "doesn't particularly care for fish." If you have the time or the inclination, the Bercy sauce may be made more substantial by starting with a basic Béchamel sauce. However, the recipe below is not only fast but undeniably delicious. Rissolé potatoes are a delectable "flash in the pan," and Green Beans Amandine can be purchased frozen. The salad is instant delight, and the dessert, of course, is a winner. Meringue shells may now be bought at your bakery.

CLAMATO COCKTAIL

Open a can and flavor to taste, or mix equal parts of clam juice and tomato juice cocktail (both available, bottled, on your supermarket shelf) and add freshly ground pepper, chives, or a dash of lemon juice.

JIFFY SOLE BERCY

1½ pounds fillet of sole
4 tablespoons butter
4 tablespoons shallots, finely
    chopped

4 tablespoons parsley, chopped
⅓ cup dry white wine
Salt
Pepper

Heat wine in a small saucepan. Add shallots and parsley and simmer until slightly reduced—about 6 or 7 minutes. Place fish in a shallow baking dish, season with salt and pepper, and dot with butter, Pour Bercy sauce over fish and bake in 325° F. oven about 5 minutes or until the fish fillets are opaque and flake when touched with a fork.

Note: You may substitute fillets of halibut or flounder for the sole. Scallions or 3 tablespoons of onion may be used if shallots are not available.

RISSOLE POTATOES

1½ pounds potatoes	Salt
4 tablespoons butter	Pepper
2 tablespoons parsley, finely chopped	

Select large potatoes, peel, and scoop out from each with a large round potato or melon ball cutter as many rounds as possible. Keep the potato balls in cold water until wanted; then blanch in fresh cold water for 5 or 6 minutes. Drain and dry them with a cloth. Heat a large frying pan, drop in butter, and when it foams add the potatoes. Lower heat and sauté slowly, shaking pan frequently, until potatoes are evenly browned. Sprinkle with salt, pepper, and chopped parsley before serving.

GREEN BEANS AMANDINE

Available in frozen packages with almonds wrapped separately to be stirred in just shortly before serving. If fresh green beans are used, however, almonds may be prepared quickly by blanching in a pan of fast-boiling water just removed from the heat. Stir round, cover, and leave them for 3 or 4 minutes. Drain off hot water, rinse, and dry. Split nuts, add to melted butter sauce, and pour over cooked green beans.

ARTICHOKE HEART SALAD WITH FRENCH DRESSING

1 large head Boston lettuce	Capers
1 basket cherry tomatoes	French dressing
1 can marinated artichoke hearts	

Decorate a bed of lettuce with cherry tomatoes and marinated artichoke hearts (canned, jarred, or frozen), cut in half. Keep well-chilled until ready to serve. Garnish with capers and bottled French dressing.

MERINGUES GLACEES CHANTILLY AU CHOCOLAT

Meringue shells   Whipped cream
Vanilla ice cream   Chocolate sauce

Fill meringue shells with a scoop of vanilla ice cream, pour over chocolate sauce, and top with a puff of whipped cream. Meringue shells may be purchased at your bakery. Chocolate sauce from jar or can is quite satisfactory for this dessert, as is the whipped cream that is sold in pressurized cans.

SATURDAY

FRENCH ONION SOUP

EASY LAMB CURRY WITH CHUTNEY

SAFFRON RICE

BREAD TWISTS

TOSSED GREEN SALAD WITH ROQUEFORT DRESSING

GAMAY BEAUJOLAIS—A LIGHT, FRESH WINE
WITH A MILD FRUITY FLAVOR

PEACH MELBA

EARL GREY TEA

A curry is almost always one of the gourmet's favorite dishes. The curry flavor is a taste not easily acquired, especially by children; however, once it is acquired and appreciated, it will provide distinct and endless pleasure, since it can be prepared around so many different bases—meat, poultry, seafood, vegetables, soup, etc. Tonight's menu is built around a meat curry, which the family now should be ready for. And since it is Saturday night and perhaps guests are in the offing, this menu will do sensationally as either a sit-down dinner or a later buffet supper. So break out your best sari. A little Ravi Shankar music will give the proper exotic note for a night that may be filled with surprises.

FRENCH ONION SOUP

There are some excellent brands of canned onion soup on the market. These need only to be heated and garnished with a toasted slice of French bread heaped with grated Gruyère cheese. Serve either in a heated large soup tureen or in individual tureens.

EASY LAMB CURRY

2 tablespoons butter	Salt
1½ tablespoons onion, chopped	Pepper
1 tablespoon flour	1 egg yolk
1 teaspoon curry powder	1 tablespoon lemon juice
2 cups stock	
2 cups lamb, cooked and cold, cut in 1-inch cubes	

Heat the butter and in it fry onion until it is golden in color. Add flour mixed with curry powder and cook, stirring for two minutes. Gradually stir in the stock and let the sauce cook until it is smooth and creamy. Add the cooked lamb, season to taste, and cover and cook for 10 minutes. Turn flame very low; and when sauce has stopped boiling, stir in the egg yolk, which has been lightly beaten with lemon juice and a little of the hot sauce. Serve immediately inside a ring of Saffron Rice with bottled chutney on the side. (For buffet purposes, the whole dish may be prepared as indicated above in a chafing dish.)

SAFFRON RICE

May be purchased partially pre-cooked and packaged for a minimum of preparation at home. Follow directions on package and arrange in a ring around Lamb Curry. Or, to prepare from scratch with raw rice: To 2 cups boiling water, add 1 teaspoon salt and 15 grains saffron. Stir in 1 cup uncooked rice. Return to boil, reduce heat to low, cover, and cook about 25 minutes or until tender.

TOSSED GREEN SALAD WITH ROQUEFORT DRESSING

Select a combination of salad greens such as lettuce, escarole, endive, watercress, chard, and a dash of tarragon. Season with salt and freshly ground pepper. Toss lightly in Roquefort Dressing.

Roquefort Dressing

Add 2 rounded tablespoons Roquefort cheese, crumbled well with a fork, to one cup French dressing.

BREAD TWISTS

May be purchased oven-ready. Serve warm and golden brown with butter pats.

PEACH MELBA

Peach halves, large (canned or frozen)	1 quart vanilla ice cream
	1 package frozen red raspberries

Place one peach half on each serving of vanilla ice cream in individual sherbet dishes. Thaw and crush red raspberries, and spoon over the top.

SUNDAY

STEAMED ARTICHOKES WITH LEMON BUTTER DIP

COQ AU VIN

POTATOES BOULANGERE

TOMATO ASPIC AND CUCUMBER SALAD WITH SOUR CREAM DRESSING

CHENIN BLANC—A DELICATE FRAGRANT
WINE SIMILAR TO VOUVRAY

CREPES SUZETTES

DEMI-TASSE

Voilà! It is Sunday, the end of a week filled with exciting culinary innovations. Time to pull out all the stops for a family who can now face Oysters Rockefeller with nary a raised eyebrow. Although the menu given above requires a little more preparation time than those of Monday through Saturday, it is indeed worth the effort for a divine denouement—which, hopefully, will also be the real beginning of more interesting, varied, and pleasurable family dining.

STEAMED ARTICHOKES WITH LEMON BUTTER DIP

Wash artichokes thoroughly with a stream of cold running water. Cut off stem from base and cut off about 1 inch from the top. With scissors trim off sharp leaf tips of outside leaves. Pull off and discard loose leaves around bottom. Stand upright in small amount of boiling salted water. Cover; simmer 25 to 30 minutes or until you can pull out a leaf readily. Drain and serve upright with small individual dishes of Lemon Butter Dip.

To eat: Tear off one leaf at a time, dip base into the sauce (holding leaf at hard top edge), draw gently between the teeth. When all the leaves are removed, cut out fuzzy "choke" (do not attempt to eat this), and eat the tender and indescribably delicious "heart" beneath with a fork.

Lemon Butter Dip

⅓ cup melted butter
½ teaspoon salt
½ teaspoon pepper

¼ cup lemon juice
2 tablespoons parsley, minced

Combine ingredients. Heat a minute or two. Pour into individual dishes.

COQ AU VIN
(Chicken in wine)

Frying chicken, cut in serving
    portions
Flour
4 tablespoons butter
Salt
Pepper

2 ounces cognac, warm
Bouquet Garni
1 cup Red Burgundy
12 small onions
4 slices salt pork, diced
12 mushroom caps

Roll chicken in flour and sauté in large skillet in butter until pieces are brown on all sides. Season chicken with salt and pepper, pour over it the warm cognac, and set cognac aflame. When flame has burned out, add a Bouquet Garni, and pour over the Red Burgundy to just cover the chicken. Cover the skillet and simmer over low heat for about 45 minutes or until tender. Sauté onions with salt pork until onions are brown. Cover and cook gently until onions are tender. Sauté mushrooms until tender. Arrange onions, mushrooms, and salt pork on warm serving platter. Place chicken on top and strain sauce over the chicken. Serve with triangles of bread sautéed in butter.

Bouquet Garni

This is the French term for a bundle of seasoning vegetables and herbs tied together for easy removal from pot. It should include celery, parsley, thyme, and bay leaf, and sometimes it *also* includes fennel, leeks, marjoram, and tarragon.

POTATOES BOULANGERE

6 potatoes, peeled and sliced
2 onions, thinly sliced
½ teaspoon salt
Dash pepper

1 teaspoon parsley, chopped
3 tablespoons butter
1 cup boiling water

Mix potatoes and onions together and season with salt, pepper, and parsley. Spread in shallow baking dish about ½ inch deep. Coat the top with butter and boiling water. Bake in 400° F. oven about 40 minutes or until potatoes are soft and crusty brown on top and water is cooked away.

TOMATO ASPIC AND CUCUMBER SALAD WITH SOUR CREAM DRESSING

1 head lettuce
1 can tomato aspic, chilled in
    refrigerator until ready to serve

1 cucumber, thinly sliced

On a bed of crisp cold lettuce, place a generous slice of tomato aspic which has been removed intact and well-chilled from can. Garnish with thin slices of ice-cold cucumber and top with Sour Cream Dressing.

Sour Cream Dressing

1 cup sour cream
2 tablespoons lemon juice *or* wine
    vinegar

Salt (to taste)
Dash cayenne
1 tablespoon chives, chopped

Add lemon juice to sour cream, season with salt and cayenne to taste. Stir in chives.

CREPES SUZETTE

⅔ cup flour
1 tablespoon sugar
Pinch salt
2 whole eggs

2 egg yolks
1¾ cups milk
2 tablespoons melted butter
1 tablespoon rum

Sift together flour, sugar, and salt. Beat together whole eggs and egg yolks and add to dry ingredients. Add milk and stir together until smooth. Add melted butter and rum. Allow batter to stand for at least two hours. Heat a small square of butter in frying pan; when it bubbles, pour in batter to make a 5-inch crêpe. Cook 1 minute, flip, and cook 1 minute on the other side. Stack them flat on top of each other until all are cooked.

Sauce

½ cup butter
½ cup powdered sugar
Grated rind of 2 oranges
Juice of one orange

¼ teaspoon lemon juice
¼ cup rum
2 tablespoons sugar
¼ cup brandy, warmed

Cream butter with sugar. Remove the thin orange-colored surfaces of the rind of 2 oranges with a very fine grater and add to butter and sugar. Add juice of one orange, lemon juice, and rum. Spread this over the cooked crêpes, roll them up, and arrange on a warm serving platter. Sprinkle with sugar and spoon over warmed brandy. Ignite and serve *flambé!*

XIV

Glossary of Food Terms

A *la mode:* served with a portion of ice cream

Al dente: cooked until just tender or barely soft

Amandine: served or prepared with almonds

Antipasto: a variety of relishes in small portions including cheese, olives, smoked and pickled meat, fish, hard-boiled egg, peppers, etc.; usually served as a first course

Appetizer: the first course of a meal consisting of a small portion of fruit, soup, juice, or fish, etc.

Aspic: a jelly made from meat, fish or vegetable stock and gelatin, used to garnish meat, fish, or chicken; often served as salad with fish, meat, etc. molded in it

Au gratin: food baked or broiled with a topping of browned bread crumbs or cheese or both, e.g., potatoes au gratin

Baste: to keep roasts and other food juicy while cooking by moistening with melted butter, fat, pan drippings, or other liquid

Béchamel: a basic white sauce of flour, butter, and milk

Bercy: a sauce (for fish) of shallots, butter, white wine, and parsley

Blanch: to put food in cold water, bring slowly to a boil, then drain; to whiten or remove skins from almonds by this method

Blanc mange: a sweet pudding made with milk or almond milk and cornstarch, flavored with vanilla or kirsch

Bouillon: a clear meat or chicken broth made from bones and flavoring vegetables

Boulangère: cooked with onions in a casserole, or with onions placed around meat during end of roasting or baking period

Bouquet garni: a combination of herbs, usually parsley, thyme, and bay leaf, tied together for easy removal after cooking

Braise: to cook meat by browning quickly in small amount of hot fat, then simmering (covered) in a little liquid

Café au lait: half hot coffee with half hot milk

Canapé: an appetizer (often served during cocktail hour) consisting of a small piece of bread or toast topped with caviar or some other delicacy (anchovy, salmon, pâté, etc.) and garnished

Capuccino: strong Italian coffee flavored with cinnamon, topped with aerated milk, grated orange peel, and nutmeg

Casserole: a heatproof dish of earthenware or glass in which food is baked and served; food thus prepared is said to be a casserole or en casserole

Caviar: roe of the sturgeon and certain other large fish, served as an appetizer

Chantilly: a dessert topping of whipped, sweetened cream and flavoring, usually vanilla

Chutney: an East Indian sauce or relish made from fruit, herbs, and spices

Cobbler: a deep-dish fruit pie with a rich biscuit or pastry crust on the top only

Cointreau: a colorless, orange-flavored liqueur

Compote: a combination of fruits, either fresh or cooked, in a sugar syrup

Condiment: something to add relish to food, usually a pungent, spicy substance served separately such as mustard, catsup, etc.

Consommé: a strong clear soup made from one or a combination of meats or fowl

Coq au vin: chicken baked in red wine with onions, garlic, mushrooms, and diced salt pork

Cream: to mash and stir around until soft, creamy and well blended

Crème de menthe: a white or green liqueur flavored with mint

Crêpe suzette: a thin dessert pancake, usually rolled or folded in quarters, heated in an orange-flavored liqueur and flamed before serving

Croquette: a mixture of chopped or ground meat, fish, chicken, potato, or vegetable, which is moistened with egg, milk or other liquid, shaped, dipped first in beaten egg, then in bread crumbs or seasoned flour, and fried

Croûton: a small piece of bread toasted or fried crisp, used to garnish soups, salads, etc.

Curry: a meat, fish, chicken, or vegetable dish flavored with curry powder, usually served with rice and a variety of condiments

Curry powder: a combination of spices and other ingredients used to make curry dishes

Cut in: to mix butter or shortening into dry ingredients by blending with two knives or pastry blender so that fat remains in small particles

Demi-tasse: a small cup of strong black coffee, usually served after dinner

Deviled: highly-seasoned food

Dredge: to sprinkle or coat with flour

Entrée: the main course

Fillet: a boneless piece of lean meat or fish

Flambé: flamed with heated brandy or other liqueur

Fold in: to add a beaten ingredient (whipped cream or egg whites) to another ingredient without loss of air by making a down, up and over motion

Garnish: to ornament a dish with something attractive and savory such as parsley, chives, etc.

Glacé: coated with icing; candied; frozen

Glaze: to cover or coat certain foods such as cold meats, fish, fruit, pastry, with aspic, or melted, spiced fruit jelly, or a thin sugar syrup

Guacamole: a mixture of mashed avocado, onion, and other seasonings served as an appetizer or dip

Hamentashen: a small, tricorn-shaped pastry filled with fruit preserve

Hollandaise: a sauce of egg yolks, butter, and lemon juice, usually served on fish, vegetables, and certain egg dishes

Hors d'oeuvre: a relish or appetizer served during the cocktail hour or at the beginning of the meal

Jambalaya: a dish of rice, herbs, vegetables, especially tomatoes and onions, and meat or fish, generally ham and shrimp

Julienne: food cut in long, thin, matchlike strips

Knead: to work dough with a pressing motion of the hands, stretching it, then folding it over on itself

Lasagne: strips of pasta baked in layers with cheese, meat and tomato sauce

Madrilene: a consommé flavored with tomato and served hot or cold

Maltaise: an orange-flavored hollandaise sauce

Marinade: a mixture of oil, acid (wine, vinegar, or lemon juice) and seasonings in which food is soaked to tenderize and add flavor; there are also dry marinades made of combinations of herbs and spices

Marinara: a highly seasoned sauce of tomatoes, garlic, and spices

Marinate: to season and tenderize by letting food stand in a marinade for several hours

Melba: a dessert of fruit, ice cream, and raspberry sauce

Meringue: a mixture of beaten egg white and sugar used as a dessert topping, usually pie; a shell baked from this mixture and filled with fruit or ice cream

Mincemeat: a finely chopped mixture, usually cooked, of raisins, apples, spices, and other ingredients, with or without meat and suet

Monosodium glutamate: a crystalline salt used in cooking to enhance flavor of meat, fish, soup, and vegetables; often sold under trade names such as MSG, Accent, etc.

Mornay: a basic white sauce with cheese, usually Swiss or Parmesan

Mousseline: a hollandaise sauce to which whipped cream is added

Paella: a dish of Spanish origin consisting of rice simmered with saffron and other seasonings, vegetables, and one or a combination of seafoods, meat, and chicken

Parfait: a frozen dessert of ice cream, syrup, and whipped cream served in a special tall, long-stemmed glass

Parmigiana: cooked with Parmesan cheese

Pasta: all varieties of macaroni, noodles, spaghetti, etc.

Pâté: a mixture of ground pork, pork fat, veal or other meat, liver, spices, and sometimes brandy, or Madeira wine, or bourbon

Pfeffernuesse: a small hard highly spiced cookie usually made at Christmastime

Pilaff: rice cooked with herbs in a seasoned liquid such as stock

Purée: cooked or uncooked food, sieved or ground into a fine pulp

Rissolé: browned in deep fat

Saffron: a seasoning used during cooking which gives a yellowish color to foods such as rice, stews, etc.

Sauté: to cook in small amount of hot fat on top of stove; also called pan fry

Scallopini: thin slices of meat, usually veal, sautéed, and served with various sauces such as wine, lemon, mushroom, etc.

Score: to make light parallel cuts in food such as pastry or ham either before or during cooking

Shallot: a small white bulb vegetable of the onion family with a delicate flavor

Shashlik: cubes of meat or fish, often marinated, alternating on skewers with vegetables such as tomatoes, onions, and peppers, and cooked over an open fire

Shish kebab: same as shashlik

Smorgasbord: a buffet of Scandinavian origin consisting of assorted dishes such as hors d'oeuvres, hot and cold meats, smoked and pickled fish, cheeses, salads, and relishes

Soubise: a white or brown sauce with onion

Soufflé: a baked dish made with a basis of eggs and white sauce, lightened by stiffly beaten egg whites

Stock: a liquid in which meat, chicken, fish, or vegetables have been cooked; used as basis for soup, gravy, sauces, etc.

Tartar sauce: mayonnaise with chopped pickles, olives, and capers added, usually served with fish

Teriyaki: a marinade of soy sauce, ginger, and garlic, for beef (and sometimes shrimp)

Torte: a cake or pastry made of eggs, sugar, very little flour, or ground nuts or bread crumbs instead of flour, which is baked in thin layers and filled with fruit jam, often covered with a rich frosting

Velouté: a basic white sauce made with flour, butter, and poultry, fish, or veal stock

Vichysoisse: a soup made of puréed potatoes, onions or leeks, cream, and stock, served cold and topped with chives

Vinaigrette: an oil and vinegar dressing with herbs.

Index

Index

See *also* Frostings (and Toppings), Cake
Saucy Baked Tomatoes, 40-41
 sauce for, 40-41
Saucy Hamburgers, 17
 spicy barbecue sauce, 17
Sauerkraut, Garnished, 167
Sausage Gondolas, 63
Sausage Specialty (Sandwich), 107
Sausages, Sweet and Sour, 53
Sautéing (pan frying), 47
Savory Grilled Chicken, 34
 sauce for, 34
Savory (Peanut Butter) Dip, 183
Sea Food Cole Slaw, 118
Sea Food Macaroni Salad, 122
Seafood Salad(s)
 Crab Meat Louis, 128
 Hearty Salmon, 126-27
 Lobster and Avocado, 127
 Sailor's (Halibut), 127
 Shrimp and Apple, 128
 Tropical Crab, 126
Sesame Seed (Pie) Pastry, 278
Shaker Loaf Cake, 220
Shaker Muffins, 88-89
 Cinnamon, 89
 Orange, 88
Shaker Spice Cake, 220
Shallow frying, definition of and procedure for, 47
Shashlik, 66
Shellfish recipes, See Fish (and Shellfish)
Shells and Crusts (Pie Pastry), 246-49
 Graham Cracker Crust, 249
 Tart Shells, 248-49
Sherbet, Lemon, 265-66
Shish Kebabs, Caraway, 27-28
Shoestring Potatoes, 297
Shoofly Pie, 254-55
Shortbread, 233-34
Shortcake, Strawberry, 76-77
Shortcut Barbecued Chicken, 64-65
Shortcut Coffee Cake, 224
Shrimp, frying procedure for, 49
Shrimp, Pineapple, 36
Shrimp and Apple Salad, 128
Shrimp Cole Slaw, 117
Shrimp Colombian, 134
Shrimp Jambalaya, Quick, 302
Shrimp-On-A-Skewer, 66-67
Shrimp Piquant, 80
Simple Party Punch, 194
Simplified Beef Stroganoff, 304
Single Crust Pie Pastry, 246, 248
6-Egg Chiffon Cake, 213

Skewered Rolls, 93
Slaw-Salami Relish, 61
Slaws, See Cole Slaw(s); specific recipes by name and ingredients
Sliced Ham With Raisin Sauce, 31
Smorgasbord, Porch, 73-75
Snack Bowl, 56
Snacks, See Hors d'Oeuvres, Dips and Snacks
Snappy Baked Beans, 37
Snow Mounds (Peanut Butter), 177
Sodas, Ice Cream, See Ice Cream Soda(s)
Sole Bercy, Jiffy, 306
Soubise Sauce, 160
Soufflé Salad, Basic, 139
Soufflés (Dessert)
 Chocolate, 275
 Vanilla, 274-75
Soup(s)
 Cold Pea, 74
 French Onion, 309
 Tomato Madrilène à la Russe, 303
 Vichyssoise, 301, 302
Sour Cream Coffee Cake, 225
Sour Cream Dressing, 313
Sour Cream-Peanut Butter Dressing, 176
Sour Cream Raisin Pie, 257
Spaghetti
 Nutty Sauce for, 186
 Parsley Butter Sauce with, 300
 Perfect, 164
 Quick-as-a-Flash Sauce, 164
Spanish Casserole of Rice, Seafood, and Vegetables (Paella), 166
Spareribs, Apple and Spice, 32
Spareribs, Apple-Glazed, 33
Spareribs, Barbecued, 64
 to grill, 64
Speedy Fluff Sauce, 276
Speedy Fruit Sauce I, 276
Speedy Fruit Sauce II, 276
Speedy Hot Buttery Sauce, 276
Speedy Hot Spicy Apple Sauce, 276
Speedy Peanut Butter Sauce, 276
Speedy Tall Summer, Cooler, 197
Spice Cake, Shaker, 220
Spice Ham and Sugar (Sandwich), Filling, 98
Spice No-Cook (Cake) Frosting, 229
Spiced Glacé Nuts, 286-87
Spicy Apple Pancakes with Caramel Syrup, 84
Spicy and Sweet French Dressing, 146
Spicy Apple Sauce, Speedy Hot, 276
Spicy Barbecue Sauce, 17, 163
Spicy Cereal Crunch, 284

Index

ACKNOWLEDGMENTS

Special thanks to Modane Marchbanks of Best Foods for the material she supplied in all categories from the Best Foods test kitchens.

All peanut butter recipes—courtesy, Best Foods, Division of Corn Products Company International, Inc.

All * recipes   —courtesy, Armour and Company

All † recipes   —courtesy, Borden, Inc.